FROM MAMMY TO MISS AMERICA AND BEYOND

This challenging book examines the relationship between cultural images and the formulation, administration and impact of US social policy on Black women. The author focuses specifically on methods by which individuals in the USA who control social institutions – in particular the mass media – operate to retain their own power advantage while at the same time maintaining African American women in a socially and economically depressed state.

K. Sue Jewell argues that the mass media play an important role in maintaining a social hierarchy of discrimination because it is the primary vehicle by which ideology is transmitted through news and entertainment. She explains how the mass media, controlled by the nation's power elite, transmit images of African American women that suggest that their values, beliefs and behaviors (and not race, gender and class inequality) are responsible for their limited access to social resources and institutions. She goes on to consider how this situation can be changed and proposes strategies for accomplishing social transformation and a reallocation of resources. She argues that the main obstacle to those wanting change is fear of reprisals from the privileged elite and their functionaries.

Fearless and passionate, and copiously supported with evidence, the book is an important contribution to our knowledge of the role of the mass media in the development of cultural imagery and its influence on US social policy. It will be of immense interest to students of media, the sociology of gender and race, and social policy.

K. Sue Jewell is Assistant Professor of Sociology in the Department of Black Studies at The Ohio State University.

FROM MAMMY TO MISS AMERICA AND BEYOND

Cultural images and the shaping
of US social policy

K. Sue Jewell

London and New York

First published in 1993
by Routledge
11 New Fetter Lane, London EC4P 4EE

Simultaneously published in the USA and Canada
by Routledge
a division of Routledge, Chapman and Hall, Inc.
29 West 35th Street, New York, NY 10001

Typeset in Baskerville by LaserScript, Mitcham, Surrey
Printed and bound in Great Britain by
Biddles Ltd, Guildford and King's Lynn

British Library Cataloguing in Publication Data
A catalogue record for this book is available from the British Library.

Library of Congress Cataloging in Publication Data
Jewell, K. Sue.
From mammy to Miss America and beyond: cultural images and the
shaping of US social policy/K. Sue Jewell.
p. cm.
Includes bibliographical references and index.
1. Afro-American women. 2. United States – Social policy – 1980–
I. Title.
E185.86.J48 1993
305.48′896073–dc20   92-11917
CIP

ISBN 0–415–08777–5
0–415–04253–4 (pbk)

To my wonderful and supportive parents,
Henry and Valerie Warren

CONTENTS

PREFACE

The focus of this book is on how those who occupy a position of power and privilege have established a social hierarchy of discrimination in which African American women have been consigned to the lowest stratum. An individual's position on this hierarchy, I contend, determines the person's access to relative rewards and the extent to which an individual is confronted with barriers (i.e. institutional discrimination) that serve to militate against acquiring societal rewards. I also believe that individuals positioned higher on the hierarchy have greater access to societal rewards and face fewer institutional barriers which preclude them from obtaining these rewards; those, like African American women, who are located in the lowest stratum of the hierarchy have limited access to societal rewards and face relatively more structural barriers which make the acquisition of societal rewards more difficult, and frequently impossible. It is my belief that race, gender and class are the primary determinants of one's position on the social hierarchy of discrimination.

Central to this book is an analysis of how the privileged in the United States control societal institutions, particularly the mass media, in order to maintain their monopoly on wealth and power, while keeping African American women in a socially and economically depressed state.

The mass media play an important role in maintaining a social hierarchy of discrimination as they are the chief vehicles by which ideology is transmitted through information and imagery. Technologically advanced societies such as the United States rely on more than force, but employ ideological hegemony to maintain a system of inequality through the consensus of the masses. In effect, mainstream media have historically served the interests of the privileged, who have defined African American women and other disenfranchised segments of the population as possessing certain values, belief systems and lifestyles that do not entitle them to receive societal resources, but account for their marginal status in salient societal institutions.

In this book I am not suggesting that the privileged in the United States do not use force, for such is certainly not the case. On the contrary, those in power and their designates have acquired and maintained control over societal resources through an established tradition of force, using any means necessary, which they have historically ascribed to those to whom they have assigned the label "radical" or, in the case of African Americans, "militant." It is quite the case that the privileged in America firmly embrace the postulate, "Win at all costs." To this group, any loss, irrespective of how minuscule it may appear to others, threatens the very existence of their monopoly on wealth and power.

Essentially, this book examines how and why those who constitute the country's power elite have constructed and maintained negative and nonrepresentative images of African American women, and how they have used and continue to use the mass media to proliferate these images which contain myths, stereotypes and assumptions that are intended to denigrate and exclude African American women from mainstream institutions and societal resources. I also explore the relationship between ideological hegemony and the effectiveness of gender-oriented social policy relative to African American women.

Finally, I propose solutions to the marginal status of African American women and their community. While employing these proposals requires one to be an activist, to understand and appreciate these solutions one need only be what I call an "equitist." That is, one must do more than embrace a philosophy of equality for all people but must be personally committed to this precept, so much so that one becomes disconcerted when institutional policies and practices, as well as individual and collective behavior, result in the unfair treatment of an individual or group of individuals. In other words, the sheer knowledge that a person has been treated unfairly should evoke a sense of disappointment and consternation, as well as a feeling that some action should be taken to correct the injustice that has taken place and to prevent the occurrence of future inequities.

It seems tenable that one must reach a certain level of social consciousness to be self-described as an equitist before becoming a social activist, as the latter dictates action and not simply attitude. Over the past thirty years, African American women and other marginal groups of individuals have increased their level of participation in societal institutions. And, although they have generally remained outside policy-making positions, they have acquired critical information regarding how systems operate and the fallacies and assumptions that support the operation of these institutions. These groups have learned that they are not intellectually or culturally inferior, and also that those who have historically occupied positions of authority, controlling the vast economic wealth and political power in the United States, are not innately superior, as they have maintained. It is therefore incumbent upon African American women and other marginal groups to continue to redefine their experiences, values, beliefs and collective expectations.

Equally important, as African American women continue to challenge institutional inequality, they must do so by enlisting the support of other disenfranchised groups, and include the use of alternative information networks in their strategies for societal transformation. For it is through these non-mainstream venues that the ideologies, policies and practices, with their inequities, irregularities and inconsistencies, that enable the privileged to maintain a monopoly on the nation's power and wealth can be exposed. Moreover, it is the systematic exposure of irregularities, inconsistencies and inequities that will erode the power base and monopoly of economic wealth of the privileged, and ultimately lead to a more equitable distribution of societal resources, thereby enhancing the socioeconomic status of African American women and their community.

ACKNOWLEDGEMENTS

I would like to thank the editor Chris Rojek for his patience and assistance during the preparation of this manuscript. I would also like to express my gratitude to Professor Jon Lockard for his willingness to permit me to include his artwork in this book and to Professor Murry DePillars for permission to include his artwork on the cover.

Finally, I wish to express my sincere appreciation to Henry Warren, Valerie Warren, Kathy Warren, Michael Warren, SiSi Jewell and Curtis T. Jewell II for their tremendous support during the entire preparation of this manuscript. I am extremely grateful for their patience and understanding, which has contributed immensely to the completion of this book.

1

THE STATUS OF AFRICAN AMERICAN WOMEN

The role of ideology and mythology

The purpose of this book is to examine factors that contribute to the social, political, economic, legal and educational disenfranchisement of African American women. Specific attention is focused on the structures and dynamics in the United States that result in African American women remaining on the periphery of mainstream society. Specifically, I examine how the privileged class uses images and ideology to maintain its social power and economic wealth, while consigning African American women to a depressed socioeconomic status. I argue that those who have a monopoly on power and wealth use the mass media and societal institutions to ensure their privileged status through the maintenance of various systems of domination (i.e. race, sex and class inequality).

Many have attempted to explain the marginality of African American women, and other groups such as African American men, Native Americans, Chicanos and poor Whites, by examining social dislocations such as poverty, unemployment, school dropout rates, out-of-wedlock pregnancy and so forth. Explanatory models that explicate the exclusion of African American women and members of their community using these factors and conditions tend to arrive at strategies for resolving such conditions that are highly ineffective. In addition, they lend themselves to social policies and programs that are incapable of significantly improving the level of participation of African American women, men and children in salient institutions in American society. One of the consequences of this approach is that it raises false hopes among African American women and other disenfranchised groups. Equally alarming is that failed social policies and programs are viewed by Whites as indicators that African American women and members

1

of their community cannot succeed even with the help of government-funded programs and a national social policy designed to remedy past and ongoing injustices.

This approach to eradicating the societal ills that confront African American women, men and children is not without some merit. Certainly, those who believe that education, social policies and laws alone will make marked improvements in the socio-economic status of African American women and their community base their convictions on the history of other racial and ethnic groups that they believe have achieved through these measures. Another more plausible explanation for subscribing to the premise that the acquisition of education, the formulation of social policies and the passage of laws, in our existing social system, will lead to the elevation of an entire disenfranchised group is because those in power establish that such a correlation exists. These measures tend to have a greater impact on individuals than on groups of individuals. Moreover, during and after the Civil Rights Movement, these initiatives had a greater impact on those African Americans who were already experiencing higher levels of participation in microcultural systems than on individuals who were outside these systems. African American women who had already begun to attend historically Black colleges benefited more from affirmative action, college grants and low-interest loans than African Americans who had little knowledge of, or participation in, such systems. Therefore, these efforts have had a differential impact on African Americans depending on their class and previous experience with accessing certain institutions either at the microcultural or macrocultural level.

It is doubtful that such initiatives alone will ever elevate African Americans as a group, because the problem that results in low levels of educational achievement, unemployment, poverty and a myriad of other problems also influences the nature of social policies and laws that are instituted. These policies, laws and practices are not designed to improve substantially the life chances of African American women and other members of their community. Rather, social policies, laws and societal institutions are intentionally designed to benefit the privileged class. Other groups who benefit from these policies do so because their race, gender and class result in their access to more societal resources. Perhaps the most common reason that individuals embrace these proposals, which focus almost exclusively on eradicating poverty, increasing levels of educational achievement and establishing social policies and laws, as necessary requisites for elevating the status of African American women and their community, is fear. This fear, which is generally suppressed, yet tends to temper activism and the strategies that activists propose to elevate the status of African American women and others, stems from the knowledge that if the real problem, that of controlling societal resources and maintaining systems of domination, is challenged, the solution becomes one of revolution rather than reform. In other words, when the goal is for African American women to achieve equality with White men in a capitalist society then another group must emerge as a replacement for African American women. Based on the prevailing ideology, there must always be groups who dominate and those who are dominated. It is believed that these elements are essential to maintain a system of competitive individualism. According to this belief – which is the foundation that supports capitalism – systems of domination breed competition, which serves as an incentive for production. Hence, should African American women achieve equality, they will be required to exploit, oppress and discriminate against another group of individuals. However, if the goal of African American women is to help construct a society where resources are allocated based on individual need and the contributions that individuals make toward creating and maintaining resources, then society must undergo monumental change. Thus, the goal for African American women, and others who seek equality for all people as well as an equitable allocation of resources, is one of societal transformation rather than reformation. The former requires eradicating stereotypes, dispelling myths and supplanting ideologies which serve as the basis for patriarchy and other systems of domination.

Many who pursue temporary and rudimentary approaches to improving the life chances of African American women and their communities do so understanding that those who have a monopoly on, and control of, power will use any means necessary to maintain their power advantage. These activists are willing to bargain and negotiate with the privileged for minor concessions, recognizing that efforts to improve significantly the life chances of African Americans will result in a major reallocation of societal resources; and a societal metamorphosis. Realistically, such an overhaul in the social system transcends the United States and the

North American continent, as it is international in scope. Dismantling the political machine that places and sustains the nation's power and wealth in the hands of a small number of individuals requires social revolution and not merely social reform. There are many who are honest, albeit naive, in believing that African American women and their community will reach parity with White males if they simply achieve a higher level of education or successfully complete job-training programs. These individuals, like the masses of Americans, are the victims of ideological hegemony in that they have been inculcated, with the effective aid of the mass media, with a belief in meritocracy. That is, the belief that an individual's rewards are commensurate with her investment. However, an individual's capacity to invest or produce is determined by certain ascribed qualities such as race, gender, family background and class, as well as achieved attributes like education and occupation. Further, those who accept this ideology ignore the fact that our social system is pre-established, with a reward structure that allocates resources based more on ascribed than achieved qualities. This line of reasoning also presupposes the fallacy that all White males are treated as equals, and includes a belief in fairness and equality. I do not accept the premise that African American women and their community will experience significant social, economic, political and educational opportunities simply by addressing symptoms of problems such as those already stated.

It is my belief that the problem confronting African American women and members of their community is the fact that a paucity of individuals in the United States have a monopoly on power and wealth.[1] Moreover, this privileged class, in constructing a system to maintain its power, has developed a belief system to explain the differential access and acquisition of various societal groups to resources and institutions in the United States. This belief system uses race, gender and class to explain achievement and why different groups of individuals have more or less access to wealth and power. In effect, race, ethnicity, gender and class are the primary factors that are used to explain differential access to societal resources. These same qualities have also become systems of division and domination which protect the interests of those who mediate societal resources and institutions.

Accordingly, Thompson states that, "ideology is more than a world view, value system or set of beliefs which members of a

4

society hold in common and which thereby serves to guarantee or underwrite the cohesion of the social order. In the last analysis its most fundamental characteristic is that it serves to maintain relations of power and domination."[2]

That is, an individual's capacity to achieve, and thus to acquire, societal resources is largely determined by racial group membership, gender and social class status. Each of these factors has an ordinal rank, with related values. For example, being male is more highly valued than being female. Race is another factor that produces division among the masses, whereby the privileged assign a higher rank to those of European descent than to individuals of non-European descent. Variations in rank are highly delineated relative to ethnic background, race and class. The social scientist's broad delineations of social class have become further divided and assigned values. Hence, the traditional three class divisions of lower, middle and upper have become further delineated into six categories, whereby each class has been further subdivided into three classes. For instance, the middle class contains the lower-middle class, the middle-middle class and the upper-middle class. Such a delineation, based on the Weberian model of defining class on the basis of life chances and values possessed by each class within the broader class, has questionable utility for scientific purposes.[3] However, this stratification system and related typologies are quite useful to the privileged who employ these models to explain why certain individuals, depending on their race, ethnic background, gender and class, have greater access to societal resources and therefore occupy higher strata because they possess certain qualities (belief, values, abilities, etc.) that those in lower strata do not possess.

These typologies also serve to divide and factionalize the masses. Essentially, those who mediate societal institutions and monopolize society's resources have developed and proliferated a belief system that supports the differential distribution of wealth and power in the United States. In effect, the privileged maintain their power and wealth by establishing a number of artificial factors and conditions that create dissension among the masses. They do so by constructing a social hierarchy of discrimination where individuals higher on the hierarchy, with whom they are more closely aligned, have relatively more access to societal resources and institutions than those who are placed lower on this hierarchy.[4] The myths and stereotypes that constitute this belief system are developed by the privileged to ensure that those outside the privileged class do not recognize their commonality and direct their dissatisfaction and disillusionment to those who control society's resources and institutions. Instead, because of these divisions, individuals with certain qualities, generally ascribed characteristics, are the functionaries who help to maintain systems of domination. These functionaries perceive themselves to be of greater worth than those who are positioned in what are defined as lower strata. Further, these functionaries, with attributes of race, gender and class which predetermine their self-worth, attempt to wield power and domination over those who possess qualities predefined as inferior. In so doing, they protect the power and wealth of the elite as well as their own relative power and material advantages.

The structures and functions that the privileged use to reinforce and perpetuate the social system, and that grant certain groups greater access to societal resources and institutions than others, require ongoing scrutiny and scientific investigation. It is this social order that places African American women at the very bottom of the social hierarchy of discrimination. In other words, who has a legitimate right to benefit from various societal resources? Although many questions are raised by the conceptualization of a social hierarchy of discrimination, one of the most crucial is: why are African American women located at the lowest rung of the hierarchy?

I believe that the determination of positioning on the social hierarchy of discrimination is based on how closely individuals approximate the race and gender of the privileged class. Some scholars suggest that the privileged class's predilection for those who resemble them is based on their desire to propagate or clone themselves.[5] According to this theory, the more a group of individuals resembles those in power the greater the likelihood that cloning can occur. Colloquially stated, like is attracted to like. Therefore, White males occupying different social classes are positioned below the highest class of White males, those who have a monopoly on power and wealth. Next, males of color are stratified according to ethnicity and skin color, with those of lighter complexion placed higher in this hierarchy than their darker-complexioned counterparts. This group is followed by White females, who share a common race with men of privilege. On the lowest level of the hierarchy are females of color who are also stratified. Like their male counterparts, ethnicity and skin color are determinants of positioning for this group. Clearly, African American women have the least common physical attributes in terms of race and gender, compared to White men who belong to the privileged class. There are, however, similarities between the privileged class's perceptions of African American women and themsleves in terms of emotional make-up, such as assertiveness, decisiveness, independence and their task orientation, meaning their determination to accomplish goals. And it is on this basis that African American women challenge the authority and privilege of, and represent a threat to, those who occupy the highest position on this hierarchy, the privileged White male. C. Wright Mills argued that members of the power elite at the top of the hierarchy have similar backgrounds. He said that because of their common characteristics and experiences they tend to trust each other, that their trust for each other increases with ongoing interaction, and that their continued association cements what they believe they have in common. Mills also believed that the power elite which is at the "top of modern society is increasingly unified and often seems willfully coordinated."[6] It should be noted that those who control power and wealth can also become victims of discrimination. However, when this occurs the perpetrators are more likely to be individuals who share their victims' power advantage, and not institutions.

THE MYTH OF MERITOCRACY

Historically, little emphasis has been placed on the use of a schema such as this to differentiate relative degrees of power and wealth. Such sophisticated mechanisms of domination are not a necessity until a society reaches the stage of development where there is a growing disparity between the upper and middle classes and those who live in abject poverty. In effect, when a society reaches a level of economic development that requires the specialized labor of its workers, pseudo-social classes, such as the working class and middle class, emerge and expand. In a capitalist society differential incentives or rewards are provided to members of these different classes, determined by the privileged class's valuation of their labor. The maintenance of such a social system is facilitated through the use of various systems of domination that include class stratification as well as other artificial divisions based on race and gender. It is also the case that force and the threat of force continue to be employed when necessary to bring about conformity and to maintain the social order. Prior to a society reaching this developmental stage, the privileged class relies more on the use of force and the threat of force to maintain its control over societal resources and to ensure conformity among the masses.

According to Gersh, it was not until the late nineteenth century, with rapid industrialization, that the disparity between the rapidly growing upper and middle classes and those experiencing dire poverty became enormous and visible.[7] It was during this period that those who were benefiting immensely from an inequitable distribution of society's resources, through the exploitation of the labor of the poverty class, realized that it was imperative to develop explanations for their wealth and the poverty of the masses. The poor claimed that they were being exploited. The wealthy proferred other explanations to counter claims by the country's poor that their labor was being exploited. In effect, those who were garnering an inordinate amount of society's resources argued that their material and monetary advantage was attributable to higher levels of intelligence and to virtues that were absent among the lower classes and non-European peoples, including African American women. Essentially, the privileged maintained that achievement, based on merit, was the basis for the fact that some individuals had greater access to, and acquisition of, societal resources than others. In addition to advancing this premise, the privileged provided financial support for the development of instruments such as standardized tests that, by design, validated this assumption.[8] Asante, employing an Afrocentric conceptual model, argues that the idea of the inferiority of non-European people, particularly Africans, was a part of European thought as early as the seventeenth century.[9]

IDEOLOGICAL HEGEMONY: A COVERT METHOD OF SOCIAL CONTROL

Gramsci's notion that ideological hegemony, and not the traditional use of arms, is the preferred method by which developed societies maintain an unjust social order has a great deal of utility in the United States and in other Western nations.[10] Gitlin discusses Gramsci's explanation of hegemony in the following statement:

Hegemony is a ruling class's (or alliance's) domination of subordinate classes and groups through the elaboration and penetration of ideology (ideas and assumptions) into their common sense and everyday practice: it is the systematic (but not necessarily or even usually deliberate) engineering of mass consent to establish order. No hard and fast line can be drawn between the mechanisms of hegemony and the mechanisms of coercion, the hold of hegemony rests on elements of coercion, just as force or coercion over the dominated both presupposes and reinforces elements of hegemony. In any given society, hegemony and coercion are interwoven.[11]

In effect it is through ideological hegemony that those in power control not only the means of production but also the production of ideas. Just as constructing tenable belief systems that enable those in power to rule with the consent of the masses is essential to maintaining an inequitable distribution of society's resources, so proliferating these belief systems is critical as well. It is the primary responsibility of the mass media to assume this latter function. Therefore the media's role in defining the entitlements of African American women and the privileged men who control society's power and wealth, individuals at two polar extremes, is a major focus of this book.

I believe that the mass media, called "consciousness industries" by Becker, are used as an instrument by the privileged to define and legitimize entitlements, by proliferating certain belief systems, based largely on myths and stereotypes.[12] These entitlements refer to the rights of certain groups within society to have greater or lesser access to its resources and institutions. When the populace accept these beliefs about entitlements, they are accepting their predetermined position on a social hierarchy of discrimination. In doing so, they embrace the belief that certain artificially predetermined factors such as race, gender and class are responsible for the stratification of various groups within the hierarchy. They also legitimize the monopoly of power and wealth by the privileged by recognizing and authorizing their right to mediate societal resources and institutions. Basically, the masses give their consent for the privileged to rule and to design social policies and laws that result in their continued monopoly of power and wealth, based primarily on race, gender and class. Accordingly, White males are placed in, and retain, a superordinate position while African American females are consigned to the lowest socioeconomic position in the United States.

In this book I examine how the mass media have systematically portrayed a cultural image of African American women, based on myths and stereotypes, that justifies the limited access that African American women have to societal resources and institutions. In addition, I explore how these cultural images are used to define African American women as a group of individuals who possess qualities that do not entitle them to access to societal resources and participation in salient institutions at a rate comparable to that of the privileged class or those who are positioned higher on the social hierarchy of discrimination.

While it is not the intent of this book to examine the media's portrayal of the privileged or those who are higher on the social hierarchy of discrimination, it is clear that the cultural images of these groups are relatively more favorable than those of African American women and others who derive relatively few benefits in our society. It is extremely important that we examine how belief systems and ideologies serve as the fundamental principle for acquiring and maintaining control over institutions and resources in the contemporary United States. Equally important is the recognition that the privileged, not an amorphous entity commonly referred to as "society," construct these belief systems. In developing these belief systems, a different set of values and norms, established by those in power, is used to interpret cultures and their members. Frequently, the privileged offer incorrect interpretations of the symbols and gestures that exist within specific cultures. Nevertheless, these interpretations are accepted by the masses although they may be rejected by those who belong to these cultural groups. It is usually the case that when members of the privileged class, or their designees, provide differential and even conflicting meanings for symbols and gestures, in contrast with those proffered by the members of these cultures, they do so because it serves their own interest. The systematic portrayal of cultural images that symbolize African American women in a nonrepresentative manner, despite the protestations of African American women and others, can only benefit the producers of such imagery as it conflicts with the interests of African American women and others who object to the nonrepresentativeness and distortions of such portrayals.

Another example of how the privileged, and the social scientists who serve as their functionaries, impose their values and norms on other cultures and expect such definitions and conceptual models to be unchallenged can be found in the historical discussion of female-headed families within the African American community. Prior to the 1960s and 1970s, when African Americans' microcultural values and institutions began to undergo change to conform to those held within the larger society, there were more African retentions such as the extended family and mutual aid networks. These were defined negatively by traditional social scientists using a European American value orientation. In traditional African cultures there exists a parallel which reveals how differential interpretive models have been, and continue to be, incorrectly employed by the privileged and the social scientists who represent their views. In traditional African societies where polygyny occurs, one might enter a compound which contains the homes of several kin. There may be four wives and one husband, each wife and her children occupying a separate house. The husband would also have his own house. If the social scientist visited the compound on a day when the husband was visiting with one wife there would be the appearance of one intact family and four female-headed homes. In the absence of knowledge regarding the mutual sharing of household duties and responsibilities, one might argue that three of the households are female-headed, and that these families cannot function at a level commensurate with that of the nuclear family. In such cases social scientists using this explanatory model are unaware of the role played by what appears to be the absent spouse and kinship and mutual aid networks. Prior to the 1960s and 1970s many African American communities resembled the African compound where single mothers received support from the absent spouse, other male relatives (i.e. fathers, brothers, uncles, etc.) and female relatives and friends. During this period that emphasized mutual dependence and collective responsibility, female single-parent families were able to exchange goods and services with members of their communities. Still, social scientists and policy-makers de-emphasized and often disavowed the role of the nonresidential father and other adult males and females, who made up a strong and reliable informal social support system. This type of conceptualization is common in the literature on the African American family. Such misnomers are common and constitute myths and stereotypes regarding African American culture.

To a large extent, African American families have been

criticized for their sense of community, cooperation and mutual sharing and caring. And with increased assimilation, African American families have been encouraged to establish and maintain nuclear families that are independent and characterized by social isolation akin to the White middle-class ideal nuclear family. The unavailability of the institutional support systems, established and maintained through social policy, that White families receive, along with a sense of alienation and systematic discrimination, have contributed to the disintegration and destabilization of African American two-parent families. Understandably, these factors have led to the increase of African American families maintained by women.

Cultural images of African American women based on stereotypes are at the very foundation of the problem of African American women's limited access to societal resources and institutions. Efforts to redefine the belief systems that are housed within these images must be an integral part of any individual or collective action to eliminate the institutional barriers and resistance that significantly limit African American women's life chances. What I am suggesting is that, when individuals and groups challenge institutions to eliminate barriers that impede the social mobility of African American women, they must do so by challenging the belief systems that maintain the innocence of the privileged and the guilt of African American women and other disenfranchised groups.

Unquestionably, cultural images of African American women convey to the larger society the message that African American women are not entitled to a greater share of resources within American society. This occurs because African American women are portrayed as not possessing the values and virtues that lead to access to resources and institutions. In order to challenge the myths and stereotypes inherent in traditional cultural images of African American women, the inconsistencies and contradictions in the institutional treatment of African American women must be exposed. It is equally important that activists challenge the innocent image of the privileged class and the societal ideology of equality and justice. A close examination of how laws, policies and practices are applied differentially for African American women compared to the privileged and others positioned higher on the social hierarchy of discrimination belies such untruths.

Shelby Steele provides an intriguing discussion of how race

relations between African Americans and Whites are based on a paradigm of innocence and guilt.[13] According to Steele's analysis, power is predicated on innocence, while powerlessness is associated with guilt. This conceptual model is also implicit in the status of the victim. In the study of victimization, the victim is perceived as innocent while the victimizer bears the onus of guilt.[14] It is always in the interest of those who mediate society's resources, as well as the ideas of its members, to maintain their image of innocence. In controlling resources and institutions in society the idea of image implies that the privileged and individuals positioned high on the social hierarchy of discrimination are entitled to the societal rewards that they possess and mediate. And that those with relatively meager resources can only blame themselves for occupying an economically depressed position, because it is reasoned that they lack the qualities that are necessary for greater access to societal institutions and resources. Any efforts to bring about significant social change that will have permanence in improving the status and life chances of African American women and their communities must include efforts to dispel traditional images of innocence and guilt.

This is no easy task for it requires access to, and influence over, one of the primary vehicles that the privileged use to maintain cultural images: namely the mass media. Using non-mainstream media presents other problems. The availability of Black media, such as the Black press and African American owned television and radio stations, and the extent to which they are able to counter the effects of mainstream media, are related to economic factors. Most African American owned media are limited in their effectiveness because of their dependence on advertising dollars from outside the African American communities. To the extent that African American media are able to retain their independence from major corporate advertisers they are in a better position to offer venues for challenging institutions and distorted cultural images. Still, those who have a monopoly on wealth and power will not concede to challenges to the institutions and resources over which they exercise tremendous control. It is therefore imperative that African American women revitalize their networks to provide the necessary support for themselves and others within their communities. Mutual aid networks must also form coalitions with other disenfranchised groups. In addition, it is of paramount importance that self-help networks continue to offer a relentless challenge to the political machine that is responsible for the downward mobility of African American women and the demise of African American institutions. It is within these networks that traditional values and belief systems support African American institutions and collective cooperativism, whereby African American women can establish and maintain unity with others in their community. It is this type of unified effort, based on traditional African values, that cannot easily be coopted or controlled by those with wealth and power.

In this book I discuss how those who monopolize wealth and power influence the mass media, cultural images, social policies and the legal system to maintain their privileged status. When the overt, and covert, methods used by those who monopolize power and wealth in the United States are revealed it becomes apparent that what those outside the sphere of power label an "old boy network" is in reality a political machine.

2

THE SOCIAL
SIGNIFICANCE OF
CULTURAL IMAGERY

Throughout the history of America social policy has been formulated with specific beneficiaries in mind. That is not to say that social policy has been intentionally formulated and implemented for the purpose of excluding certain groups of individuals. Rather, one of the primary goals of social policy is the inclusion of various groups of individuals; it is formulated with specific beneficiaries in mind and may result in meager benefits for other groups of individuals. For the most part, social policy is designed to ensure the provision of goods and services to predetermined groups of individuals. Accordingly, contenders for social and economic resources are quite competitive as they seek to influence social policy decisions. Most do so to enhance further their own socio-economic status.

While special interest groups develop strategies and tactics to influence the formulation of social policy, there is a plethora of other factors, often obscure, that contribute to the development of social policy. Although the literature is replete with diverse analyses of social policy, including factors that contribute to its formulation, implementation, administration and impact, little is written about the latent factors that have a subtle yet profound influence on the construction of social policy. In the absence of such information a thorough understanding of the dynamics that lead to the formulation of US social policy is incomplete. It is also the case that many factors that affect the formulation of US social policy seriously impact upon its implementation. Thus, the extent to which policies and practices are able to produce desired ends is determined largely by factors that are indistinct. There exists a sufficient body of evidence, albeit relatively untapped, that reveals the historic significance of latent factors that are inextricably woven into the construction and implementation of US social policy.[1]

Specifically, the formulation of social policy is based on underlying assumptions about the prospective groups of individuals who are targeted as benefactors. These assumptions tend to define and characterize the moral character, values, beliefs, behaviors and general lifestyle as well as the standard of living of the intended beneficiaries of social policy. Unquestionably, the outcome of such an assessment is that groups of individuals are categorized and labeled as to their legitimacy as beneficiaries of various social policies. While there are social, economic and political advantages to the ordinal ranking of beneficiaries of social policy, these assumptions and beliefs that define whether specific groups of individuals are entitled to benefit from social policy are constructed and proliferated through cultural images, with the aid of the mass media. The extent to which these images persist over time is a function of the media's capacity to purvey imagery that supports or refutes these underlying assumptions and beliefs, and how effectively this is done. In effect, cultural images emerge that can either facilitate or militate against the efforts of certain groups to exert a favorable influence on social policies. Negative imagery purveyed by the mass media can adversely affect the formulation of social policies that can enhance the quality of life for certain segments of the population.

Throughout this chapter I examine how social policy and the mass media have had a profound impact on the socioeconomic status of African American women and their participation in major societal institutions. Specifically, I explore how individuals who monopolize social power and economic wealth have historically formulated social policies and laws to retain their power advantage. Equally important is their use of the mass media to construct and reinforce cultural images that define the extent to which they and other segments of the population, particularly African American women, are entitled to societal resources and benefits that will enhance their socioeconomic status. My thesis is that there are individuals in the United States who have a monopoly on societal resources, and included in the resources and systems over which they have control are the mass media.[2] I also argue that their economic and political power advantage is maintained and enhanced largely through hegemony;[3] that through the effective use of the mass media, groups that control private and public capital establish for themselves and the masses the belief that those in power have a legitimate right to the resources and institutions over which they have a monopoly. They also contend that they are entitled to be beneficiaries of social policies and laws that enable them to retain their power advantage. Clearly, they assure the populace that such policies and laws, which bestow privileges upon the wealthy, are also designed to enhance the lives of the masses. One of the by-products of monopolizing a society's resources is a need to explain why certain persons are wealthy, others live in abject poverty, and the majority of citizens earn modest incomes. One of the most common arguments used by the privileged to explain the unequal allocation of resources in the United States is that certain groups in society have limited resources due to flaws inherent in themselves or in the culture in which they have membership. Therefore, cultural determinism is cited as the primary determining factor in the acquisition of wealth and power.[4] Accordingly, African American women, and members of other racial and ethnic groups, who have limited access to economic wealth and political power have only themselves to blame.

THE ROLE OF THE MASS MEDIA

The mass media become the vehicles by which such information is transmitted. Thus, the mass media, as instruments of those who control private capital, have systematically proliferated cultural images of African American women that attribute their depressed socioeconomic status to individual and cultural deficiencies.[5] Such deficits are said to be an integral component of cultural values, beliefs and behaviors. In other words, the fact that African American women in the United States have not reached parity with other race–sex groups is frequently attributed to individual and cultural shortcomings and not to societal barriers and structural conditions.[6]

The more frequently the mass media purvey cultural images that attribute the socioeconomic status of African American women to their own lifestyle, the more the wider society believes that social policies and legislation are unable to improve their life chances and increase their participation in major societal institutions. In effect, such images, which place culpability on individuals and not institutions, result in the denial that racism, sexism and classism are largely responsible for the status and functioning of African American women in societal institutions. My thesis that groups that mediate societal resources also control the production of ideas is certainly not novel. Marx argued that those who own the means of production also control the production of ideas.[7] To be sure, the most expedient method of maintaining a monopoly on political power and economic wealth, in a capitalistic society that emphasizes freedom and civil liberties over the use of physical force, is with the consent of the masses.[8] Otherwise, power and economic wealth must be forcibly maintained through military might, as in the case of dictatorships. However, in a postindustrial society that is built on the principles of freedom of choice and the will of the people in determining social policy, laws and govern- ance, it is critical that those in power continue to have their power legitimized by the masses. Consequently, as Gramsci argues, hege- mony, the ability of those who have political power to rule based on the consent of the masses, is the vehicle by which the privileged are permitted to establish policies and laws that ensure their power advantage.[9] Receiving the consent of the majority enables those with power to maintain the status quo. This translates into the retention of social power and the authority to continue to influ- ence social policy and legislation, which guarantee the successful competition of certain groups while limiting the ability of African American women to compete for the same prestige goals. Thus, cultural images are embodied with values that establish the extent to which certain groups of individuals have a legitimate right to receive specific societal benefits, goods and services.

The role that the mass media play in proliferating cultural images that define the extent to which various segments of the population are entitled to social policies that will improve their access to, and acquisition of, societal resources cannot be over- emphasized. The media's role in influencing social policy is an area that warrants critical analysis. British researchers and theoreticians have made significant contributions in this area. Considerable attention has been given to the social power of the mass media.[10] In addition, how the mass media affect the proliferation of ideas and images, thereby perpetuating private capital, is another phenomenon which serves to enlighten any analysis of the media's impact on social policy.

It is my thesis that, while those with social power construct disparate cultural images of diverse groups in society, it is the

18

media that is the powerful force responsible for the transmission and perpetuation of these images. And because those who control capital also wield significant control over the mass media through ownership and financial support (i.e. through advertising), the mass media are more likely than not to coalesce the interests of those with power and wealth. Hence, on balance, the mass media have historically demonstrated a propensity for purveying the materially privileged more favorably, while those with access to, and in possession of, meager resources experience relative devaluation based on images projected by the mass media.[11] Because these images include definitions and assumptions regarding the legitimate rights of individuals to benefit from social policies that will enhance their standard of living, the mass media tend to define those with social power as more deserving of the societal resources made available by social policies than members of other socioeconomic classes. Hence, a "continuum of entitlement" is the gauge for determining levels of entitlements for disparate groups of individuals within society. This continuum is the basis for the allotment of societal resources and benefits to groups of individuals. In effect, those controlling capital are at one end of the continuum and defined as the most deserving, while those with the least amount of capital are at the other end of the continuum and defined as the least deserving. The extent to which these groups and those in between (i.e. the middle and working classes) are capable of influencing social policy also decreases as one moves from left to right on the continuum. According to Karenga, people who possess social power shape the world in their own image and interest at the expense of those without power.[12]

Determining which groups possess a monopoly on social power and economic resources is neither capricious nor largely a function of achieved status. Instead, ascribed qualities also significantly influence one's life chances and the likelihood that one will have membership in this privileged class. Perhaps the most salient factors that affect an individual's quality of life, each of which is predetermined at birth, are race, gender and social class. Despite the fact that the literature is replete with debates on the race/class issue, there is substantial evidence that race, class and gender are the interactive factors that significantly affect one's life chances in the United States.[13] Undoubtedly, these factors influence the facility with which one can acquire achieved quality of life indicators such as occupation, income and education. On the other hand, when race, gender and social class are considered in conjunction with occupation, education and income, it is fairly obvious that a social hierarchy of discrimination exists that influences an individual's life chances. While it is commonly believed that the acquisition of social power and economic wealth is a function of the possession of achieved qualities, it is typically the case that those who are materially privileged are first endowed with qualities such as family background, race, gender, class, etc. that are ascribed. It is these qualities that influence their privileged status.

How does a society form ideas, images and definitions about various social classes and the extent to which they are entitled to share society's resources? What are the societal beliefs regarding factors and conditions that contribute to upward mobility? In other words, where does the notion originate that our system of stratification in the United States is predicated on a class rather than a caste system? Clearly, there are favorable cultural images associated with individuals who are members of the upper and middle classes. By contrast, the image of members of the underclass is not one that would be coveted. Sowell states how uncommon it is to hear rich people referred to as "a team of masses" irrespective of how many there are per square mile. He asserts that wealthy Park Avenue neighborhoods are more densely populated than many inner-city slums, yet the former are never labeled or perceived negatively. However, the poor living in highly populated areas are commonly depicted in such an ignominious manner.[14] This is particularly true when accounts are given of conditions that affect African American women and their families living in poverty. Typically, they are depicted by the media as living in inner-city slums, in overcrowded housing that is drug-infested, and with deplorable overall living conditions. Clearly, these images are a function of the high level of visibility of African Americans who are impoverished. Generally, African Americans are more likely to dwell in inner-city urban communities while their White counterparts tend to reside in rural communities. Still, the question must be asked: Why do the media selectively portray African Americans in poverty, an act which perpetuates racial stereotypes and cultural assumptions about African American women and their children who are poor? This is problematic since the work ethic is believed to be the primary basis for acquiring wealth in American society. Accordingly, it is believed that individuals who become wealthy and experience upward mobility do so because of hard work. By contrast, it is commonly assumed that individuals who hold an economically depressed status do not subscribe to a strong work ethic, and that those who are impoverished have a disaffection for work. Thus, a stigma is associated with social and economic programs that are designed to provide America's impoverished with the basic necessities of life. The fact that a sizable percentage of the poor in the United States consists of women and children has done little to reduce society's lack of empathy for those who belong to the underclass. Generally, culpability is attributed to the absent father and the female head for the economic impoverishment of the family. Compounding this problem is race and gender. The fact that a disproportionate number of African American poor families in the United States are headed by women has resulted in an even harsher conception of the poor and African Americans. In fact, there are many in our society who possess a cultural image that identifies all poor people in the United States as African Americans. The accepted cultural image of the typical welfare recipient is the African American mother and her charges.

This negative and distorted conception is largely a function of assumptions that are made about the causes of poverty, namely the absence of a value orientation that includes the work ethic. This conception also includes racial stereotypes that characterize African Americans as individuals who devalue work and do not possess the intellectual faculties that are necessary to secure job skills, employment and the income to climb out of poverty. These images, definitions and labels attribute the depressed socioeconomic status of African American women to the possession of innate qualities and the absence of a work ethic and other prescribed social conventions, such as a strong, viable family structure. Inherent in these cultural images of African American women is the belief that they have a proclivity for performing tasks of domesticity, not in their own families, but working for others. The pervasiveness of the image of African American women eager and content to perform domestic tasks and other affective functions has received adequate treatment in the literature.[15] Associated with this cultural image is a justification for the meager wages earned by African American women, and others, who work as domestics and in predominantly and historically female-dominated occupations. Therefore, it is believed that the subsistence wages received in these low-income-generating occupations

21

are acceptable and augmented by the intrinsic satisfaction derived by women in these positions, and that they are unable to perform well in other occupations. And to legitimize the minuscule wages that African American women receive as domestic servants is the widely accepted notion that African American women have a biological affinity with and a maternal instinct for performing affective functions, such as domestic duties and rearing and caring for their children and those of their employers. Hence, according to the mammy image, the domestic's duties are expected to result in a form of remuneration that provides meager income but is replete with intrinsic rewards. This intangible reward is generally expected to supplement and even counterbalance the low wages that accompany domestic service. This rationale has been used to justify the low wages of African American women, who have historically been overrepresented in domestic service, as well as those who are employed in other low- to moderate-paying female-dominated occupations such as teaching and social work.

While little is agreed upon by social scientists there is consensus that the activities, policies and practices regarding the poor and their treatment in England throughout the sixteenth and seventeenth centuries impacted tremendously on the way in which Americans during the colonial period developed programs to address the needs of society's dependents. The Elizabethan Poor Laws that distinguished between the deserving poor and the undeserving poor, and established local governmental responsibility for caring for the poor, have had a tremendous influence on the societal conception and response to the poor in the United States.[16] Moreover, there is considerable evidence that beliefs that surfaced during the colonial period in America about the causes of poverty continue to exist. That is, during the seventeenth century it was held that poverty in America occurred because of individual misfortune on the part of the head of the household. During that era poverty was a function of occupational hazards, such as working in seafaring, or early death caused by war or diseases, some of which resulted from plagues. Considering poverty a function of misfortune, and economic solvency a consequence of hard work and frugality, is inextricably related to capitalist ideology. Indeed, the liberties, at least in theory, that are characteristic of our free-market system dictate that all people have an equal opportunity to acquire economic wealth based on their own skills and effort. The only exception to this tenet were slaves. The consequence of this ideology is most profoundly manifested in the extent to which society's members believe that individuals who constitute the nation's poor are entitled to receive societal resources to ensure their survival and to improve their socioeconomic status. That is, social welfare policies that are designed to address the needs of the poor are consistently criticized, and not too infrequently condemned. In effect, as long as the poor are seen as being unproductive by choice, because of an aversion to work or limited intellectual capacity, there will continue to be societal resistance to social policies that will be effective in substantially elevating the socioeconomic status of the poor, in general, and African American families headed by women who are engulfed in poverty in particular.

The mass media are vital to the transmission of information that defines favorably those who possess private capital. Moreover, it is the media that perpetuate beliefs about the requisites needed for individuals to acquire and maintain capital. In other words, the mass media influence strongly accepted beliefs regarding why certain individuals are wealthy and others are in abject poverty. These beliefs are deeply embodied in cultural images regarding the various groups of individuals in society, and the mass media are the most impressive and powerful vehicles for the transmission of these cultural images.

The rapid growth in technology in the communications industry has increased the significance of the mass media, particularly the electronic media, in proliferating ideas and images to the masses. The use of television for educational purposes, not to mention programming designed for children and youthful populations, places television in a critical role as a chief socializing agent. Therefore, the mass media become somewhat of an inorganic reference group member. The media can and does validate and legitimize one's relative worth to society, as an individual and a member of a particular racial or ethnic group. Perhaps the most significant aspect of the media's role in constructing images of society's members along the lines of race, ethnic group, gender, social class and other ascribed categories is that it does so using diametrically opposed categories.[17] Collins states that these categories in society are ordinal, meaning that categories are ranked as higher or lower, and better or worse. Thus, certain races are defined as better than others, men are more valued than women, and so forth. These "dichotomous oppositional differences" are subjective and arbitrarily defined by those who control wealth and social power.[18] Once these images are constructed and systematically purveyed by the mass media they become an integral part of American culture.[19] Essentially, the mass media are used to proliferate and legitimize these images. After repeatedly purveying images that characterize groups of individuals in a certain fashion, whether positive or negative, these images become firmly rooted in American culture. Hence, images of societal groups become symbols of those groups and their members. These images gain acceptance by the wider society and, in some cases, by members of the culture to which they are ascribed. Certainly, not all members of any cultural group accept images and definitions that are constructed by individuals who possess power and wealth; yet there is evidence that many of these definitions and images are internalized by members of various cultural groups even when the definitions are negative and adversely affect their status and social and economic well-being.

One reason for the acceptance of cultural imagery defined by those who control wealth and power is the scarcity of imagery constructed by the members of specific cultural groups themselves. When various groups do construct and generate imagery of their own societal group they frequently lack venues for purveying these images to others. Still, as some argue, many cultural images that have been constructed for the purpose of symbolizing various societal groups are accepted by members of those groups primarily because they have differentially defined the meanings associated with the qualities that these images possess.[20] For example, mammy and Aunt Jemima are images that have historically symbolized African American womanhood. While many of the characteristics attributed to these images were defined negatively and carried negative connotations within the larger society, they were not defined as such by African American women themselves. Specifically, the verbal aggressiveness of the mammy and Aunt Jemima images has been defined, by those in society who monopolize wealth, as a masculine characteristic. According to Gilkes, aggression is one characteristic that challenges and threatens patriarchy.[21] Thus, women who manifest aggression are defined negatively. Such definitions are designed to raise doubts about African American women's femininity and womanhood. However, African American women have rejected such definitions. By contrast, aggression is defined as a favorable and necessary quality for the survival of African American women, their families and community. This is particularly true since female-maintained families have evolved as a survival mechanism, and such a familial arrangement with the female as the head of the household requires in part that African American women exhibit aggression to survive and progress. In Chapter 3 a more detailed examination is provided of how the cultural images that symbolize African American womanhood are defined differentially by those with power and wealth (who initially constructed these images) and by the African American women portrayed by these images.

MEDIATING IMAGES AND SOCIETAL RESOURCES

In his writings Marx established quite succinctly the relationship between individuals who control societal resources and their control over the ideas transmitted to the masses.[22] Marx recognized that, in order for a select group of materially privileged people to maintain their control over the means of production, they would also have to mediate the production of ideas. Gramsci also argued that the control of power and wealth is inextricably related to the ability of those in power to maintain their power advantage by gaining the masses' acceptance of why society is stratified, based on certain reasoning.[23] Gramsci advanced the notion that, as societies become more technologically advanced, it is no longer acceptable or feasible for them to maintain their political and material advantage simply by force.[24] Instead, it becomes important for the socially and economically advantaged class to develop a rationale for why different members in society are advantaged while others are disadvantaged. Not only does this affect the acquisition of wealth but its retention as well.

The importance of ideological hegemony cannot be understated as it is responsible in large measure for the stability of the United States government, despite severe economic downturns that adversely affect large segments of the African American and Hispanic populations, and sizable numbers of poor Whites as well. As mentioned earlier, Gersh states that during the period prior to World War I members of the power elite in America felt the mounting pressure from various members of society to explain why there were so few members of the upper class, an expanding middle class and a class of individuals unable to derive anything but meager benefits from their labor.[25] Long before this period, explanations had abounded regarding the enslavement of African Americans and the fact that African American women that were treated as a separate and distinct category with no linkage to their male counterparts. The separateness of African American women that resulted from identifying this group independently of their males was for the purpose of exacting economic profits from their labor independently of their mates. In contrast, European American women were valued along with their children as a family unit based on the husband's ability to produce. Because African American men and women were not expected to derive benefits from their labor but were to generate wealth for their masters, it was not expedient to consider African American women as dependents of anyone other than the slave master or, after emancipation, their employer, for whom they were also expected to generate wealth.

It is of little surprise that the power elite began to justify its wealth and the relative wealth of the middle class as being based on innate intellectual ability, a strong work ethic and frugality. The mass media, especially the print media – magazines, newspapers, books – and later radio and television, were major vehicles for transmitting these theories regarding the unequal distribution of wealth and power in a land of copious resources. Emphasis was placed on intelligence to explain why wealth was disproportionately possessed by certain ethnic groups rather than others. Gender was also an important criterion in determining which individuals were most likely to acquire wealth and social power. But constructing images of various groups in society was not a sufficient tool on its own for legitimizing the wealth and power of a few and the abject poverty of many. To substantiate further the role of intelligence as a determinant of wealth and power, members of the elite provided financial support to, and otherwise commissioned, designated academicians to corroborate their theory that intelligence was the basis of the aristogenic class to which they purported to belong. To do this, the mass media were once again used as a vital instrument for convincing the masses that standardized intelligence tests, which were innovations at the time, provided unequivocal evidence that those who controlled society's resources did so justifiably because of their superior intelligence. Through a process of selecting for inclusion in intelligence tests items that reflected high levels of performance along certain ethnic and gender lines, and excluding questions where performance was higher for disadvantaged members of society, this privileged group developed a rationale for the unequal distribution of wealth and power that continues to be accepted by the vast majority of society's members.[26] Thus, a social hierarchy of discrimination was created and seemingly validated objectively.

Because race, class and gender serve as important criteria for determining power and wealth, African American women and other women of color occupy the lowest social and economic position in the United States. Not surprisingly, African American males are not too far removed from the socially, educationally and economically disenfranchised group of African American women. Interestingly, although cultural images that purport to explain low levels of educational achievement and social and economic mobility for African American women and their male counterparts are accepted by various segments of the population, another important factor has been added in an effort to explain why a growing number of European Americans are economically disadvantaged. The media have systematically informed these individuals that, while intelligence plays a significant role in their limited resources and lack of social mobility, the presence of African Americans in the labor market and throughout American society prevents other members of society from ascending the socioeconomic ladder and enjoying the guarantees provided by the American Constitution and the Bill of Rights. For instance, the American public is regularly exposed to images of African American women as welfare recipients, procreating large numbers of children without the benefit of fathers who are willing and able to care for their offspring. Implicit in these images is the message that through their welfare dependence, African American women are deriving benefits from tax dollars while others are being deprived of societal resources. It is held by those who construct and control the proliferation of cultural images that most members of society are more entitled to the resources they are being denied than are African American women and their children. Using cultural images, those in power have constructed the image of welfare as being primarily an institutional support system for African American females and their charges.

This argument frequently results in a welfare versus warfare debate that has become so inextricably woven into the fabric of our society that it has a most pernicious effect on poor women and their children throughout our society. In effect, in the United

States individuals are forced to choose between supporting system-created dependent women and children or the Department of Defense and its affiliates to ensure the security of the country. And with few exceptions billions of dollars are annually allocated for defense. The reason for this set of priorities is that defense spending results in benefits to the privileged who, through stock ownership, control the corporations that receive government defense contracts.

Imagery and socioeconomic status

Constructing images that provide explicit definitions of who is entitled to what benefits in society is a rather complex undertaking. While many of the tenets of entitlement have remained constant over time, there are changes on the basis of race, ethnicity and gender as to which groups of individuals are entitled to specific societal resources. That is, the basic conditions for amassing large quantities of societal resources are fairly constant. The majority of resources are legitimized for upper class European American males, and other groups are then arranged in terms of entitlements along racial, ethnic, class and gender lines. Greater attention must be paid to how the social hierarchy of discrimination is structured and functions to give certain groups differential access to wealth and power. While there are always examples of a few select individuals who achieve in spite of their relatively low position on the hierarchy, their numbers remain small and relatively insignificant. Still, the privileged point to those individuals who have achieved beyond societal expectations, as examples for others to follow. However, the number of African Americans who experience high degrees of success are insufficient to support the arguments that others within these disadvantaged groups can also experience the same level of success if they are willing to undergo changes in their individual and cultural values, belief systems and behaviors.

Throughout the larger society, images also vary according to social class. Both the print and the electronic media purvey disparate images of men and women who are members of different socioeconomic classes. Cultural images related to social class reflect the presumed values, beliefs and behaviors of individuals who occupy diverse strata. While there are those who question the appropriateness of assessing the value of these images, there is

28

consensus among members of society that certain images are more positive than others. It is fairly obvious that images tend to be more positive when they depict middle and upper class members, while images of the underclass are considered far less positive. The fact that there are positive cultural images along social class lines has a direct bearing on other cultural images. Again, the construction and proliferation of cultural images takes on a greater level of complexity. One of the consequences of the construction of images that define certain groups of individuals as positive, based on social class, is that such images are not interpreted independently. Instead, there are multiple cultural images that symbolize groups of individuals based on their social class, racial and ethnic group, gender and other physical qualities and emotional make-up. Cultural images are also constructed regarding weight, societal definitions of attractiveness, etc. Despite the existence of different cultural images based on membership in diverse groups, images associated with social class are extremely powerful. That is not to say that images related to racial and ethnic group membership are any less impactful on society; however, to the extent that cultural images reflect stratification within various racial and ethnic groups, images take on a more positive quality when individuals who belong to one of the disadvantaged racial or ethnic groups are also members of the middle or upper class. For example, the upper middle class Cosby family is portrayed more favorably than the lower-income families portrayed in the sitcoms "Good Times" or "Sanford and Son." While African American women across all socioeconomic levels experience race, gender and class discrimination, African American lower-income women are likely to be denied more opportunities due to the interlocking effects of race, gender and class than are middle-income African American women.

There are certain fundamental characteristics of the cultural images associated with social class, in that individuals who belong to higher social classes are portrayed by the media as possessing virtues such as hard work, intelligence and moderate consumption that are believed to lend themselves to the acquisition of status symbols that confirm their upper class status. Cultural images are not static; the dynamic nature of cultural images is largely a function of economic exigency. One of the most dynamic images has been that of European American females who have been characterized at different periods in history by their labor market participation. During the development of the frontier in colonial America, during both world wars, in the 1970s and today, cultural images portray White females as workers outside as well as within the home. During other periods in history (1950s and 1960s), American White females were portrayed as housewives. Again, these cultural images have been directly related to the necessity for European American women to contribute to the development and stability of the family and the country. Cultural images of European American women have also been constructed based on social class. Unquestionably, the southern belle, with her social and material advantages, was considered a more positive cultural image than her middle and lower class counterparts.

Throughout the history of America images that symbolize African American women have been distinguished on the basis of age rather than social class. It was not until the decade of the 1980s that media images of African American women differentiated more systematically between working class and upper middle class African American women. Situation comedies were the first television programs that purveyed African American women in middle class environments. Prior to this period middle class African American women were rarely seen on television, with the exception of an occasional program such as "Julia" in 1968. "The Cosby Show," originating in the 1980s, has been credited with setting a precedent by portraying an African American family as members of the upper middle class. Later, "A Different World", a sitcom that evolved from "The Cosby Show," provides a plethora of middle and upper middle class college females and an occasional adult African American female. The characteristics of this new image of African American womanhood are quite similar to those of her White counterpart. Although a detailed discussion of this emergent image is presented in Chapter 3, it is fair to say that the middle and upper middle class African American woman's emotional make-up is decidedly different from that of poor and working class African American women, who have been portrayed as representative of African American women. The physical characteristics of the middle and upper middle class image of African American women are also more consistent with those of the image that symbolizes European American women. Because of this resemblance in terms of physical and emotional make-up, critics have argued that these images, like earlier images depicting African American women, are distorted and unrepresentative of real-life African American women. Aside from cultural images of African American women portrayed on television sitcoms, images are also constructed and purveyed through television via commercials, news, documentaries and special programs.

Imagery and its consequences: perceptions and expectations

The fact that images are assigned different values is of extreme importance when considering the status, availability, accessibility and acquisition of resources by various groups in society. Cultural images of diverse segments of the population not only reflect the extent to which groups possess resources but also reveal, whether real or imagined, how favorably one group compares with others in terms of possessing the requisites to acquire wealth and social power. Another critical function of cultural images is to create certain perceptions and expectations regarding a group's likelihood of contributing to and participating in key societal institutions. One underlying assumption is that certain groups of individuals have made and continue to make greater contributions to society, therefore they are entitled to receive a greater share of the nation's wealth than others, who are perceived either as making a smaller contribution or even as a drain on the social system. Accordingly, individuals belonging to the latter group are perceived as having little personal or social worth and are believed to represent a burden on society.

Cultural images contain definitions of groups of individuals that can be ranked on a continuum according to their degree of positive or negative connotations. In addition, cultural images with their inherent assumptions regarding the physical, emotional and social characteristics of diverse societal groups lend themselves to perceptions and expectations. Therefore, cultural imagery results in individuals developing stereotypic views of different groups of individuals within our society. Whether the cultural images, with their assumptions, are accurate or false has little bearing on the extent to which these images are accepted and internalized by society at large, and by the societal groups that the images purport to represent. It is important to note that these images have a profound influence on the status and functioning of the groups of individuals they define. Further, cultural images contribute to social distance between society's members, making it difficult for those outside the mainstream to develop networks that will

31

increase their access to societal resources. This is especially true if societal groups are separated by different racial and ethnic backgrounds or by social class. W.I. Thomas's statement, that "If men define situations as real, they are real in their consequences," is certainly applicable to the construction and perpetuation of cultural images.[27] In many instances, cultural images of African American women and other disenfranchised groups have been distorted and generally uncharacteristic of individuals belonging to this group; yet these images have had a profound influence on other people's perceptions and expectations of African American women. For example, in spite of the fact that African American women have gradually been abandoning domestic service jobs for clerical and retail sales positions, the media continue to portray African American women performing domestic functions. The shift that is reflected in images of African American women on television is that they are now seen performing tasks of domesticity in their own homes, instead of carrying out domestic duties in the homes of employers, as maids and cooks. This is indeed a shift in role portrayals that transcends social and economic class. Although the African American woman, Claire Huxtable, in "The Cosby Show" is scripted as a lawyer she is rarely seen practicing law but is usually portrayed either in a nurturing role or performing some other affective function in the home. Away from home, Claire is usually seen taking part in a social function or an activity involving her children.

One of the problems associated with those who live and interact outside the cultural groups for which they construct images is their inability and unwillingness to validate such images with the individuals who are being portrayed, even though these cultural images can adversely affect those who are represented by them, as well as other members of society. In the case of the former, when images have little or no empirical correspondence, members of cultural groups that are inaccurately portrayed must develop mechanisms to refute these images and to ensure they are not internalized by impressionable youth. In effect, the negative and distorted images that are systematically purveyed often conflict with and contradict the values, beliefs, norms and behaviors of the societal groups that they are designed to represent. Here the media take on the role of a competing socializing agent. When this occurs, adult members of these groups have the horrendous responsibility of minimizing the effects of the images that the media transmit. This activity of assuaging the impact of negative and inaccurate imagery is crucial since internalizing the characteristics of these images may serve to impede the psychosocial development and cultural group identification of youth. This is particularly confusing since Cooley argued that individuals form their self-concept based on the looking-glass self, seeing oneself as one is viewed by others.[28] Many psychologists in the Africentric school maintain that if African Americans in general, and women in particular, see themselves as they are seen in the media, then it is questionable whether they will develop positive self-concepts and reference group identification. Likewise, images of African American women have also warranted that African American women reject and reconstruct cultural images symbolizing African American womanhood. In so doing, the cultural imagery of African American women is redefined and reconstructed by African American women themselves. Hebdige and others have explored the ways in which disenfranchised groups resist mainstream ideologies, as did African American women before the aftermath of the Civil Rights Movement.[29] Increasingly, African American feminist intellectuals have also been in the vanguard of efforts to replace inaccurate cultural imagery with images of African American women that are more representative of this population.[30] This process has not occurred in any formal, standardized or consistent manner yet it has been effective, mainly because of the informal venues which served as vehicles of communication. Nevertheless, a majority of African American women are seldom provided with an opportunity to participate in redefining the cultural images that are representative of them.

The consequences of inaccurate and negative imagery for members of the societal groups that these images are meant to represent are fairly obvious. Still, there is evidence that African American women rely on informal mechanisms within their own cultural group to construct positive images of themselves. And, as venues for the proliferation of these images are not as numerous within the community of African Americans, informal social support networks are the primary vehicles for the transmission of cultural images of African American women. That is not to say that traditional mainstream cultural images of African American women are not internalized by any African American females. Such a presumption would be untenable. However, it is the case that African American women have historically relied on a strong sisterhood for the construction of cultural images that symbolize African American women. Similarly, they tend to rely on the same source for the formation of their self-concept. The fact that corrective measures have been operative within the African American community, enabling African American women to define and redefine their own cultural images, has little if any impact on the perceptions and expectations of other members of society who have no basis for evaluating cultural images of African American women to determine how accurate and representative thay are.

It is also the case that cultural images influence role expectations. If members of other cultural groups become accustomed to seeing a certain cultural group possessing certain characteristics or engaging in specific behaviors, a role expectation is developed. And validation exists whenever members of the cultural group exhibit the characteristics attributed to them by cultural images constructed by a select group of individuals who control power and wealth. It is alarming when one considers how damaging these images have been in depriving the African American woman of opportunities, societal resources and the recognition of her value as a human being and contributing member of society. One of the results of distorted images of African American women is that other individuals may have difficulty recognizing the inaccuracy of these images, even when they see and interact with African American women whose values, beliefs, behaviors and physical and emotional make-up provide irrefutable contradictions to the cultural images that generally symbolize African American women.

3

CULTURAL IMAGES AS SYMBOLS OF AFRICAN AMERICAN WOMANHOOD

Society is replete with cultural images based on race, ethnicity, gender and class. When race, ethnic background, gender and class are combined, a plethora of diverse cultural images emerges. For example, the cultural image of African American women is different from that of European American women, Hispanic American women, Native American women and Asian American women. It is the case that while cultural images of most racial and ethnic groups have changed over time, the cultural images of African American women have changed only minimally. When changes have occurred they have been slight modifications in physical characteristics, while changes in emotional make-up have been extremely slow to surface. This is true despite the protestations of many groups, including African American feminist scholars, artists, academicians and others who have criticized traditional as well as extant images that symbolize African American womanhood. Most efforts to ensure that cultural images symbolizing African American womanhood have empirical correspondence and are representative of African American women began during the decade of the 1970s. It was during the Civil Rights era that academicians and others challenged the mass media and societal institutions to improve images and adverse social conditions viewed as exploitative and negative relative to the African American community. Because of a predilection for employing African American women, rather than men, in domestic jobs as well as in the movie industry, distorted images of African American women were more pronounced and visible, and African American activists directed their efforts toward demanding that distorted cultural images of African American women be redefined.

Research on cultural images of African American women has revealed that, until the 1980s, there were essentially four categories in which African American women have been portrayed. They are mammy, Aunt Jemima, Sapphire, and Jezebel or the bad-black-girl.[1] While other images of African American women have been purveyed by the media, they have been episodic, whereas the foregoing images have been systematically presented as symbols of African American women, both young and old.

The emergence of new images of African American women during the 1980s was accompanied by two practices. On one hand, the media would introduce more positive and representative images of African American women yet, simultaneously, include one of the old stereotypical images of African American women. The other practice was to introduce an image reflecting the strengths and positive qualities of African American women and then, later, seek to invalidate the positive attributes of this image. Hence, the media were not satisfied with the construction of positive and representative images of African American women but engaged in the destruction of such images, an action which served to validate traditional stereotypic images of African American women. The method by which the mass media became involved in the construction and destruction of images which symbolized African American women was exemplified in their treatment of Vanessa Williams, the first African American woman to be crowned Miss America. This is discussed later in this chapter.

IMAGES AND ORIGINS

Images that symbolize African American womanhood have, with few exceptions, been defined as negative by African American scholars.[2] These images, which are believed to have evolved during slavery, portray African American women as the antithesis of the American conception of beauty, femininity and womanhood. As such, some argue that the media's efforts to masculinize African American women, assigning them physical attributes and emotional qualities traditionally attributed to males (who possess power and wealth) is directly related to the extent that African American women represent a threat to those in power.[3] This threat to male prerogative is a function of the African American woman's refusal to accept gender roles constructed by men in power and the related positions of subordination to which women, in general, have been consigned. Consequently, the images of African American women that the mass media have purveyed have been diametrically opposed to those that define womanhood in general. It has also been suggested that since these images were constructed during a period of slavery they were designed to invalidate rumors and beliefs that slave owners had an interest in female slaves beyond their capacity to provide manual and reproductive labor. After all, the exaggerated features, comedic quality and masculinized characteristics of these images challenge the assumption that slave owners were sexually attracted and abusive to their female slaves. Generally, when sexual liaisons did occur between the female slave and the slave owner, the compelling image of the bad-black-girl, or Jezebel, was used to explain this relationship. That is, slave owners who privately coerced their female slaves, or surreptitiously offered them harsh alternatives if they were unwilling to submit to their owner's sexual whims, attributed these liaisons to the hypersexuality of the female slave who was purported to be the aggressor or seducer. Therefore, the bad-black-girl image as a symbol of African American women has been used to depict the African American woman as an eager, available and willing sexual partner for her slave owner and for other males, with relative degrees of power and wealth, in American society.

IMAGES OF AFRICAN AMERICAN WOMANHOOD

Mammy

The image of mammy as a symbol of African American womanhood is inextricably integrated into the folklore of American culture.[4] As a symbol of African American womanhood, the image of mammy has been the most pervasive of all images constructed by the privileged and perpetuated by the mass media. Although the image of mammy originated in the South during slavery it has permeated every region of the United States.[5] How and why this image came to symbolize African American womanhood is a pertinent question.

The image of mammy is so deeply rooted in American culture that it can be found in virtually every form of print and visual media. The importance of the mammy image cannot be understated, for it represents the African American female adult just as the bad-black-girl is representative of the African American female youth and young adult. Further, the mammy image serves as the basis for the image of Aunt Jemima, which has also come to

37

characterize a group of African American females who are distinguished by occupation, emotional qualities, physical make-up and behavior.

Historically, the mass media in the United States have portrayed the African American woman in a stereotypic fashion, projecting characteristics of mammy that suggest submissiveness towards her owner (during slavery) or her employer (following emancipation). Moreover, she displays aggressiveness in her relations with other African Americans, particularly males. Other attributes that mammy possesses include physical features that in Western culture are associated with masculinity. Her comportment connotes satisfaction and contentment with her station in life, wherein she is consigned to performing domestic duties.

The evolution of the mammy image can be largely attributed to some female slaves being assigned the arduous responsibility of performing domestic duties for the family of the slave owner. Although female slaves performed a multiplicity of duties on the plantation, from working in the fields as laborers, to assuming the primary duties for the slave owner's household, it is this last function, that became the foundation for imagery that symbolizes African American womanhood. One may ask why this function rather than other forms of labor performed by the female slave, was chosen to represent African American womanhood. There may be many plausible explanations; yet it is clear that portraying African American women as mammies served to challenge critics who argued that slavery was harsh and demeaning. After all, female slaves were depicted as being happy and content with their duties as servants. They were portrayed as having socially acceptable master–servant relationships; and as women they were merely assuming domestic roles which were culturally prescribed for individuals of their gender. All women, even the privileged, were expected to perform some of the duties assigned to mammy. Upper class women and those who were members of the middle and lower classes were expected to be affective, nurturing their husbands and children. Other women in society, who were without material privilege, were expected to assume the same functions as mammy, to contribute to the social and economic survival of their families. The most obvious difference is that female slaves were expected to perform these functions without pay and for a minimum of two families, the slave owner's and their own. Frequently, female slaves also performed domestic duties for unrelated men, women and children residing in the slave quarters. The fact that the image of mammy has some of the qualities genuinely possessed by African American women does not justify the embellishment and distortions of many of the physical attributes of mammy, nor is this a rationale for the systematic portrayal of this image, nor for the fact that it has been generalized to African American women.

When the physical and emotional make-up of mammy is examined it is clear that she is the antithesis of the American conception of womanhood. She is portrayed as an obese African American woman, of dark complexion, with extremely large breasts and buttocks and shining white teeth visibly displayed in a grin. Most portrayals of mammy depict her wearing a drab calico dress or the type of uniform worn by domestics. The former attire was that usually worn by female slaves. The slave owner's investment in caring for slaves was governed by a desire to maximize profits and minimize the costs of slaves' clothing, food and board. Unpretentious clothing, referred to as "Negro clothes," was considered appropriate and expedient for meeting the minimal needs of the female slave and lessening the extent to which she was perceived as a threat to her mistress.[6]

Aside from her plain clothing, mammy was almost always depicted wearing a headscarf, more commonly called a head rag. The headscarf was worn not only by female slaves who worked as domestics but by other female slaves as well. Wish provides considerable insight into the use of headscarfs by female slaves.[7] He states that slaves were provided with clothing on their arrival in America: "Women were given two dresses of striped cotton, three shifts, two pairs of shoes and were supplied with handkerchiefs, which the men frequently and the women nearly always wear on their heads." The fashioning of handkerchiefs into headscarfs can be traced to Africa. The wearing of headgear arises from an African custom that necessitated the covering of the head, particularly in religious ceremonies but also on other occasions.[8]

In a culture that devalues women of large stature, mammy's obesity is responsible, in part, for the comedic nature of the character. Banner's extensive research on the evolution of American standards of beauty reveals that women of large proportions have been considered beautiful during various periods in American history.[9] Nevertheless, women who are extremely overweight are defined as matronly and humorous if they are mature adults, and humorous if they are young adults. In either case, they are not only perceived as humorous but are expected to humor others. Even during periods when women of large stature were defined as attractive, their weight was expected to be proportionate, and not grossly disproportionate as in the case of mammy. Again, there is a differential set of definitions that are culturally determined. Being large in physical stature has been defined as aesthetically appealing during different periods in history and in certain cultures. In developing countries, including many on the continent of Africa, a woman who is large in size is considered affluent and physically attractive. In such instances, being stout reflects one's ability to eat well, which means being financially solvent. Further, in countries where there is widespread poverty, famine and malnutrition, being large symbolizes individual survival as well as upward mobility. Nevertheless, the physical size and make-up of mammy make it highly unlikely that she would conform to any known cultural standard of beauty, femininity or womanhood on the basis of the physical features that have been portrayed by the media in the United States.

Two of mammy's most endowed features are her breasts and buttocks. This should not be surprising as these two qualities are considered desirable, particularly by males, in the United States; and it is a known fact that males who occupy positions of power in our society control societal institutions and influence ideas. Thus, it is fairly obvious why this group has carefully included physical features that it finds appealing in all women. Both breasts and buttocks are enlarged in all images that symbolize womanhood.[10] However, in mammy these features are extremely exaggerated. The unusually large buttocks and embellished breasts place mammy outside the sphere of sexual desirability and into the realm of maternal nurturance. In so doing, it allows the males who constructed this image, and those who accept it, to disavow their sexual interests in African American women. Therefore, when slave owners were sexually involved with female slaves, the implication was that it was the result of the sexual advances of the female slave and not the slave owner. Portraying mammy as an overweight female was not coincidental. Actresses such as Louise Beavers and Hattie McDaniels, African American actresses who portrayed mammy and Aunt Jemima, were selected for these roles for more than their acting ability. In fact, one of the conditions for employment was that they be overweight. According to Bogel, Louise Beavers, who portrayed mammy in the 1920s and 1930s, was forced to consume inordinate quantities of food in order to maintain her weight at 200 pounds. This was necessary in order for her to maintain her acting career, playing mammy roles in movies.[11]

J. A. Rogers' discussion of the European male's fascination with and admiration for the Hottentot Venus provides additional insight into the attribution of oversized breasts and buttocks to mammy. Rogers indicates that the celebrated Hottentot Venus was brought from South Africa and exhibited nude in Europe. He asserts that there was a preoccupation with the large buttocks and breasts of the African females in the culture from which the statue originated. Further, Rogers states that the Hottentot Venus was such a sensation that her projecting buttocks set a fashion trend that culminated in the invention of the bustle, a large pad worn over the hips of European women.[12] So it is no coincidence that mammy is well endowed with large projecting buttocks, although her exaggerated size is generally perceived as an anomaly rather than viewed with admiration.

Mammy's large bosom has been described as a haven or safe comfortable place for men to lay their heads. Verta Mae likens mammy's large bosom to that of popular symbols of womanhood, such as Jayne Mansfield or the Gibson Girl. She contends that mammy is a prototype of the pin-up girl who, like these other images of womanhood in popular culture, is there for the gratification of the privileged males who constructed these images.[13] Verta Mae adds that Gyland Kain, in his poem "The Blue Gorilla", says, "The big ample bosom of mammy is as American as apple pie. And that everybody wants to rest in the big, soft, warm haven of mammy's black bosom."[14]

Another characteristic of mammy are her shiny white teeth, which she displays constantly. The conspicuousness of mammy's teeth can be attributed to several factors. First, during slavery, Europeans and Americans were impressed by the soundness of slaves' teeth. The continuous displaying of teeth, in a grin or smile, suggests satisfaction or contentment, which was important to slave owners. It was customary for slave owners and proponents of slavery to perpetuate the myth that slaves were content with their status; and therefore the institution of slavery was harmless, and even benevolent, since it provided for the material and spiritual needs of those who would otherwise remain uncivilized. This is consistent with Steele's notion of innocence associated with those in power.[15] The sign of contentment represented in mammy's grin, smile or laughter allowed slave owners to maintain their innocence. In so doing the privileged who initiated and controlled the institution of slavery could retain their power, which was predicated in part upon their innocence. Finally, exhibiting one's teeth in the form of a grin, and at inappropriate times, is comedic in nature as it implies a pathetic individual with limited intelligence whose sole purpose for existence is to serve and entertain others.

Europeans expressed curiosity and amazement at the structure and overall good condition of slaves' teeth. This was extremely important to slave dealers and prospective buyers who reasoned that teeth were an indicator of the healthiness of a slave. Gilberto Freye states that considerable rivalry and conflict ensued between the mistress and the female slave because the mistress was frequently jealous of the female slave's teeth.16 In Portugal, female slaves were chosen to be wet-nurses because they met the Portuguese hygienists' standards for good dental hygiene. This occurred during a period where sound teeth were uncommon among the colonists.

The emotional make-up of mammy resembles traditional gender roles associated with masculinity. While she is portrayed as fiercely independent, aggressive and powerful, parameters for mammy's behavior are clearly established. Generally, aggressive behavior tends to be prescribed for mammy's relationships with other African Americans. When mammy is portrayed as a servant to Whites she is not afforded the same liberties; and when she oversteps these boundaries she is reprimanded and remanded to her obsequious status. For example, mammy's verbal assertiveness is tolerated when she is giving advice to her mistress or employer. In such instances she assumes a caring and nurturing role. However, when she is perceived by her mistress or employer as "pushy" she is quickly admonished and returned to her position of submissiveness and subordination. The indignation and presumption that is expressed by mammy towards her mistress and her youthful charges represents the only socially acceptable outlet for her occasional feelings of frustration and discontent. One cannot deny that female slaves who worked in the slave master's house were keenly aware of the role expectations required of them. Still, bruises and scars, sometimes representing permanent disfigurement, are among many indicators that female slaves refused to exhibit the blind loyalty, docility and tractable behavior that characterize the mammy image. On the contrary, slave narratives reveal that many subtle and overt forms of resistance were undertaken by female slaves.

One cannot deny the influence of subliminal messages on young African American females. If young African American females internalize rather than reject these images, they would find it acceptable to emulate the behaviors of mammy. If this had occurred on a large scale whereby African American women were aggressive in the home and timid and submissive in the workplace, it is likely that the progress that African American women have experienced since emancipation, and especially over the past thirty years, would not have been realized.

The primary reason that African American women refused to accept mammy and other cultural images constructed by those in power is that they, unlike many other groups in society, depended little on the privileged to define them until the 1960s and 1970s. Instead, African American women looked to other women, who made up mutual aid networks, to define African American womanhood. Because these networks were comprised of friends, neighbors and kin, African American women were able to give, and receive, ongoing information regarding qualities that contributed to and symbolized African American womanhood. Generally, those qualities referred to being well-groomed, sharing and caring, assuming the primary responsibility for nurturing children, spouses, relatives and friends and ensuring the survival and progress of the race. Although African American women were rarely affected by the definitions of womanhood encompassed by the mammy and other cultural images constructed by privileged males, members of the larger society have been affected by these images. Accordingly, these images have influenced societal perceptions, beliefs and expectations regarding African American women.

The gradual decline of these networks in the aftermath of the Civil Rights Movement raises questions about the influence of external factors on defining African American women. Efforts to revitalize informal social support systems among African American women may counteract external influences and increase the likelihood that African American women will rely more on each other than on those outside their culture to define who they are.

The portrayal of mammy as an individual content with performing tasks of domesticity and caring for the socialization and emotional needs of children and adult family members in her owner's or employer's family, while relegating the needs of her own family, was quite common. Images such as mammy have had historical significance because the occupational choices of African American women were significantly limited until the 1960s, and even today there are still numerous barriers which keep African American women in predominantly female occupations. The belief that African American women provide their most valuable function working in service occupations, particularly as domestics, has been pervasive in the United States. It has long been recognized that occupational choices were severely restricted for African American women until after the Civil Rights Movement. Prior to that time African American women generally had two career choices. They could become a domestic or a teacher. Consequently, African American families forced to make a choice would opt for sending their daughters, rather than their sons, to college. After all, African American males had considerably more occupational choices as skilled and semi-skilled factory workers. Despite relatively high rates of occupational mobility for African American females between 1960 and 1980, they continue to be over-represented in domestic service jobs. In 1980, African American women still accounted for 52 per cent of all private household cleaners and one-fourth of those employed as maids. African American women have experienced upward mobility against seemingly insurmountable odds, by rejecting this and other cultural images and defining and redefining their roles, capabilities and aspirations in society.

African American feminist scholars were among the first to encourage African American women, both within and outside academia, to define and redefine their own values, attitudes and behaviors. In addition, African American women have been encouraged by these same feminist scholars to construct and reconstruct cultural images that are consistent with their own experiences, interests and cultural expectations.

Aunt Jemima

Another cultural image that has historically symbolized African American womanhood is that of Aunt Jemima. This particular image, which evolved from the mammy image, is very similar in terms of appearance. The primary distinction between mammy and Aunt Jemima is that Aunt Jemima's tasks of domesticity are usually limited to those of a cook. She is portrayed as extremely jolly, and, according to Bogel, she is also cantankerous.

44

Sapphire

The similarity between mammy, Aunt Jemima and Sapphire is related more to their emotional make-up than to any other qualities that they possess. The fierce independence of mammy and the cantankerousness of Aunt Jemima, in conjunction with a proclivity for being loquacious, headstrong and omniscient, combine to make up Sapphire.

The Sapphire image of African American womanhood, unlike other images that symbolize African American women, necessitates the presence of an African American male. When the Sapphire image is portrayed it is the African American male who represents the point of contention, in an ongoing verbal dual between Sapphire and the African American male. Her sheer existence is predicated upon the presence of the corrupt African American male whose lack of integrity, and use of cunning and trickery provides her with an opportunity to emasculate him through her use of verbal put-downs. In so doing, Sapphire demonstrates her virtues and morals compared to those of her mate as she exposes the lack of virtues and morals of the African American male. The most notable characteristic of Sapphire is her sassiness which is exceeded only by her verbosity. She is also noted for telling people off, and spouting her opinion in an animated loud manner. Because of her intense expressiveness and hands-on-hip, finger-pointing style, Sapphire is viewed as comedic and is never taken seriously. She usually has an ally, another African American woman who shares many of the same characteristics. Generally, the supporting female character is played by a more mature African American woman who is portrayed as a mammy or Sapphire's mother. African American males, like others in society, usually do not take Sapphire seriously and refer to her constant bossiness by saying, "You're always running your mouth."

The Sapphire image has no specific physical features other than the fact that her complexion is usually brown or dark brown. She is a mature adult whose build is moderate to stout.

The most popular Sapphire image was portrayed by Ernestine Ward, in the Amos and Andy series, who played a character known as Sapphire. Her husband, Kingfish, played by Tim Moore, was the man who fulfilled the male requirement for the Sapphire image in this television series.

Jezebel/the bad-black-girl

Jezebel, more commonly known as the bad-black-girl, is a cultural image that is portrayed as a mulatto or a fair-complexioned African American female, who possesses features that are considered European. Thin lips, long straight hair, slender nose, thin figure and fair complexion are the physical characteristics that make up this image, which conforms more to the American standard of beauty than any of the other images. The bad-black-girl is depicted as alluring, sexually arousing and seductive. She fulfils the sex objectification requirement of White womanhood, although she is portrayed as a less naive, more worldly seductress. The bad-black girl reinforces cultural stereotypes regarding the hypersexuality of the African American female, who yearns for sexual encounters. This image has appeared on television as well as in the movies. In the 1980s Jackee, one of the stars of the television sitcom "227," gained tremendous popularity for her portrayal of the bad-black-girl in her character, Sandra Clark.

The tragic mulatto, discussed by Bogel, played by Dorothy Dandridge and Lena Horne among others, meets all of the requirements of the bad-black-girl. However, she is so close to being White that she attracts a White male who would marry her thus becoming her Prince Charming. The unfortunate revelation is that there are no Black fairy tales with the proverbial happy ending. Consequently, what is tragic is that the mulatto cannot enter into the blissful state of matrimony with her White male suitor because she possesses at least one drop of Black blood.[17]

Many of the aforementioned cultural images that symbolize African American womanhood have undergone some modifications; yet, in spite of the introduction of a few cultural images that reflect the strengths of African American women, these traditional cultural images persist.

It is clear that while there are individuals who conform to these traditional cultural images such images are not representative of African American women as a collective. Moreover, one of the most damaging and adverse effects of these images is that they are portrayed with various qualities that are negatively defined by the privileged who have constructed them; yet many of the same attributes are defined positively by African American women. Because characteristics such as independence, aggressiveness and decisiveness are defined by those in power as qualities associated with masculinity, they are exaggerated and defined negatively when they are associated with images that symbolize African American women. If these attributes did not represent a threat to male privilege they would not be defined negatively by those in power. For example, when aggression is attributed to mammy it is defined as being fiercely independent. In the case of Sapphire, omniscience is reduced to her being a comedic know-it-all, while her verbal aggressiveness is defined as "running-off-at-the-mouth."

Finally, many of the characteristics that mammy possesses such as her attire, shiny white teeth, headscarf and so forth are defined differently depending on the historical time period and culture.

TOWARD POSITIVE CULTURAL IMAGERY

The efforts of those who have argued for critiquing and redefining cultural images of African American womanhood have met with limited success. The most significant visual results were apparent in the 1970s. The mammy and Aunt Jemima images were first to undergo modification. When this occurred there was an increase in the portrayal of the bad-black-girl image.

Interestingly, the increased opportunities for African American actresses were characters in movies that came to be known as blaxploitation films.[18] These movies of drugs, crime and passion in the inner city replaced the traditional films that included African American characters, produced by White film makers. These African American film makers were equally guilty of portraying the same negative cultural images of African American women that had been criticized when the producers were White.

Because of the demands of African American activists, changes in cultural images of African American women were increasingly apparent during the decade of the 1970s. Artists such as Professors Murry DePillars and Jon Lockard had a tremendous impact on the development of positive imagery of African American women. DePillars' depictions of Aunt Jemima and that of Jon Lockard clearly reject the mass media's exploitation and distorted portrayals of African American women.[19] The subtle changes in images of African American women involve their physical characteristics; the emotional make-up of these images has been fairly constant. The exception is the new images introduced in "The Cosby Show" and "A Different World," both Cosby television productions, which emerged during the 1980s. The mammy and Aunt

47

Jemima images were modified in the 1970s. In the case of Aunt Jemima, her complexion was lightened, her size was slightly reduced, her head rag was replaced with a head band and she smiles instead of grins.[20] Again, in the 1980s, Aunt Jemima was modified again by the Quaker Oats company on whose pancake box and other food products her face appears. She is more modernized. The head band was removed and she was reduced in size even more.

Like the Aunt Jemima image, mammy was contemporized as she appeared in television sitcoms. She also became smaller in size and lighter in complexion, and her head rag was removed. Contemporary mammies did not always work for Whites. In the television sitcom "Good Times," Ester Rolle, who played Florida, worked as a domestic for a White family. This program resulted in a spin-off called "Good Times" in which Ester Rolle, as Florida, was the star of a show that focused on her own family which lived in a low-income housing project, yet had good times. In this series she also worked outside the home as a maid. Other contemporary television mammies who had their own families were Theresa Merritt in "That's My Momma", also starring Clifton Davis; Nel Carter who played Nel, a live-in housekeeper for a White male single-parent family in "Gimme A Break;" and Shirley Hemphill in "What's Happening." When still other contemporary mammies emerged, they too exhibited these physical changes and usually retained their occupation as a domestic; yet their emotional qualities remained intact. Modern mammies remained quick-witted and continued to be strongly opinionated. The maid, Florence, played by Marla Gibbs on "The Jeffersons'" offered a new twist in that she worked for an affluent African American family where the husband, George Jefferson, one of the stars of the show played by Sherman Hemsley, was a successful businessman. She was permitted to be verbally aggressive because her employer was an African American male. Also unique was that Florence represented a synthesis of two combined images, that of mammy and Sapphire, and she evoked considerable laughter by constantly putting down and insulting her employer, Mr Jefferson. In this sitcom, Isabel Sanford plays Louise Jefferson, George Jefferson's wife. The character she plays also represents a synthesis of mammy and Aunt Jemima, as she is large in stature, and also of Sapphire, for her verbal put-downs of her husband, George. The other main female character was Helen, played by Roxie Roker, an affluent

African American neighbor whose husband was White. This character did not conform to traditional cultural images of African American women.

During the 1980s Bill Cosby, the comedian and educator, introduced positive imagery of African American women, reflecting numerous strengths such as intelligence, an achievement-orientation, career mobility and warmth. Phylisha Rashaad plays Claire Huxtable, a lawyer, while her husband Cliff, played by Bill Cosby, is an obstetrician. This new image of an African American woman is one in which the character places her family before her profession and enjoys co-parenting with her husband. While the affluence of this upper middle class African American family is not enjoyed by a majority of African American women, nor their mates and children, Hill and Scanzoni's research supports the idea that the values, aspirations and family dynamics of African American families more closely approximate those of the Huxtables than the traditional cultural images of African American women and their families.[21] Because this image is so new, and continues to be overshadowed by traditional cultural images, it is inaccurate to label this new, and infrequently seen, image as one that symbolizes African American womanhood.

Other positive images of young African American females appear in the sitcom "A Different World," also produced by Bill Cosby. The young female characters who appear in this sitcom reflect the strengths of middle class college-aged African American females. Although the young African American females in this sitcom are on a historically Black college campus, their values and behaviors are characteristic of working and middle class African American youth. As stated earlier, other television sitcoms in the 1980s in which African American women are portrayed included "227" and "Family Matters," both of which include at least one traditional image along with images reflecting the strengths and values of African American women. In the 1990s, aside from the Cosby-produced sitcoms, other television sitcoms which portray images of African American women are the series "The Fresh Prince of Bel-Air" and "Roc." In "The Fresh Prince of Bel-Air," Will Smith, a young rapper, stars as the character, Will Smith. Janet Hubert-Whitten who plays his aunt, Aunt Viv, is an upper class African American female who is down to earth, yet maintains a lifestyle unlike that of the average White or African American female. The Banks family, including husband, wife, son and daughter, are far removed from the reality of the overwhelming majority of Americans, irrespective of race or ethnicity. "Roc," by contrast, is a sitcom about an African American family in which Eleanor, a nurse, played by Ella Joyce, is married to Roc, a sanitation worker, played by Charles Dutton. Such families, in which the wife's occupational status exceeds her husband's, while the husband's income generally surpasses his wife's, is not uncommon among African American families.

Changes in the portrayal of African American women on television have been slow to occur and, like progress in other areas, the changes that have occurred are in direct response to the demands and initiatives of African Americans. If it had not been for the efforts of Bill Cosby, the introduction of the first positive images of African American women would not have occurred. The conclusion which can be drawn from this is that, in spite of the ongoing demands that were placed on producers to construct and portray positive images of African American women, there was little positive response until Bill Cosby initiated the construction and portrayal of these images. It is clear that African Americans must continue to play an integral role in challenging negative images and in constructing and purveying positive and constructive cultural images themselves. Despite the ire which the idea of self-help generates among some activists it continues to play a vital role in efforts to effect social change for African American women and their community.

THE BLACK MEDIA

When self-help efforts are considered as a method of improving the portrayal of positive images of African American women, a discussion of the Black media is inevitable. To this end, the role of the Black media in portraying positive and representative images of African American women warrants serious consideration. The Black media have been instrumental in portraying images of African American women that transcend socioeconomic class. However, the Black media, like their White counterparts, have also been criticized for having a predilection for portraying African American women with physical characteristics that conform more to European than African standards of beauty. Moreover, the Black media, particularly African American movie producers, have been challenged for portraying African American women in the image of the bad-black-girl. In 1986 considerable debate ensued over the film *The Color Purple*, which was a highly controversial film depicting African American women and men in stereotypical roles. The theme of the bad-black-girl was portrayed by the character Shug Avery, while the African American male was portrayed as a brute in his conflict-ridden relationships with the characters portrayed by African American women. A growing number of young African American male film producers in the 1990s have also perpetuated the bad-black-girl image in such movies as *Harlem Nights* produced by Eddie Murphy and *A Rage in Harlem* produced by Kerry Boyle and Stephen Wooley. Other film producers such as Spike Lee have also portrayed African American females using the stereotypical bad-black-girl image, as in the case of Lee's film *School Daze*. However, there is room for optimism as young film makers develop higher levels of race consciousness. Such is the case in Spike Lee's film *Jungle Fever* which reflects varied images but includes some positive images of African American women. However, John Singleton's *Boyz n the Hood* depicts the inner-city African American male as disrespectful of African American females, calling them "hoes" and "bitches." Making such statements continues the process of devaluing African American women, and contributes to negative societal perceptions of African American women.

African American women must individually and collectively assume a proactive position, defining and redefining images that are reflective of them. These cultural images must be disseminated throughout the African American community and the larger society. African American women should give recognition to the producers of images that conform to these definitions, and negative sanctions should be imposed on those who continue to portray non-representative and stereotypic images of African American women.

In the main, the Black media have had a tremendous impact on the presentation of balanced and accurate portrayals of African American women. They have done so in spite of limited financial resources and the mass media's constant attack on the legitimacy of the Black media. It is the role of the Black media that has contributed in large measure to reinforcing positive and empirically represent-ative images of African American womanhood. Therefore, it is extremely important that African American women and members of their communities collaborate with the Black media to identify means of ensuring the media's survival. This is particularly important in view of the economic crisis which confronts the Black media and other institutions within the African American community.[22]

THE MEDIA'S ROLE IN THE CONSTRUCTION AND DESTRUCTION OF AN IMAGE: A BLACK MISS AMERICA

On 18 September 1983 it was considered a *fait accompli* that the cultural image of African American women had undergone a permanent 180-degree turn when the first African American woman was crowned the 1984 Miss America. The most coveted title for young women in America was finally bestowed upon Vanessa Williams, an African American female.

African American women expected this precedent-setting event to have a positive effect on every medium that was used as a vehicle to transmit images. Further, many believed that, since an African American woman had been accepted as America's symbol of womanhood, African American women would gain greater acceptance throughout society. While there were those who made reference to Vanessa Williams's European features, it was the first time in American history that an African American woman of any hue had been selected to represent womanhood in the United States. Still, there were individuals who expressed their doubts over the motives of the pageant officials who had bestowed one of the most honorific titles, for a young woman, in the United States upon an African American woman. Some attributed this occurrence to the waning public interest in the Miss America pageant due to the feminist movement's impact on society, whereby beauty pageants are considered demeaning because they reduce women to sexual objects. Others maintained that the sexual revolution of the 1970s had reduced societal guilt and inhibitions, and this had lessened the pageants voyeuristic appeal. Those who advanced these views contended that an African American Miss America was needed to inject enthusiasm and to renew interest in a dying pageant. Despite different explanations for this occurrence, few questioned Vanessa Williams's qualifications in all areas of the competition. It was also common to hear statements regarding other African American women who, in previous years, were also qualified but were not selected to reign as Miss America. Thus, it was generally agreed that the social climate was conducive to Vanessa Williams being the first African American woman to earn this title.

The mainstream media began to portray very positive images of the new Miss America, yet there were many who felt that this historic event was too good to be true. Before the end of her one-year reign, this sentiment or, more aptly stated, this fear was borne out. The media covered Vanessa Williams's activities on almost a daily basis; but near the end of her reign a rumor surfaced that nude photos of a pornographic nature had been taken of Miss Williams prior to her participation in the pageant. The basis for the controversy was the fact that, before contestants could participate, they were required to sign a statement indicating that they had not engaged in behavior that would defile the image of the pageant or conflict with the moral conduct considered appropriate for an individual selected to wear this crown. The rumors continued to spread, aided by the mainstream media, on a daily basis. Simultaneously, pageant administrators assured the public that there was no truth to these rumors. On 23 July 1984, Vanessa Williams met with reporters during a press conference and admitted that the nude photos had been taken but that she had never given consent for their release. The photographs were purchased by Robert Guccione, publisher of *Penthouse* magazine, and later distributed throughout the country in one of the most successful editions ever printed.

Of the many questions that arose regarding the media's role in revealing this information, the most persistent, perhaps because of its rhetorical nature, was whether the same series of events, including media disclosures and financial exploitation, would have occurred if Miss America had been White. A related question was whether the media went on a witch hunt in their efforts to destroy the image they helped to construct. These questions, for which there were no forthcoming answers, did nothing to stem the scathing and hostile verbal attacks initiated and instigated by the mass media. In effect, the mass media that had been successful in constructing a positive image of an African American woman also contributed to the destruction of this image.

Interestingly, the first runner-up in the 1984 Miss America pageant, the year that the first African American held the title of Miss America, was also an African American, Suzette Charles. Therefore, in the remaining two months of Vanessa Williams's reign as Miss America, Suzette Charles wore the Miss America crown. While these months were uneventful for Suzette Charles, the second African American crowned Miss America, the media continued their flagellation of Vanessa Williams during this period.

In the year that followed, subtle and implicit comparisons were made between the 1984 winner and Arlene Wells, the 1985 Miss America, a White female from Utah. The new Miss America was

53

touted to be a paragon of virtue with high moral standards. The pageant was reported to have selected Arlene Wells to elevate the image of the pageant which some suggested had been tainted by Vanessa Williams.[23]

Later in 1990 and 1991, African American women were crowned Miss America. The title was held by Debbye Turner and Marjorie Judith Vincent, respectively. In 1990, the media, through an article in one of the tabloids and later over the wire service, attempted to besmirch the image of Debbye Turner, the 1990 winner of the Miss America pageant. The rumor that she belonged to a religious cult was unable to undermine her reign. This effort to destroy the positive image of the third African American woman to hold the title of Miss America was unsuccessful.

The Black media's handling of the problems that led to Vanessa Williams, the first African American crowned Miss America, abdicating her title was decidedly different than that of the mainstream mass media. There was greater sensitivity to, and support for, Vanessa Williams on the part of the Black media. The supportive nature of the Black media was exemplified by Susan Taylor, editor-in-chief of *Essence*, a magazine oriented toward African American women. In her commentary, Susan Taylor offered the understanding and support that is characteristic of the sisterhood and mutual aid network established by African American women.[24] This type of media coverage, which provided factual, nonjudgemental information, also emphasized that Vanessa Williams did possess strengths, most of which were being disavowed by the mainstream media. The Black media pointed out that Miss Williams's infallibility in one area should not be interpreted as representing the total person that she was. The Black Media's refusal to contribute to the destruction of Miss Williams's image was supported throughout the African American community. In so doing, the Black media reflected an understanding of the mass media's historical role in using distorted and negative cultural images as symbols of African American women. Therefore, the Black media made a personal statement regarding their continued favorable valuation of Vanesa Williams, and an even broader political statement regarding the maintenance of positive cultural images of African American women.

4

IMAGERY OF AFRICAN AMERICAN WOMANHOOD

Underlying conditions – social and economic considerations

THE ECONOMIC MOTIVE

There are plausible explanations as to why slave owners depicted African American women in four major categories (discussed in the preceding chapter), each the opposite of the American conception of womanhood. In each case cultural images were constructed based on embellished truths, and each image was designed to justify the treatment that African American women received during slavery. Equally important, cultural images of African American women, while generalized to African American women in America, failed to represent accurately the myriad differences in African American women throughout the United States. The purpose of these images was to justify an economic system that was based on slave labor, including the reproductive labor of female slaves. The masculinizing of the African American female occurred in real life, on large plantations and small farms wherever female slaves were found. Sojourner Truth's renowned speech delivered at a women's rights convention in Akron, Ohio, in which she asked the question "Ain't I a woman?", is evidence that where possible the slave owner, unlike the female slave, made little if any distinctions between female and male slaves; particularly those whose labor was confined primarily to the fields.[1] To do so would have mitigated the value of the female slave's labor. If slave masters had recognized gender differences among slaves the treatment of females slaves would have been less harsh. Thus, the assignment of tasks would have reflected the belief that women's labor should be lighter than that of males because of differences in musculature and the traditional conviction that women in general possess less physical strength and endurance than men.

Clearly, such an acknowledgement would have had a profound impact on the division of labor, levels of production and profits derived from slave labor; the economic profitability of slavery did not allow for such a differentiation of gender differences for male and female slaves. Sex stratification relative to the division of labor occurred more frequently in slave quarters, where women performed domestic duties and men worked in non-domestic areas, than in the fields.[2] Similarly, where male and female slaves worked for endless hours as domestics in the master's house, the division of labor was also stratified based on gender.

Essentially, cultural images were constructed by propertied men, and purveyed by the media that they influenced to maintain the system of slavery. The question then becomes why these images were perpetuated following emancipation. It is tenable that the cultural images of African American women were important to the economic order to keep African American women and others outside the economic mainstream. Again, the economic motivation for images that define African American women as domestics, and consign them to perform menial tasks that others in society are reluctant and unwilling to perform, is significant as such images lead to societal perceptions and expectations that African American women who fill occupational positions other than those defined by cultural images are in status-discrepant positions. Along with this argument are underlying assumptions regarding the qualifications of individuals who are in occupations that do not conform to stereotypes that have been given credence by popular imagery. For example, are African American women perceived as qualified to be accountants, lawyers, physicians and college professors?

SOCIAL FACTORS

Aside from the economic motivation theory, cultural images of African American women have a social basis as well. Social stratification in our society is clearly predicated on a number of factors, some of which are ascribed while others are based on achievement. To that end, defining African American women within the four categories, all of which are negatively defined by our society, places the African American woman in a lower social stratum relative to others within the United States. One of the consequences of this rank ordering is that when one examines achievement, conclusions are made as to why certain groups of individuals exist in one stratum rather than another. Thus, assumptions are made that individuals who rank low in terms of social class do not possess the necessary skills, values and belief systems that would enable them to compete successfully for societal goals. This type of reasoning lends itself to the attribution of responsibility for lack of social mobility exclusively to individuals. It does even more than place the onus on socially and economically depressed groups for their failure to acquire culturally defined symbols of success; it exonerates societal institutions and its controllers from any culpability.

It is also the case that some progressive thinkers, like their more conservative counterparts, are likely to identify social explanations for the continued socially depressed status of Black women. Progressives feel that African American women occupy a socially depressed position because they are culturally disadvantaged, and are engulfed in a social system that they are ill-equipped to access. The same logic is advanced by social conservatives, the difference being that progressives believe the government should assume greater responsibility for elevating the status of African American women. By contrast, conservatives place the total responsibility for upward mobility on African American women themselves. Neither progressives nor conservatives recognize the fact that, regardless of the nature and number of skills acquired, and whether African American women accept a mainstream value system, African American women, and other disenfranchised women and persons of color, will continue to remain outside the mainstream until those who control societal institutions become less rigid and more equitable. Assigning African American women to a lower social class relative to men and women of other racial and ethnic groups is evident throughout society. First, African American women occupy the lowest occupational status and income group compared to others in the United States. Second, the social welfare system, which is perhaps the most stigmatized and despised of all government funded programs, is erroneously defined as a system for African American women and their charges. While a detailed examination of the social welfare system and the pejorative connotations associated with African American women recipients is discussed in a later chapter, it should be noted that African American women who are recipients of social welfare services are also defined as contributing to the social, economic and cultural degeneration of American society. Those who place the entire cultural decline on the backs of African American women do so by pointing to concomitants of being in a socially depressed position, i.e. high teenage pregnancy rate, high school dropout rate, delinquency and so forth. Exponents of this perspective extend their argument that African American women are responsible for problems that confront their families and the entire African American community to include the belief that African American women who head families with incomes below the poverty level not only subscribe to but transmit a culture of poverty. To them, African American female-maintained families are pathological and pathogenic.

It should also be noted that the images that symbolize European American women and women who belong to other racial and ethnic groups are not accurate representations of these groups either. In fact there is an abundance of evidence that cultural images of these groups of women have also been constructed with many of the same economic and social motives in mind. Succinctly stated, images of women in general have been developed, according to some, for the purpose of retaining traditional gender role definitions that are necessary to maintain the status quo and, therefore, are unlikely to upset the existing balance of power and economic wealth.

There are yet other social factors that explain why cultural images of African American women are the opposite of definitions of womanhood and fail to conform to definitions that African American women ascribe to the same images.

One fairly obvious result of cultural images that assign African American women to a relatively low social stratum, by virtue of the occupations, behavior, appearance and assumed level of intellectual ability of these images, is that they serve to elevate the status of other groups of individuals in society. It became fairly apparent that the inception of Negro chattel slavery would elevate the status of individuals who had, prior to the introduction of what John Hope Franklin termed this "peculiar institution," themselves occupied a socially depressed status. As such, poor Whites and women in general were elevated, simply by social convention, to a status above the slave. This became increasingly apparent as the abolitionist movement escalated and the poor small farmer, driven out of business and into the mountains by the large planter because of the invention of the cotton gin, joined the abolition movement to end slavery. The small farmer who was forced to move to non-arable land and live in abject poverty, while the large planter continued to amass wealth and live in luxury, became incensed and joined the abolitionist movement. However, the large planter used prejudices that were based on the status differentiation of the small farmer and the slave to cause small farmers to defect from the abolitionist movement. Hiring the small farmer as an overseer of the slaves, the large planter encouraged the small farmer to abandon the abolitionist movement. This strategy was successful and the small farmer recommitted his support for the southern slavocracy. The economic incentive cannot be de-emphasized, however, and neither can the fact that the small farmer's commitment to the abolitionist movement was tenuous simply because of his desire to remain in a stratum above the slave. Without the slavocracy the small farmer would have been forced to return to occupying a lower position within the social system.

Unquestionably, the arbitrary divisions, along the lines of race, gender and social class, established by those who have a monopoly on power and economic wealth, create conflict and divisiveness among groups of individuals whose race, gender and social class are different. In effect, these differences lead to what has already been described as a social hierarchy of discrimination. The conflict that ensues over the allocation and acquisition of societal resources, based on who – according to cultural images, definitions and perceptions – is entitled to these resources, is sufficient to prevent the same groups of individuals from challenging those in power. This same privileged class has cleverly planted the seed of hegemony, and used the mass media to cultivate the hegemonic ideology that certain groups of individuals should have greater access to, and be in possession of a disproportionate amount of, societal resources. They reason falsely that their control over these vast resources occurs because they are innately endowed with certain mental faculties and socially imbued with the cultural values necessary for obtaining and mediating these prestige goals. It is, therefore, no coincidence that service occupations are considered appropriate for African American women; unskilled and semi-skilled labor is considered appropriate for African American males; masonry, carpentry, plumbing and the trades are defined as jobs suitable for working class White males; being a homemaker is defined as appropriate for White females; and high-status positions like physicians, lawyers and business ownership are defined as occupations for White upper class males. While these occupational groupings are gender and race based there are traditional occupations that are gender-specific. For example, nursing, social work and non-college teaching have historically been defined as female occupations. By contrast, the trades, medical doctors, lawyers, judges and college professors were considered male occupations. Cultural images have been very useful in perpetuating cultural beliefs and gender role expectations along these lines. These cultural beliefs are so enmeshed in American society that, in spite of the occupational mobility experienced by women over the past 30 years, when women are in positions historically occupied by men, and men are in occupations dominated by women, they are perceived as being in status-discrepant positions.

Cultural images that reinforce beliefs that certain groups of individuals are entitled to more or less of society's resources simply because of their gender, race or social class serve as the basis for class conflict and also result in order forms of intergroup conflict. Marx, Gramsci and others argue strongly that those with power and wealth deliberately establish these arbitrary divisions for the purpose of creating conflict among society's other contenders for wealth and power. Furthermore, the conflict based on these arbitrarily constructed divisions becomes never-ending as intergroup conflict and competition emerges and is sustained between women and men on the basis of race, ethnicity and class. In addition to intergroup conflict, intragroup conflict and competition are also fueled by cultural images of African American women. To the extent that cultural images that symbolize African American womanhood are accepted by members of the African American community, these images do little to contribute to co-operation, unity, positive reference group orientations and self-concepts. Fortunately, African American women have other sources of cultural definitions and images that emphasize strengths, macrocultural and microcultural contributions and characteristics that, while defined as masculine by the originators of such images, are redefined as positive by African American women.

It is the case, however, that there is a value system, identified earlier by James Weldon Johnson in his *Autobiography of an Ex-Colored Man*, in which light skin color and other features associated with European Americans are more highly valued than the darker complexions and features categorized as African American, within the larger society as well as in the African American community.[3] Johnson's assessment appears to have merit today. It appears that the value imputed to these physical characteristics is economically based, as in the larger society. Accordingly, those women in possession of the most highly valued features, categorized as European American, are the most likely among their cohorts to compete successfully for societal goals. In the United States there is no legal system like that in South Africa, which designates certain civil liberties to people based on racial mixture and apparent skin color; yet, in the United States there has been, and continues to exist, an informal system that rewards African American women whose features and skin color most resemble European Americans. During the civil rights era African Americans engaged themselves in a process of redefining African American qualities and culture. In the aftermath of this period, there remains an acute awareness of how insidious messages continue to define African Americans' qualities, culture and experiences based on European American values, norms and belief systems. There is definitely a need for strategies that will negate the effects of such subtle but forceful messages.

There is some evidence that at least one traditional cultural image of African American womanhood was integrated into African American culture. While there is no official rite of passage for young African American males making the transition from adolescence to adulthood, there are some forms of conduct that characterized this transition prior to, and somewhat following, the Civil Rights Movement. "Playing the dozens" is a part of this process. Today there are still African American youths who engage in the practice known as "playing the dozens." Essentially, verbal gymnastics and duals are an integral component of African American male maturation. While practiced principally by adolescent and young adult African American males, on occasion African American young females and adults engage in verbal dueling. This practice, associated with courtship during slavery, was a method by which young African American male slaves attempted to impress females, by displaying their verbal adeptness at using rhymes, put-downs and comedic forms of jest. Those most adroit with verbal tenacity obviously made the greatest impression on the prospective female paramour. Unlike other forms of verbal dueling, "playing the dozens" is directed more at joking and verbal put-downs of a male's female relatives.[4] Generally, the mother of the males involved in "playing the dozens" becomes the focal point of such verbal sparring.

One example of how images of African American women have had a microcultural influence can be found with the image of Aunt Jemima. One of the most common statements made by young men "playing the dozens" used to be "Hey man, ain't ya' momma on a pancake box?" Stated rapidly this statement sounds like, "Aunt Jemima on a pancake box?" Typically, statements such as this resulted in hilarious laughter and served as the precipitator of the next series or round of verbal put-downs. The phenomenon of "playing the dozens," which was largely a practice for adolescent African American males, transcended all socioeconomic levels within the African American community. Today, this practice is virtually nonexistent among the African American middle class, although it is sometimes practiced by inner-city male youth. It is likely that the Civil Rights Movement and to some extent the feminist movement have resulted in greater sensitivity to, and awareness of, the overt and subtle messages that are inherent in such statements, which were once accepted and even considered comedic yet gain little acceptance today. Racial consciousness may have been raised during the 1960s and 1970s, resulting in the decline of "playing the dozens." Yet the commercialism of the 1980s gave rise to what may have been the last vestige of this practice, when "playing the dozens" eventually gained national visibility among young African Americans and the larger society. This occurred when recording artists in the 1980s produced a hit record entitled "Yo Momma." Like earlier forms of "playing the dozens" that had occurred within the confines of the African American community, this song became a hit throughout the United States. Interestingly, this practice continues today and is most visible in rap music.

Whether such statements about African American womanhood are viewed by the African American males who express them as negative is questionable. It appears that such statements are an integral part of a process of establishing new social boundaries to the relationship between African American mothers and their male children. As the African American youth begins to make the transition from adolescence to adulthood, such statements, sometimes deprecating, redefine the mother–son relationship as one where the son assumes greater independence from, and begins to challenge, female authority. A parallel exists in the process of maturation for African males, a *rite de passage*, in many contemporary African countries. The formal transition involves young males who are taught customs, cultural values and beliefs, and includes circumcision. When the African male completes the ritual his relationship with his mother is no longer the same as it was prior to the ritual. The African son is now in a position to function with greater independence and requires less supervision from his mother. A similar relationship emerges, albeit over a longer period of time, when African American males are in transition from adolescence to adulthood.[5]

Again, while there is little evidence that young African American males who once participated in regularly "playing the dozens" consider this practice denigrating to African American females, it is also the case that not all African American females define such verbal exercises as offensive. The fact that this practice was inextricably woven into the fabric of African American culture suggests that for a large segment of the population verbal put-downs of African American females, mainly mothers, was viewed as comedic and harmless.

It is through African American feminist scholarship that the cultural imagery that finds its locus in popular culture is subjected to critical analysis. Redefining cultural images of African American women is an ongoing process. It is recognized by African American feminist scholars that it is in the interest of African American women to redefine qualities attributed to them that are perceived as threatening to patriarchy. The gradual disappearance of "playing the dozens" is not happenstance. The fact that this practice is engaged in, to a limited degree, by lower-income African American males is likely to be a function of raised levels of social consciousness among the African American working class and middle class. For these groups, there is a greater awareness through formal education that African Americans, both males and females, must examine cultural imagery and behaviors that detract from rather than enhance positive self-concepts and social interaction. However, while the practice of "playing the dozens" occurs infrequently compared to the pre-Civil Rights era, the use of sexual pejoratives to describe African American women has been popularized by some African American male rappers through the record industry. While it has long been recognized that the mass media are important transmitters of cultural images and ideology, the recording industry and its venues, radio, audio and video tapes, records and discs, were certainly not considered likely agents for transmitting cultural images of African American women.

Some African American female rappers have attempted to combat these negative messages as well as to take a proactive approach to redefining African American womanhood. They communicate positive messages regarding self-respect and their expectation for mutual respect in their relationships with others, particularly in male/female relationships.[6]

Some contend that cultural images of African American women are reflective of characteristics that threaten patriarchy. The characteristics that are most likely to challenge the ideology that supports male superordinance, such as strength, endurance, perseverance, the willingness to accept challenges and to compete in the civilian labor market, increase the number of competitors for valuable, yet purportedly scarce, rewards – namely, jobs, collegiate degrees, and other prestige goals of our society. Historically, such values and qualities have been attributed to those who have a monopoly on economic wealth and social power. Others have been said to possess such qualities in varying degrees depending on ascribed variables: gender, race, ethnicity, family background and achieved factors like education, occupation and so forth. The fact that African American women possess characteristics that those who construct cultural images associate with masculinity is primarily a function of their African heritage; African ancestors not only performed the affective functions generally assumed by women – domestic duties, child-rearing, nurturing – but also the instrumental functions, the breadwinning, associated with masculinity. However, it cannot be denied that the harsh realities of slavery and of continued social and economic hardships, due to race, gender and class discrimination, have necessitated that African American women possess qualities such as strength, endurance, problem solving, competition, assertiveness and other traits that ensure their own survival and that of their community. In effect, those who possess power and wealth, because of their desire to allocate societal resources inequitably based on race, gender and social class, are largely responsible for the socioeconomically depressed status that African American women occupy. The ongoing challenges that African American women face as a result of occupying the lowest socioeconomic position have resulted in the African American woman's increased strength and endurance and other qualities that evolve when an organism is involved in an ongoing struggle for survival. Thus, while those who possess economic wealth and social power negatively define the cultural images that symbolize African American womanhood, they define these qualities positively when cultural images symbolic of themselves possess the same characteristics.

The paradox is that as long as African American women must assume responsibilities for themselves and their families, due to a social and economic system that limits opportunities for African American males and females, they will continue to possess the qualities that threaten patriarchy. Clearly, these qualities are not gender-related as they occur naturally in any society. Rather they develop as individuals are placed in situations and positions, either voluntarily or because of circumstances, that warrant skills that will enable them to overcome challenges and obstacles to their survival. Characteristics that are developed and enhanced for the purpose of survival are those that result in an organism having the capacity to protect and provide. The more that individuals must overcome challenges in these two areas the greater the likelihood that these skills and abilities will be developed and manifested. Defining these characteristics negatively by suggesting that they are gender-based will not bring about their extinction. On the contrary, if those who possess power and wealth are interested in ensuring that African American women reject the threatening characteristics that they possess then those in power must eliminate the need for such qualities. To do so, would mean that those who are socially and economically privileged would no longer be able to maintain their advantaged status by limiting the opportunities of others, including African American women.

Even if this were to occur, it is highly unlikely that African American women would lose all characteristics that are threatening to a patriarchal society. The emotional make-up of African American women has evolved and reflects an African retention. And while the African American woman's strength may have become even more heightened by her struggle for survival and social justice, it is still the case that such characteristics have their origin in precolonial African societies, where African women reigned as queens and participated in, and even controlled, industries. However, it would be untenable to suggest that if cultural limitations were lifted from African American women, thereby enabling them to participate more fully, and with greater parity, in societal institutions, then the need for some of the characteristics that African American women possess would not have the same utility. In other words, if African American males had greater opportunities to perform the provider and protector functions, there would be less need for African American women to possess characteristics and skills associated with these functions. However, as long as African American women must assume responsibility for maintaining families, sometimes independently of a husband; challenge employers to adhere to fair standards of employment without regard to race, gender and class; and protest various forms of discrimination in housing and education for their children and themselves, then those in power should anticipate that African American women will continue to possess characteristics that they perceive as a threat to patriarchy.

One of the goals of African American feminism is the task of redefining cultural imagery that symbolizes African American women. In addition, critiquing, criticizing and replacing the Western ideology that provides a rationale for the hierarchical system of status, wealth and power, based on race, gender and social class, is a task that all African American women must undertake. One of the major initiatives of African American feminism is not simply responding to normative paradigms that characterize African American women as pathological, but formulating an African American feminist ideology.[7] It has long been recognized that developing an African American feminist ideology that reflects the values, belief systems and world view of African American women is essential. While it is important to identify limitations of existing feminist thought and the extent to which it is reflective of African American women's needs and interests, African American women are continuing to move forward with developing and refining an ideology that presents the values, beliefs, norms and experiences of African American women. A primary component of developing an African American feminist ideology is rejecting traditional cultural images of African American women with their inherent negative definitions. One of the most positive aspects of this undertaking is the collective recognition among African American feminist scholars that many of the qualities that have been attributed to African American women – aggressiveness, independence, and being task-oriented – are positive. In the past, African American women, on an individual basis, have not denied that they possessed characteristics that are defined as masculine, according to Western culture's definitions of masculinity. They simply do not accept this definition that has been imposed by those outside their culture. The task of African American feminists and women throughout the United States is to develop an ideology that not only rejects the notion that African American women must conform to a culturally constructed model of womanhood, based on Western ideology, but to establish tenets and a philosophy of African American womanhood. The quest for equality, along with the capacity to exhibit aggression, independence, mutual sharing and collective responsibility, understanding and an unfettered determination to validate her accomplishments, in spite of institutional resistance, points to the uniqueness of African American women. Certainly, their history, contemporary experiences and status do not place them in the dependent and helpless category of the "lady." Equally, their compassionate and empathic qualities are not captured in the term "woman", once used interchangeably with "wench" to address the female slave of African descent. Instead, African American females, with their resilience and commitment to assuage the pains of struggle and oppression for themselves and their communities, are more appropriately called gentlewomen.

Increased levels of race and gender consciousness contribute immensely to the growing awareness among African American women of the impact that cultural images of African American womanhood have on social interaction with individuals internal and external to the African American community. I have discussed elsewhere how internalizing negative cultural images of African American men and women can have a divisive effect on male/female relationships among African Americans. Moreover, cultural images of African American women have also served as the basis for establishing employment standards for African American professional women. Dumas's research reveals that African American female professionals are expected to include nurturing tasks and related affective functions in their professional job responsibilities.[8] These additional responsibilities are likely to contribute to work-overload and burnout and adversely affect how well they perform, for which they are employed and evaluated. In this way the mammy image gives rise to unrealistic and counterproductive employer expectations of African American professional women. In spite of the fact that cultural images of African American women appear to impact upon microcultural male/female relationships as well as employer and co-worker expectations of African American women professionals, they have had a negligible effect on the self-esteem of African American women.

The fact that African American women have been able to insulate themselves from negative cultural imagery is both admirable and astonishing. The ability to reject cultural imagery that systematically reveals that members of a particular group, by virtue of their race, gender and class, do not meet the necessary requirements to be defined as valued members of that group cannot be taken casually. African American women's refusal to capitulate to Western culture's image of African American womanhood is no minor accomplishment. If African American women did not have strong social networks, kinship bonds and a history of defining self-esteem that is based primarily on a reference group comprised mainly of other African American women, it is likely that they would have attempted a transformation in their emotional make-up, whereby they would have replaced qualities that Western culture associates with masculinity with those that are said to represent the Western conception of womanhood.

The mutual support and reinforcement that African American women maintain can be observed on a daily basis as they interact with each other. The discourse between friends and even acquaintances is generally uplifting and supportive. African American women, young and old, are complimentary in their discourse. They frequently invoke a social closeness by interacting in close physical propinquity, touching and offering positive compliments to each other about the most minute accomplishments. The words "girl," "honey" and "girlfriend" are frequently used by African American women when addressing each other. These forms of address are expanded depending on the popular culture. For example, "diva" is a term which surfaced in the 1980s and 1990s and African American women sometimes address each other in this fashion. For example, a friend may call another friend on the telephone and begin the conversation with "Hi, diva, what are you doing today?" While adult African American women acknowledge and respect the maturity and wisdom of each other they systematically recognize the beauty, vitality and fresh ideas of youth when they address each other as "girl," a form of address that transcends age and social class for African American women. The mutual sharing of concerns related to male/female relationships, parenting, child-rearing, birth, death and ongoing forms of societal inequities serve to cement firm relationships between African American women kin and non-kin. The permanence and strength of these relationships have been subjected to challenges since the 1960s as mainstream value orientations emphasizing social isolation, independence and competition conflict with the mutual dependence, collective responsibility and cooperation which undergird the informal social support system that African American women have historically maintained. The ultraconservatism and reactionary character of the 1980s and 1990s, marked by the recision of liberal social policies, the erosion of social and economic gains and the disintegration of African American two-parent families, has served to revitalize and strengthen the mutual aid network, established and maintained largely by African American women.

In spite of the fact that African American women have relied on an informal social support system, a sisterhood, to withstand negative definitions, I am not suggesting that all African American women have rejected all Western cultural images of womanhood. To do so, would be to deny that African American women, like others in society, are interested in obtaining the rewards that are forthcoming when women conform to cultural images. After all, one of the objectives of cultural imagery is to legitimize and perpetuate stereotypes, as well as to encourage individuals to embrace certain values and belief systems and to exhibit certain behaviors. Through systematic exposure to cultural images, individuals are expected to conform to, emulate and internalize the characteristics, values, beliefs and behaviors of these images or to reject them and to accept those images that are diametrically opposite. Even for the most economically advantaged African American women, inequities based on race have rarely resulted in African American women assuming the emotional make-up inherent in the Western cultural image of womanhood. The uniqueness of African American women's experiences in the United States has resulted in the evolution of a woman who has the ability to assume some qualities traditionally associated with womanhood as well as those attributed to masculinity. The African American woman's facility for discriminately displaying behaviors associated with cultural definitions of masculinity and womanhood has contributed to her androgynous character. This is also the case for African American males. In both cases, African American women and their mates have exhibited role adaptability as men and women share in the performance of tasks that are gender-based. In other words, as Hill has pointed out, African American women and men have historically performed both instrumental and affective functions.[9] Still, in certain milieux, African American women and men also assume traditional gender roles. In effect, the division of labor within African American families has not been based on the same level of sex segregation as that which characterizes European American families. It is not uncommon for African American women to defer to African American males in their home. For example, there are African American women who continue to serve their mates food at dinner and other meals. Exhibiting coy and dependent behavior in prescribed situations is not uncommon among African American women during courtship and marriage. Moreover, African American women living in segregated communities also depend on their mates to protect them, even though that protection is usually structurally limited to the confines of the African American community.

Subsequent to the Civil Rights Movement it became apparent that the anticipated social and economic opportunities had not become available to African American men and women. This is particularly significant as African American males had anticipated that, if institutional discrimination were eliminated or at best lessened, their participation in societal institutions would be greatly increased. Along with increased participation would come greater economic solvency. Ultimately, African American males expected to assume traditional gender roles, enabling them to become the chief breadwinner in their families. They reasoned that this would result in African American wives assuming traditional supportive roles while decreasing their breadwinning function. Specifically, African Americans projected that African American women would begin to perform more affective functions and fewer instrumental ones, like their White counterparts. African American women were going to be expected to assume a supportive role and become dependent upon their spouses, who were planning to conform more to the traditional masculine gender role of provider and protector.[10] When these social and economic opportunities failed to come to fruition, African American males and females continued to perform both instrumental and affective functions, and were forced to modify their expectations of being able to assume traditional gender roles. The fact that social policy failed to result in the expected outcome has caused dashed expectations, frustration and conflict for many African American couples.[11]

PERPETUATING IMAGES: THE ELECTRONIC VERSUS PRINT MEDIA

The media have been effective instruments for conveying and proliferating cultural images. One of the most important questions regarding the media as a means of transmitting cultural imagery is their availability and influence on various segments of the population. On the surface it appears as though the media are equally available to all individuals who wish to use them as a means of communicating ideas, events and imagery. However, not all individuals have equal access to the mass media. And what is even more apparent is that it is those in power who influence the media, and who determine in large measure what will and will not be transmitted, how it will be presented and when it will be purveyed. There is considerable debate over whether the media act as their own independent agents or whether they represent the interests of their owners and the corporations whose advertising dollars provide the financial support to sustain them. It is certainly plausible that the mass media are influenced by a multiplicity of sources in terms of determining which images will be transmitted. What is most important is identifying the source with the most significant influence over the imagery that the media purvey. There is little doubt that those who have ownership in any particular medium help to determine the content and format of material and the audience to whom its message, whether in print or visual form, is targeted. Others who contribute to the content and format of the information and images that are transmitted include advertisers, audience, media personnel and so forth.

Historically, the general population has relied upon the print medium for its messages and specific cultural images. It was not until the early twentieth century that the electronic media, primarily radio and later movies, became the important vehicles for transmitting cultural images. Later, around the 1950s, television became more widely available and gradually became the most impressive and influential medium.

It is important to examine how significant each medium has been in terms of its portrayal of cultural images of African American women. Because the print medium, in the form of

71

comics, literature, newspaper articles and magazines, has had the greatest longevity it is this medium that was originally responsible for proliferating and perpetuating cultural images of African American womanhood. Initial images of African American women were based on stereotypes developed largely by slave owners attempting to justify the institution of slavery and, equally important, seeking to provide a rationale for their refusal to recognize gender differences in the treatment of slaves.

There is a plethora of print media that have portrayed African American women using one of the four cultural images. These have been critiqued and criticized in great detail by African American women scholars.[12] Early caricatures of African American women were not only based on cultural images that characterize African American women, but exaggerated these images so that they resulted in grotesque characters that, some argue, contributed even more to the denigration of African American women.[13] The electronic media, beginning with radio and film, continued to perpetuate the cultural images of African American women that had initially appeared in print. When one weighs the impact of the print and electronic media, relative to the extent to which they have been available to African Americans for the purpose of purveying positive cultural images of African American women, it is clear that the print media have been more accessible. Thus, although mainstream print and electronic media have both portrayed cultural images of African American women from a cultural ethnocentric model, African Americans have had more opportunities through the print media to portray African American women from a microcultural perspective. The print media have been more likely to portray African American women using a greater range of cultural images, largely true because African Americans have had what is commonly referred to as the Black press throughout a large part of their existence in the United States. The first reported Black newspaper was entitled *Freedom's Journal*.[14] It was first published in 1827. Before the outbreak of the Civil War in 1861 there were seventeen newspapers, narratives and books published by African Americans.[15] In addition, African American artists and writers, despite having limited resources, have written and disseminated poems, articles, newspapers, journals and books, and also produced paintings. Through various print media African Americans have constructed and proliferated their own cultural images. Therefore, cultural images of African American women that conflict with and contradict those developed and portrayed by the mainstream media have been, and continue to be, purveyed by the Black press and members of the African American community. Nevertheless, there are limitations to the visibility and availability of cultural images portrayed through the Black media. After all, the resources of the Black press have never paralleled those of the mainstream media.[16]

The Black press is targeted, almost exclusively, to an African American audience. Consequently, while the African American community benefits from the Black press's ability to define and redefine cultural images of African American women, members of other racial and ethnic groups have generally had to rely on the cultural images of African American women depicted by the mainstream media. The fact that the Black press is available within the African American community does not mean that it has the same impact on the community for which it is largely intended. The most common form that the Black press takes is the weekly newspaper. This presents an obvious limitation regarding its capacity to address current issues and daily events that occur within the African American community. There are also geographical limitations – the Black press usually operates within a local market and cannot adequately address issues and events that occur on a global level. Operating within a restricted market also serves to limit financial support for the Black press. In the case of weekly newspapers, limited advertising dollars affect both content and format. Still, through the Black press, African American artists and writers have sought, and utilized, a variety of resources for the purpose of transmitting information and positive cultural images to members of the African American community.

In spite of the fact that the Black press and African American artists and writers transmit positive cultural images of African American women, members of the larger society rely almost exclusively on the mainstream media for cultural images of African American women. Consequently, the cultural imagery of African American women that the dominant media purvey has become firmly rooted in American culture. The fact that African American women and others have raised objections to these images has done little to eliminate either the images or their impact upon the societal perception of African American women. In fact, American artifacts such as Aunt Jemima and mammy dolls, cookie jars and postcards are an integral part of American popular culture,

73

particularly in the southern region of the United States. Clearly, the South's lengthy involvement in maintaining slavery resulted in the development, and greater acceptance, of mammy and Aunt Jemima artifacts. Many believe that the mammy and Aunt Jemima cultural images of African American women are comforting and satisfying to various segments of the United States, who associate nurturing, caring and the performance of domestic tasks with African American women, because of these images.

Two major historical periods in the United States represented large-scale efforts to purvey images of African Americans, including African American women, from a microcultural perspective. The Harlem Renaissance in the 1920s was the first major effort among African American artists and writers to infuse African heritage and the experiences of African Americans in their artistic works.[17] These artistic expressions gained widespread acceptance from those with an interest in art, within the African American community as well as the larger society. Obviously, not many members of the wider society were aware that African American artists and writers were purveying cultural images of African American women that sometimes differed from those portrayed by the mainstream media. It was, and remains, the case that art appreciation is not a quality possessed by the vast majority of Americans in the United States. Thus, one can expect that it is even more rare to find considerable interest in art reflecting African American culture among the majority of society's members. The most widespread and vocal protestations about the mainstream media's portrayal of African American women occurred during the Civil Rights Movement when artists and writers not only offered vocal protestations but their works criticized the systematic distortions and exploitation of cultural images of African American men and women. They demanded that the mainstream media purvey cultural images of African American women that reflected their strengths, contributions and intellectual abilities. African American activists demanded that traditional cultural images of African American women that were stereotypical, demeaning and exploitative be eliminated.

The electronic media have been more consistent in portraying African American women using traditional stereotypical cultural imagery than the print media. Because of limited access, and the prohibitive costs associated with owning a radio station or producing television programs or movies that contain positive cultural images of African American women, these media have not been the major vehicles for purveying positive and representative cultural images. Generally, African Americans unable to afford television stations or to broadcast their own programs over major networks must rely on radio and cable television to convey information and images. These venues are limited for transmitting positive cultural images of African American women and other disenfranchised groups. For example, radio is no longer considered a viable medium for reading stories that enable audiences to imagine and visualize each character. Moreover, cable television has only limited utility as it is not available to large numbers of viewers across the country. In fact, in many communities cable programming must be purchased at a monthly fee that is not widely affordable. More importantly, even if one can afford to purchase cable television there is no guarantee that the cable company will offer African American oriented programs. Yet, it is through such programs that one is most likely to view cultural images of African American women that are positive and representative of African American women in the population.

Efforts of African American women, and others, to replace traditional cultural imagery with positive cultural images of African American women have met with minimal success. Still, some advances have occurred, although these changes have not resulted in the mainstream mass media systematically purveying an increased number of cultural images of African American women that have been legitimized by the women themselves. Changes that have occurred have generally been initiated by African Americans, who have relentlessly challenged the mainstream media to make more positive and representative cultural images of African American women.

5

CULTURAL IMAGERY OF AFRICAN AMERICAN WOMEN AND EMPIRICISM

SOCIAL DEMOGRAPHIC CHARACTERISTICS

In 1990, out of a population of 246,191,000 there were 30,393,000 African Americans; 16,138,000 were females and 14,255,000 were males. African Americans represented 12.1 per cent of the population in the United States. The sex ratio imbalance, which reflects nearly 2 million more African American females than males, has a decided effect on African American women in terms of dating, courtship and marriage.[1]

In 1960, the median years of education were 7.7 years for Black males and 8.6 years for Black females. By 1975, the effect of the US Supreme Court's ruling in *Brown* v. *the Board of Education* and the government's affirmative action edict had begun to make a significant increase in levels of educational achievement for all African Americans. In 1975, the median years of education had risen to 10.7 and 11.1 years for African American males and females, respectively. By 1980, African American males and females had reached parity in years of school completed; the median period of education for both sexes was 12 years, compared to 12.5 years for Whites. By 1990, African American males had a median of 12.7 years of education compared to African American females whose median period of schooling was 12.8 years. The median period of education in 1990 was 12.9 years, the same as for White males and White females.[2]

College enrollment figures also reflect growth over the past thirty years. The number of African Americans enrolled in colleges, particularly in predominantly White institutions, was lauded as an indication of the success of affirmative action. When increases in the numbers of African American college students are subjected to greater scrutiny, however, it becomes evident that African American females, not African American males, made major gains in attending colleges and universities during the 1960s and 1970s. In 1960, of the 134,000 African Americans enrolled in college, 48 per cent were African American males and 51 per cent were African American females. African American male enrollment continued to diminish over the next twenty years, while African American females' college enrollment increased dramatically. By 1980, 688,000 African Americans were enrolled in institutions of higher education. Of this number, 278,000 or 40 per cent were males and 60 per cent were African American females. In 1988, of the 752,000 African Americans attending colleges and universities, 455,000 (60 per cent) were African American females and 297,000 (40 per cent) were African American males.

Changes were also registered in the percentage of high school graduates attending college from 1970 to 1988. Increases in the percentage of African American males and females completing college occurred between 1980 and 1990. The proportion of African American male college graduates rose from 7.3 per cent in 1980 to 16.7 per cent in 1990. African American females graduating from college increased from 8.6 per cent in 1980 to 14.5 per cent in 1990. Corresponding figures for Whites show that 26.9 per cent of White males and 17.3 per cent of White females graduated from college in 1980 compared to 32.1 per cent of White males and 25 per cent of White females in 1990. From 1970 to 1988, the percentage of African American female high school graduates attending college increased from 24.1 per cent to 30.5 per cent. During the same period, the percentage of African American male high school graduates attending college decreased from 28.7 per cent in 1970 to 25 per cent in 1988.[3]

Between 1976 and 1981 African American females made advances in three degree levels, the baccalaureate, doctorate and professional. During this period African American females experienced an 8 per cent increase in baccalaureate degrees, a 29 per cent increase in doctorates and a 71 per cent increase in professional degrees. The only area in which a decline occurred for African American women was a 12 per cent decrease at the master's degree level.[4]

African American women are now represented in larger numbers in the White collar occupations, although the largest percentage of African American White collar employees are in clerical, technical, retail sales and administrative support positions. Specifically, 39.7 per cent of African American females and 45.7 per cent of White females were employed in technical, sales and administrative support occupations, while 27 per cent of African American women compared to 16.1 per cent of White women worked in service occupations. African American women were less likely than White women to be employed in managerial and professional specialty type occupations. Only 18.8 per cent of African American women compared to 27.4 per cent of White women worked in managerial and professional specialty type occupations in 1990.[5]

In effect, African American women and their White counterparts continue to be overrepresented among service workers. The noticeable distinction is that African American women tend to be employed in service occupations, that have incomes at or near the poverty level, i.e. hospital aides, food service workers, etc. Conversely, White women working in service occupations earn higher incomes as dental hygienists, social workers and so forth.[6]

In addition to working in service jobs that generate lower salaries, African American women are also overrepresented in clerical positions that yield the lowest salaries. For example, African American women who work in clerical jobs are generally clerks, clerk typists, data entry operators, telegraph operators and intermediate clerks. Higher-paying clerical jobs, such as legal secretary, word processor, bookkeeper, administrative assistant and lab technician are jobs in which African American women are underrepresented.[7]

According to census data in 1989 African American female workers earned $11,524, 98.2 per cent of the income of White female workers ($11,724). This reflects a slight widening of the income gap from 1979 when African American women earned $10,183, 99.6 per cent of the median income of White women workers ($10,219). It should be noted that African American women tend to work more hours (37.8 per cent more hours annually) and are more likely to have longer job tenure than their White counterparts. Therefore, comparing salaries between African American women workers and White women workers requires qualification that suggests that the disparity in income for African American and White women workers continues to exist. The 1989 earnings of American women represent 75 per cent of the income of African American males who earned $15,320. White women's income continued to be considerably less than that of White men who earned $22,158 (53 per cent) in 1989.[8]

In spite of the social and economic gains that African Americans experienced in the 1960s and 1970s, they continue to be overrepresented among the impoverished class. In 1989, African American families were 3.5 times as likely to be poor as White families. Further, in 1989 the percentage of African Americans with incomes below the poverty level (31 per cent) was three times that of Whites (10 per cent) and only one percentage point lower than the proportion of African Americans (32 per cent) with incomes below the poverty level in 1980. An inordinate proportion of African American women who head families (46.5 per cent) are poor, compared to 11.8 per cent of African American married-couple families. By contrast, 25.4 per cent of White families headed by women and 5 per cent of White married-couple families in 1989 had incomes below the poverty level.[9]

A major factor contributing to the growing number of African American families headed by women is the increase in marital disruption that has occurred among African Americans and White American couples. In 1990, two out of three marriages to African Americans ended in divorce compared to one out of two marriages that were disrupted by divorce for White couples. The proportion of African American families headed by women increased between 1980 and 1990 from 40.3 per cent to 43.8 per cent. By contrast, the proportion of White families headed by women rose from 11.6 in 1980 to 12.9 in 1990. Married-couple families accounted for 55.5 per cent of all African American families and 85.7 per cent of White families in 1980 and 50.2 per cent of African American and 83 per cent of White families in 1990.[10]

In addition, separation remains high among African American married couples. Another factor that contributes to the disproportionate number of African American families headed by women is the growing number of never-married African American women with children. Over the past twenty years there has been an increase in African American women who maintain a permanent status of never married. There are many theories that purport to explain the high percentage of female-maintained families, ranging from high rates of unemployment for African American males to sex ratio imbalances for African American males and females, but little has been undertaken to attenuate the problems leading to and resulting from female-maintained families. This situation is exacerbated for African American women as their rate of remarriage is lower than that of White women. In addition, the prerequisite for marriage – a job – is more easily achieved for White males than for African American males. In 1990, the unemployment rate for African American males was 11.8 per cent, which was more than twice the rate of unemployment for White males of 4.8 per cent. African American women had a rate of unemployment of 10.8 per cent compared to the unemployment rate of 4.6 per cent for White women in 1990.[11] Clearly, income or socioeconomic status are important determinants of marriage and remarriage as well. Despite an unemployment rate for African American males that has remained almost 2.5 times that of White American males since the Great Depression, African American females continue to have a rate of unemployment higher than that of White males, White females, and African American males. It is also important to note that, in 1990, the civilian labor force participation rate for African American women (57.8 per cent) and White women (57.5 per cent) was only slightly higher for the former. African American males, like White males, have higher rates of participation in the civilian labor force than African American women and White women. In 1990, African American males had a lower civilian labor force participation rate (70.1 per cent) than White males (76.9 per cent).[12]

Given the depressed socioeconomic status of African American females it is little wonder that their families are adversely affected by the inequities associated with the conditions that they face. The fact that an inordinate percentage of African American women have incomes below the poverty level and are outside mainstream institutions accounts for the precarious position of African American women and children. Accordingly, one out of two African American children, compared to one out of five children in the general population are poor. Further, in 1990, 51.2 per cent of African American children lived in female single-parent families whereas 16.2 per cent of White children resided in female-headed families.[13]

In addition, the absence of effective affirmative action policies at the national level and in public and private sector companies results in African American women experiencing racial and gender discrimination. Boston argues that one of the modal forms of labor market discrimination is not "differential wages paid to equally productive Black and White workers, but rather the

80

differential access to employment and differing rates of occupational mobility."[14] When African American women are employed they, like their White counterparts, are generally employed in traditionally female occupations that offer low wages. Essentially, African American women tend to be victims of occupational segmentation. That is, they are employed in occupations where they acquire skills that have limited utility throughout the company or organization. In such cases, job skills that are acquired and refined are not viable outside of the organizational division or occupation in which the African American woman is employed. Examples of these occupational enclaves are highly visible in both the private and public sectors. Therefore, it is reasonable to assume that the highest percentage of African American women within private corporations are found in the area of human resources; in institutions of higher education African American women faculty are in African American studies departments or other non-traditional academic units such as ethnic studies or women's studies; and in government professional positions, African American women are hired in departments of community development or human services. I am not suggesting that positions within these occupational areas are of no utility to the agency or organization. However, I believe such positions rarely provide African American women with marketable job skills that can be used in other divisions within the firm.

In addition, African American women have not increased their marketability to enable them to be competitive in an American labor force that is now largely a service-oriented industry requiring sophisticated and complex technological skills. What has occurred is that African American women, despite moderate occupational advances over the past 25 years, continue to assume marginal positions in terms of their careers. This is true for African American women professionals and non-professionals. In both instances, African American women have lower earnings than any other group of individuals in the United States. Basically, although African American women have increased numerically relative to their participation in institutions from which they were excluded before the Civil Rights Movement, they continue to occupy a relatively low occupational status within these institutions. Equally important, African American women workers remain outside the decision-making process. This is perhaps a double-edged sword in that the most efficient and expeditious methods by which African

American women can expect to increase their earnings, and thereby elevate their socioeconomic status, is to be in a position to affect policies. The fact that African American women remain outside the policy-making process in salient institutions in American society means that they have difficulty ensuring that their own interests and needs are articulated and met. Consequently, African American women have had to rely on other disenfranchised groups and socially conscious individuals to integrate the African American women's agenda with that of other disenfranchised groups who are in a better position to effect organizational decision-making. And while there is evidence that others can act as advocates for African American women, it is also true that African American women's virtual exclusion from policy-making positions within societal institutions presents a dilemma and an obstacle to their need for social equality.

Jones raises similar questions when she explores the decline in the rate of African American women's participation in the civilian labor force. Jones contends that the following factors influence women's decisions to enter and to remain in the labor force:

1 If they have high earning potential related to educational attainment;
2 If they contribute to a large percentage of the family income;
3 If they are in good health;
4 If older children are in the home;
5 If they have prior work experience.

Noting that African American women meet these factors that determine women's decisions to enter the labor force, she attributes their decline in labor force participation rates to institutional biases that result in truncated career mobility.[15]

Fulbright states that African American women meet the structural conditions Kanter enumerates which act as a disincentive to labor force participation. In effect, when Fulbright studied African American female managers she found that nearly 50 per cent experienced obstacles to their mobility during their careers. Specifically, women who worked in staff positions, jobs viewed as peripheral to the company's business, experienced the following mobility inhibitors that Kanter described: corporate pyramid structures in which available positions decrease as one gets closer to the top; securing dead-end jobs, or positions with a short career ladder; and movement through the wrong route into a job that usually has many job opportunities but results in a person who has not acquired the job skills essential for taking advantage of the job opportunities that exist. Those who worked in line positions, perceived as critical to the company's business, reported mobility inhibitors related to race or gender discrimination. This was true despite the fact that these women had selected career tracks purported to lead to mobility within the organization.[16] Thus, structural impediments that result in disparate salaries, limited career mobility and the unavailability of positions, despite the posting of affirmative action disclaimers, contribute significantly to African American women's decline in labor force participation rates. Recognizing that there are ceilings placed on occupational mobility serves to heighten the frustration that African American women experience in the labor force. Nevertheless, it is interesting to note that African American women continue to hold positive attitudes toward work.

IMAGERY AND CAREER SUCCESS

The facts that African American women are overrepresented in low-paying jobs, are experiencing a decline in labor force participation and have incomes lower than those of White males, African American males, and White females are irrefutable. It is also the case that cultural images appear highly related to factors that contribute to the depressed economic and occupational status of African American women.

Cultural images that depict African American women as domestics, whose chief function is to provide nurturance to adults and children, influence occupational outcomes. Career tracking does not begin in institutions of higher education, nor within the labor force. Instead, career tracking, while influenced by early educational screening, is formally initiated overtly in middle school and in high school. The role of guidance counselors and teachers is invaluable to the student's career decision-making. And even when parents have high career aspirations for their children, students are frequently compelled to rely on school personnel, counselors and teachers, to advise them what courses they should take to prepare themselves for specific career tracks. This is particularly true when children have little access to adult role models who work in diverse occupations.

Cultural perceptions of their students, based on race, gender and class stereotypes, influence guidance counselors and the advice they give to students in planning their careers. It is not uncommon for African American women to report that they were advised in high school to pursue a secretarial career rather than a career that would have necessitated a college degree. Generally, African American women who relate such experiences are those who, for a number of reasons, discounted such suggestions of a guidance counselor and matriculated to a college or university. In most cases when African American women indicate that they were advised to secure employment in a clerical occupation and not an institution of higher education, they state that the guidance counselor suggested that the student did not possess the ability to attend college. Test performance and academic tracking may influence suggestions made by guidance counselors, leading students away from career tracks that will result in higher pay and the student realizing her potential; but living in a culture where there are more images reflecting African American women in professional occupations is likely to influence the perceptions of teachers, counselors and educational administrators when they consider the types of jobs for which African American women are suited.

Hughes discusses problems that professional African American women encounter when they occupy status-discrepant positions.[17] The African American female doctor, lawyer or judge is likely to engender surprise from the public who are unaccustomed to seeing African American women in such occupations. Again, these expectations exist when African American women are students, deciding which career track to pursue. Research indicates that there is a paucity of role models who are managers in corporations for African American women to emulate; therefore, it is extremely important that cultural images that consign African American women to domestic and service positions be replaced. African American women are likely to receive input from their significant others that supports their capacity to actualize their potential, yet one cannot underestimate the effects of cultural images on establishing cultural perceptions, especially stereotypes that affect educational and career tracking at all levels of education. Inarguably, teachers, guidance counselors and other pertinent school personnel develop expectations of various groups of individuals based on cultural images and the assumptions that underlie such imagery.

The fact that cultural images, underlying assumptions and stereotypes of various groups of individuals affect the expectations that teachers have of their students is well documented. For example, female students have been encouraged to pursue careers in traditionally female occupations such as teaching and nursing, while male students are encouraged to pursue a broader variety of career options. White males are more likely to be encouraged to become scientists, engineers and medical doctors. Kunjufu and others also report that teachers are more willing to accept competitive and aggressive behavior in White males while discouraging the same characteristics in White females, African American males and African American females. Some argue that African American males are expected to demonstrate aggression within limits.[18] The boundaries that are acceptable for African American males to exhibit aggression are confined to the sphere of athletics. On the other hand, African American women are geared toward service-related occupations.

In all cases there is a plethora of cultural images that support stereotypes regarding the intelligence and occupation of individuals based on gender and race. It is not happenstance that African American males are generally depicted as athletes, while African American women are purveyed as domestics, White women are shown as housewives and White males are portrayed in numerous occupations, but generally shown as successful professionals or businessmen. On the surface one may question whether art is imitating life or the converse. In fact, both are taking place. What is occurring is that cultural images are used to transmit certain values, expectations and ideologies which reinforce occupational segmentation. Ultimately, the purpose of these images is to ensure that those who control societal institutions and resources are portrayed as the legitimate mediators of society's wealth. The fact that other groups of individuals are rarely portrayed in the highest status and prestigious occupational positions results in the existence of societal expectations in which all other groups are peripheral to key occupations in the United States. African American women and others who are purveyed and viewed as outside critical occupational positions reinforce the status quo. In so doing, these images ensure the existing distribution of societal resources, including wealth, power and other prestige goals of our culture. The continued allocation of society's resources, in which a small percentage of individuals control societal institutions and resources, is at the root of the inequities that individual groups face in their participation in, and exclusion from, societal institutions. Thus, while the function of all institutions is to maintain the status quo through the cultural transmission of norms, values, belief systems and behaviors, the mass media are the main instruments by which societal institutions undertake and complete this process of perpetuating the social order, also known as socialization.

The process by which cultural images influence African American women's career success occurs not only on a macrocultural level as described above, but also takes place within the microcultural environment. Accordingly, African American institutions, especially the African American family, have a tremendous responsibility attempting to define African Americans; this falls particularly on the women who, as in other cultures, are the primary socializing agents for African American children. It is important that African American women perceive themselves positively, and are perceived as such by their offspring and others within the community. In view of the growing significance and influence of the mass media, particularly television, African Americans who define themselves differently from the cultural images purveyed by the mainstream media must compete with images and ideologies that often contradict those embraced by many African American women, men and children. There are two levels on which cultural images purveyed by the mainstream media are likely to have an adverse affect on career opportunities for African American women. These images affect both educators and employers; both groups control rewards for African American women and wield significant influence over their careers.

Historically, African American women have been able to make strides, albeit slowly and gradually, in both occupational and economic areas. They have done so by accepting and overcoming inexorable social and economic conditions, and by maintaining a strong sisterhood, or strong informal social support system. Some believe that mutual aid networks, whereby African American women exchange invaluable goods and services, including advice and information necessary for the development of positive self-concepts, is an African retention, one that withstood the harsh realities of slavery and contributed greatly to the fortitude and resilience of African American women throughout their existence in the United States. Integral to the mutual aid network and strong kinship network was the accepted belief that African American women could overcome the most arduous challenges and maneuver and access societal institutions. African American women have guided and directed their children's educational experiences, worked as dual earners with their spouses and maintained frequent social interaction with their female significant others, especially family and close friends. Unlike others in American society, the African American female relied almost exclusively upon her female relatives and close friends for her personal identification. She was able to reject, for the most part, the mainstream media's definitions of womanhood and replace them with definitions constructed by other African American women who made up her significant others. Therefore, although African American women were compelled to work outside the home, they generally used the knowledge they acquired to enhance their children's educational achievements and employment opportunities. Dill describes how African American female domestics used information to assist their children in accessing systems.[19] The African American woman, by virtue of working for White employers in their homes, was privy to information denied to those outside the mainstream. Possessing critical information has enabled African American women to access certain organizations and institutions within society. Where African American women work as domestics and in other low-paying occupations they have used their knowledge and "connections" with Whites to enable their daughters and sons to elevate themselves to an occupation and economic status above their own.

During the Civil Rights Movement African American women had their hopes and aspirations for greater opportunities increased. They anticipated that government policies, including affirmative action, educational grants and loans, government funding for small businesses and the like, would have resulted in unlimited opportunities for African Americans, including African American women. It was during this period that African American women made their greatest occupational gains and the income gap between African American women and men was substantially narrowed. However, during the same period the mutual aid network, with its strong emphasis on a sisterhood of women helping each other, began to experience a decline. Several factors contributed to the decline of the mutual aid network. First, this system of exchange was operating under increasing demands but the resources of its members were limited. Next, the government began to usurp the role of the Black church which had always been in the vanguard of the movement for social change. Further, a new value system, reflecting the views of those who control society's institutions and wealth, began to replace traditional values that were intrinsic to African American culture.

I have discussed the decline of mutual aid networks elsewhere; yet, it is important to note that the diminution of these significant social support systems has to some extent resulted in African American women being influenced to a greater degree than in the past by cultural images and ideologies.[20] Today, African American women have more competing socializing agents that influence the development of their self-concept and self-esteem, and those of their children. The emotional support, advice and strategies for coping with the inequities that African American women face were once provided by the sisterhood that undergirded mutual aid networks. Racial group identity has even been found to be more greatly influenced by such informal systems than by factors external to the African American community.[21] When African American women were confronted with racial and gender discrimination they developed coping skills, mechanisms and strategies for overcoming these forms of overt and covert injustices.[22] Because of the decline in mutual aid networks during the 1970s, and greater participation in societal institutions, African American women have had to rely on macrocultural and microcultural institutions more than informal social support systems. In the case of macrocultural institutions, there is considerable evidence that indicates the relative ineffectiveness of social service agencies in assisting African American women to resolve various forms of discrimination. Generally, institutions designed to provide relief for discrimination in such areas as the legal system require inordinate outlays of time and money. Moreover, representatives of these systems are frequently perceived as being more sensitive to the perpetrators of discrimination than to the victims of social injustices. In fact, the 1964 Civil Rights Act places the burden of proof on the alleged victim of discrimination. Civil Rights proponents are cautiously optimistic that the new 1991 Civil Rights Act will facilitate discrimination litigation for employees and other victims of race and gender discrimination.

Other organizations such as social welfare agencies and community mental health systems have also been perceived by African

American women as being unable to relate to their problems and permitting stereotypes to influence policy and practices in relating to African Americans in general and African American women in particular.[23] If African American women were able to rely more on mutual aid networks they would receive the necessary support to challenge formidable obstacles within the civilian labor force. Because of bureaucracy and the outdated policies and practices of enforcement agencies such as the Civil Rights Commission and the Equal Employment Opportunity Commission, African American women need strong, collective, informal support systems to provide them with emotional, financial and legal support if they are to challenge successfully such social injustices. In the past, African American women relied heavily, especially during the Civil Rights Movement, on microcultural noninstitutional and institutional support systems to combat racial injustices. While few African American women filed complaints and grievances regarding sex discrimination in the past, few would argue that the discrimination that African American women have experienced historically was exclusively racial discrimination. In many instances when African American women have filed complaints of race discrimination it is highly plausible that they have been the victims of sex and sometimes class discrimination as well. Still, African American women were able to rely on the support of a mutual aid network and other men and women in their communities were well equipped to withstand and to challenge social injustices.

Today, race, sex and class discrimination are far more covert than in the past. One major problem confronting young African American women is being able to recognize the various forms that discrimination takes. Failure to discern discrimination accurately can result in individuals blaming themselves for their inability to compete effectively in the labor force. In addition, when individuals do not have access to effective strategies and approaches for successfully challenging race and sex discrimination, they may become frustrated and believe that they are helpless to do anything about it. Such beliefs are likely to result in a pattern of occupational flight instead of fight. Thus, instead of learning effective methods of challenging race and sex discrimination in education and employment, African American women may believe that they are powerless to effect positive changes in these milieux. This contributes significantly to the decline in the labor force participation rates of African American women. Exchange theory sheds considerable light on the declining labor force participation rates of African American women. Exchange theory holds that individuals will seek to maximize their rewards and minimize their costs.[24] Clearly, in view of pay inequities, occupational segmentation resulting in low-paying jobs, short-career ladder positions, and other forms of racial and sex discrimination, a growing number of African American women have decided not to enter, or to remain in, the civilian labor force. Despite the fact that African American women have historically been the victims of interlocking forms of overt race, sex and class discrimination, the more covert forms of institutional discrimination that are common today have an equally devastating effect.

The institutionalization of race and gender discrimination makes it difficult to prove that injustices have occurred. Therefore, individuals who believe that they have been discriminated against are compelled to engage in a reflective three-stage cognitive process. First, the individual must determine if discrimination has occurred or if there is another explanation for the behavior that has taken place. Included in the process of determining if discrimination has occurred, one must rule out individual or cultural differences for the act that appears to be discriminatory. In other words, did the individual fail to secure employment because of biases held by the employer, or because of the company's qualifying criteria, or was the failure to obtain a job a function of the individual's own qualifications? If the African American woman concludes that she was not the victim of discrimination then the cognitive process is complete. On the other hand, if she decides that she has experienced discrimination this mental process continues. Second, African American women must determine the nature of discrimination. Was the discrimination based on race, sex or social class? While all forms of social injustices have the same effect, that is they exclude individuals and limit their opportunities to achieve goals, there are different strategies that are employed depending on the nature of discrimination, the perpetrator of discrimination and the milieu in which discrimination occurs.

For example, when African American women experience gender discrimination they are more likely to find the most empathic group of individuals to be other women. Moreover, strategies that have been proven to be effective in remedying sex discrimination are likely to be advanced by women who have experienced sex discrimination. That is not to say that individuals

90

who have been the victims of race and class discrimination are not able to make recommendations and to offer strategies for addressing other forms of discrimination. However, there is reason to believe that a collective of individuals who have experienced specific types of discrimination, and therefore know the overt and covert forms which discriminatory practices take, are also familiar with the methods of resistance that are entrenched within institutions. Furthermore, women who experience sex discrimination are equally aware of the tactics, approaches and networks that have proven to be viable in resolving gender discrimination. One of the myths that Diane K. Lewis cites to explain African American women's lack of involvement in, and advocacy for, feminism is the belief that race discrimination is more likely to affect their lives adversely than sex discrimination.[25] Despite efforts to segment and identify the nature of discrimination that one is a victim of, it is not always possible to do so. When discrimination takes a multiplicity of forms it is even more difficult to make the initial determination as to whether one is a victim of discrimination, and them to make the second decision about what form of discrimination one has suffered. Aside from the legal necessity for such information, it is important for individuals who suspect that they are the victims of social injustice to engage in this process.

Finally, a remedy, strategy or approach for alleviating discrimination must be sought. It is not until the first two stages of this process are complete that the African American woman can attempt to seek remedies for the discrimination which she has experienced. This process is complete when an individual can begin to identify a solution to problems arising from discrimination. This usually entails eliminating the obstacles to goal attainment and social relations that result from discrimination. Members of other disenfranchised groups enter into similar cognitive processes, but the fact that African American women are likely to experience several forms of discrimination exacerbates the inexorable consequences of oppression.

While one cannot make the case for overt discrimination, which was the rule rather than the exception prior to the Civil Rights Movement, particularly in the South, it is obvious that simply because discrimination has become covert does not mean it is any less devastating to the victim. The mere fact that individuals must engage in an ongoing reflective process to determine if the treatment they receive in society is a function of racial discrimination, other biases or individual idiosyncrasies means that new insidious patterns of discrimination are equally as abusive and debilitating.

Clearly, the institutional nature of all forms of discrimination makes it more difficult to challenge. Because discrimination today is more difficult to observe and measure than in the past, it is easier for employers to deny the existence of racism, sexism and classism. Therefore, it is more difficult for African American women to establish its existence and to seek remedies and relief for discrimination. One of the major weaknesses inherent in the 1964 Civil Rights Act was that it placed the burden of proof on the victim. In effect, the emergence of a more covert form of discrimination that is difficult to prove means that the passage of the Civil Rights Act of 1964 represented the historical "compromise" that Bell discusses.[26] He posits that policy-makers and legislators have historically made compromises to accommodate the masses. Such compromises prevent the masses from believing that those outside the mainstream are receiving preferential treatment. The veto of the 1990 Civil Rights Bill by President George Bush, which would have placed the burden of proof on the employer rather than the employee, is but another example of the institutional impediments that contribute to an increasing number of African American women remaining outside, and leaving, the civilian labor force. The perception among African American women that other societal institutions impede instead of facilitate their careers also contributes to the disenchantment and ultimate withdrawal from mainstream institutions. Moreover, the mainstream media are largely responsible for systematically bombarding African American women with images that reflect a differential valuation and treatment of individuals along race, gender and class lines.

To facilitate the identification and substantiation of various forms of discrimination, undercover or covert tests are being used by various federal government departments. According to the Urban Institute, the Equal Employment Opportunity Commission and the Federal Reserve are among government agencies considering using covert tests to uncover biases. The findings of such tests reveal the dramatic economic impact of race and gender discrimination. The most glaring example of discrimination was reported in the purchasing of an automobile. The results of an undercover test reported in 1990 showed the average profit on an $11,000 car deal was as follows:

White male	$ 362
White female	$ 504
African American male	$ 783
African American female	$1,237

It is little wonder that African American females occupy the lowest socioeconomic status in the United States as the findings of this study reveal how African American women are more adversely affected by discrimination than any other group of indivdividuals in our society. Hence, African American women are not only victims of pay inequity but their purchasing power is significantly reduced by discriminatory practices in the marketplace.[27]

The mass media have been quite successful in displaying differential lifestyles of various members of society; and correlating these lifestyles with superfluous qualities such as race, gender, class and American standards of beauty. The growing experience of relative deprivation is largely a function of the mass media and societal institutions in which the differential progress of participants is associated with their sex, race and gender. Therefore, it is difficult to convince African American women that they can be all that they have the potential for becoming. Such ideas were successful in ensuring high levels of motivation, drive and goal-oriented behavior when African Americans were consigned to separate physical and social environments. In spite of the appearance of boundaries being removed during the Civil Rights era, African American females and males cannot honestly be told that they can be all that they have the potential for being, because this suggests that they have the same life chances as their White counterparts and such is not the case. This was only true in the past because African American children realized that they functioned in separate worlds, and they could excel only within limits. Today, limits are concealed under an ideological hegemony that suggests that African American women like other groups of individuals can achieve at the same rate. Therefore, African American women are told that they have themselves to blame for their inability to compete successfully in society. The mainstream media and policymakers should be challenged to remove the invisible barriers that belie employers' advertised claims: "Help wanted, women and minorities are encouraged to apply. We are an affirmative action, equal opportunity employer." This pronouncement is untrue in far too many employment situations. African American women outside the labor force must develop effective strategies for dealing with the hypocrisy associated with ideological hegemony and discrimination in education and employment, as well as within other societal institutions.

It is not possible to separate the interrelationships between cultural imagery, familial stability and the depressed socioeconomic status of female-maintained families. While I have examined the effects of media-transmitted images on African American male/female relationships elsewhere, one cannot ignore the impact of cultural images on establishing and maintaining positive and constructive relationships between African males and females.[28] Among stereotypes of African American women, that of the Sapphire image, which portrays the sassy, emasculating African American woman who is constantly putting down her mate, is one of the few images of African American women that depicts the African American woman as having a mate. Interestingly, although the African American woman is seen here with a mate the relationship is depicted as conflict-ridden. The African American male is portrayed as one who does not conform to America's definition of masculinity. Typically, the cultural images of the African American male imply that he is lazy, conniving, dishonest and, like his female counterpart, has a greater capacity to be comedic rather than intelligent. Because these cultural images have been systematically purveyed by the mass media it is reasonable to expect that they have had an adverse effect on African American male/female relationships. The ability to reject and prevent such imagery, that reflects African American males and females interacting in ways that produce conflict, by disrupting relationships, has largely been a function of microcultural institutions and informal processes within the African American community. That is, as long as the African American church, predominantly African American administered schools and the African American family collectively defined cultural images of African American males, females and microcultural institutions, emphasizing their strengths, then images purveyed by the mainstream media had little impact on the stability of African American male/female relationships. In fact, the most significant invalidation of traditional cultural images of African American males and females purveyed by mainstream media can be attributed to the highly visible real-life individuals who lived in the African American community. In addition, African American males and females refuted stereotypic images, thus, gender role expectations were not significantly influenced by the cultural images of African American males and females purveyed by the mainstream media because it was a common belief that the mainstream media and their images represented racial biases that were prevalent throughout the larger society. In fact, African Americans understood that they lived and interacted in separate worlds and that the mainstream media, and the interests they represented, were in conflict with their own interests and cultural definitions.

The ability of African Americans to disregard such imagery has been more difficult to sustain since the Civil Rights Movement. In the aftermath of the Civil Rights Movement, African Americans anticipated increased opportunities to participate in mainstream institutions. During the early phases of the Civil Rights Movement there were many indications that African Americans would experience, in fact, unlimited opportunities to achieve parity with their White counterparts in virtually every societal institution in the United States. One of the conditions for, and projected outcomes of, integration was the view espoused by integrationists that African Americans should adopt the values, beliefs and behaviors of White middle class Americans. Therefore, African Americans underwent a transition in which they began to embrace values, beliefs and behaviors that were characteristic of the White middle class. African American males and females were expected to measure their self-worth, beauty, femininity, masculinity, relationships and institutions against a new set of criteria which the privileged attributed to the White middle class. Accepting a new barometer for measuring relationships, in conjunction with the decline of microcultural institutions and informal systems that had insulated African Americans from mainstream cultural ideologies and imagery, African American male/female relationships, including those within the confines of the family, began to experience instability.

The facility and success with which African American males and females had developed their own ideologies and cultural images which contradicted those that prevailed in the larger society had guaranteed the survival of the African American family, the most salient social and economic institution within the African American community. Unemployment and sex ratio imbalances notwithstanding, it is the case that African American male/female relationships are adversely affected by traditional cultural images

95

that establish gender role expectations that cannot easily be fulfilled by either African American males or females. Just as it is unreasonable to expect that African American males, in general, have the capacity to be the sole breadwinner or to experience unlimited career mobility, it is equally untenable to expect African American women to exhibit passive and submissive behavior in their relationship with their mates and aggressiveness in the workplace. In each situation there are factors external to the individuals that militate against conformity to these White middle class norms. First, in the best case scenario where the African American male has the mental acuity, credentials and network his ascent up the career ladder is still mitigated by racial discrimination, a factor over which he has no control. Moreover, African American women, through a combination of African lineage and the inexorable conditions of American exploitation, oppression and discrimination, have acquired strength, endurance and problem-solving abilities that the mainstream culture defines as masculine qualities. In the past, refusal to accept these definitions and their propensity to substitute these images for microcultural images that define African American males and females from a perspective of strength resulted in the cooperation, stability and edification of African American women and the African American family. To a large extent the fact that these images have greater acceptance by African American men and women has contributed to the instability and disintegration of these relationships within and outside marriage.

Obviously, the increased percentage of African American marriages that are dissolved through divorce and separation has adversely affected the socioeconomic status of African American women. Moreover, the social support that one anticipates from one's mate cannot serve as a buffer for African American women seeking to climb the career ladder. Given the stresses associated with working in the labor force, and the realization that occupational pressures are exacerbated for African American women who are the frequent victims of race, gender and class inequities within the workplace, maintaining a stable and supportive familial environment is essential. However, when African American women are faced with unstable and unsatisfying work and marriages they are not likely to function at an optimal level in either milieu.

Moreover, in the most favorable conditions it is still likely that African American women will experience role strain since they are expected to provide nurturance in addition to their job-related duties in their professional employment. Clearly, when one is evaluated by a broader set of standards it is bound to impact upon how well a person will carry out her other responsibilities in other relationships. Thus, when African American women are expected to perform duties beyond the scope of their job description they must make adjustments in their families or neglect their own personal needs and interests to accommodate the desires of others. This is true if they wish to be positively defined by those within their work and familial environments.

Aside from the social and psychological devastation of divorce, African American women experience significant economic changes in their standard of living with marital disruption. Understandably, since a disproportionate number of separated and divorced African American women have children, they have a tremendous need to work. However, because of the responsibilities of single parenting it is the single parent who has the greatest need to develop her career. She is also faced with more impediments that prevent career development and shorten her ascent on her career ladder. Specifically, separated, divorced or never-married African American women with children must assume the primary responsibility for child-rearing, home management, children's education, health and a multiplicity of other issues related to parenting and performing the functions assigned to the family. And while the African American female head may be better able to rely on a kinship network, the decline in the informal social support system that includes individuals other than kin increases role strain and her ability to develop a career that will elevate the socioeconomic status of the family that she heads. In effect, she is frequently caught in the throes of a vicious cycle that perpetuates poverty, by precluding the acquisition of marketable job skills that would ensure career development.

And for a sizable proportion of the adult African American female population, cultural images wage even further assaults by reducing them to a state of ignominy; the African American woman whose income is below the poverty level and who maintains her family has been portrayed by the mainstream media as symbolizing the most stigmatized status in America, namely the "welfare recipient." It is within the sphere of social welfare that those who control wealth and power have been able to increase significantly their possession of both by establishing a hegemonical paradox for

97

the masses, of warfare versus welfare. When the media associate warfare with national and individual security and welfare with the moral turpitude of a group of individuals who can be identified by race, gender and class, it is little wonder that society in general has developed contempt for the system known as welfare as well as for African American women who have erroneously been defined by the mainstream media as its largest number of recipients.

6

GENDER-ORIENTED
SOCIAL POLICY
An agenda for improving the status of
African American women

SOCIAL POLICY: UNDERLYING ASSUMPTIONS

There have been numerous national social polices formulated
since the 1930s. Some of these policies have been designed to
ensure that goods and services will benefit certain populations and
their needs. Still other policies and social and economic initiatives
were developed and implemented to ensure that the specific
interests of other groups of individuals are met. For example,
social security was designed to ensure that retired persons will
receive monetary benefits; while unemployment compensation is
designed to provide individuals, temporarily outside the civilian
labor market, with income suitable for meeting their basic needs
and, to some extent, their financial obligations. The needs of
women can also be met through social policies and social and
economic programs. These needs arise from functions and roles
that have been traditionally assigned to women in general and
African American women in particular. Social policies that are
geared toward women must respond to needs which result from
cultural values, belief systems and practices that consign these
groups of individuals to the lowest socioeconomic status because
of their race, gender and class. African American women have
many of the same needs as their White counterparts. However,
because of the intersection of race, gender and class inequality,
African American women experience discrimination, exploitation
and oppression in the most inexorable fashion, and their need for
institutional support is greater. To the extent that social policies
are considered gender-oriented policies they must be designed to
facilitate women in performing functions to which they have been
assigned. Policies must also eliminate the structural barriers that

99

prevent women from receiving remuneration appropriate to their personal and professional efforts and investments. Further, the goal of gender-oriented policy must be to ensure that women receive equity and support from societal institutions that will increase their level of participation and give them equal access to opportunity structures that are available to the most privileged members of our society. It is not sufficient to establish a goal for African American women, and women of other racial and ethnic groups, to strive for parity with White males. To do so ignores the role that class plays in determining entitlements and differential access to societal resources and institutions. After all, it is a mistake to believe that all White men have equal access to societal resources. The social hierarchy of discrimination affords some groups of individuals greater access to societal resources and opportunities than others. This hierarchy is constructed so that societal rewards are more available to those individuals who are positioned higher on the hierarchy; while societal rewards become less for individuals who are lower on the hierarchy. While position on the hierarchy is determined largely on the basis of race, gender and class, there are other factors that increase an individual's access to societal rewards and reduce the number of structurally imposed barriers that must be overcome to achieve these culturally defined goals. Included among these factors are physical attributes such as attractiveness, height and weight. Nevertheless, it is important to note that race, gender and class are the primary factors that determine one's placement on the social hierarchy of discrimination. Accordingly, White males are given the greatest access to societal resources. And White males who are born into upper class families are positioned on the highest level of the hierarchy and therefore have the greatest access to societal resources compared to other groups of individuals. Thus, they are more likely to exhibit greater effort in protecting the social order that grants them significantly more opportunities to access societal resources and institutions relative to other groups in society.

Upper class males also have acquaintances and affiliations that guarantee the intergenerational transmission of power and wealth to each successive generation. The same is true of middle and working class males. The network of family, friends and acquaintances ensures that successive generations benefit from the achievements of their predecessors. By contrast, African American women tend to be placed on the bottom of this hierarchy.

Therefore, African American women who are born into poverty have least access to societal rewards, a position shared by other women of color such as Hispanic women and native American women, who are also positioned at the lowest level on the social hierarchy of discrimination. The fact that there is no tradition of power and wealth for African American women means that there is usually no opportunity to transmit an influential network and resources to successive generations. African American women who have incomes below the poverty level, other African American women whose middle class status is tenuous, and those who are dependent upon government employment have few resources and contacts to transmit to their offspring.

Because of the privileged class's use of race, gender and class they have been successful in convincing groups positioned higher on the hierarchy that they are a privileged class and possess qualities that account for their higher positioning and greater access to societal resources and institutions. These same groups are inculcated with stereotypical beliefs that others who are lower on the hierarchy have less access to opportunities because of innate qualities, race, gender, intellectual inferiority, etc. Those positioned in higher strata are also inculcated with the belief that those who are at the highest level of the hierarchy are there because they, like those immediately below them, share similar valuable qualities, including the most visible which are race and gender. The privileged justify their greater access to, and control over, societal resources by arguments surrounding merit and work ethic. They contend that those who work hard and are intellectually able will be rewarded commensurate with their efforts. It is imperative that those who comprise the middle and working classes, the majority of Americans, embrace these beliefs. Their failure to accept these tenets would radically challenge and alter the status quo and existing inequitable distribution and monopoly of wealth and power. If the majority of White middle and working class men recognized the fallacy inherent in this logic and realized that they, like people of color and White women, are also victims of discrimination and exploitation, there would be a revolt of such enormous proportions that the existing social structure in the United States would be dramatically altered. Because most individuals either do not know that they are discriminated against or feel powerless to challenge the inequities that exist, they are willing, either overtly or tacitly, to support the existing social

101

structure with its policies, laws and practices that perpetuate and enhance the privileged class's monopoly of wealth and power. Thus, the relative ease with which the privileged class is able to retain its control over societal resources is through ideological hegemony – convincing the masses that the privileged are entitled to the societal resources they control. Accordingly, the populace through the electoral process gives its consent to political leaders, who are strongly influenced by and connected to the privileged, allocating the public's tax dollars to whomever and in whatever ways they deem appropriate.

Historically, institutions were designed to support and meet the needs of males in the privileged class. In addition, social policies and laws have been formulated to protect the wealth, power and other resources which this class possesses. These systems have been based on cultural myths and erroneous beliefs that justify giving some groups of individuals greater access to institutions and societal resources. These myths attempt to explain why gender, race and class are important determinants of the extent to which individuals have differential access to societal institutions and resources. Explicit and implicit to these myths are theories and tenets that support the domination of various groups over other groups. According to these fallacious explanatory models, males have greater access to societal institutions and resources than females because of their intellectual capacity. The differential access of whites to societal institutions and resources is attributed to their higher intellectual capacity, stronger work ethic and greater adherence to personal morals such as moderation in consumption, frugality, and so forth, compared to African Americans. Similar types of arguments are used to explain the relatively lower level of institutional participation and overall achievement among members of lower socioeconomic classes.

Clearly, women were not expected to be the main benefactors of societal institutions or resources. The goals of the feminist movement focus on the extent to which women have been excluded from participating in societal institutions and limited in their access to societal resources.[1] Likewise, African American women and members of their community have historically been excluded from institutions and resources in the United States. Indeed, the purpose of the Civil Rights Movement was to address the marginality of African American men, women and children. The absence of institutional support for African American women

102

and their community contributed to the formation of mutual aid networks. Further, African American institutions such as predominantly African American schools, churches, the family and Black-owned businesses provided basic goods and services to ensure the survival and progress of African Americans, their culture and institutions. Two important questions which must be answered are: When did institutions within the larger society begin to address the need of African American women? Second, how effective have macrocultural institutions been in meeting the needs of African American women?

Institutions within the United States should be accessible to all of its members, including African American women. The fact that societal institutions have failed to address the needs of African American women can be better understood by examining what the specific needs of African American women are. It is also important to explore similarities that African American women and White women share by virtue of their gender, and the differences in their needs because of the interacting effects of race, gender and class discrimination.

African American women, like women from other racial and ethnic backgrounds, are expected to perform affective functions, particularly those associated with child-rearing and socialization. Other traditional female roles assigned to women, including African American women, include performing domestic duties such as cleaning, cooking, washing and ironing clothes; and wifely duties that entail providing emotional support and companionship for their mates. In addition, African American women have the informally assigned responsibility of guiding and directing the educational careers of their children, a function that is generally assumed by husbands in White families. Because one-third of African Americans have incomes below the poverty level, and a disproportionate percentage of these individuals are single women and children, African American women are faced with a multiplicity of problems associated with poverty. For example, African American women with incomes below and slightly above the poverty level cannot afford medical care, or adequate housing, food and clothing. Other needs include job training, education and child care. And since African American women tend to be victims of gender, race and class discrimination, they need policies and laws that will expand existing practices, rules and regulations that have been designed to include other groups in society, while

103

increasing the probability that African American women are excluded. The unemployment and underemployment of African American men and women places the African American family in a financially strained relationship. The fact that in 1989 African American married-couple families earned $30,650, only 78 per cent of the median income of White married-couple families ($39,208), is but one example of how labor market discrimination affects the standard of living of African American families.[2] Macrocultural institutions were challenged during the 1960s and 1970s to increase the level of participation of African Americans. Specific needs of African American women were not separated from those of all African Americans. However, since the Moynihan report attributed problems confronting the African American population to the African American female single-maintained family, many believed that social policies and social and economic programs would significantly improve the socioeconomic status of African American women, men and others with incomes below the poverty level. When one reviews the gains over the past 30 years it becomes obvious that, while changes did occur, the controllers of institutions continue to refuse to increase significantly the level of participation of African American women.

SOCIAL POLICY AND AFRICAN AMERICAN WOMEN

There are many areas that one can examine to determine the extent to which social policies have impacted upon African American women. Because the needs of African American women and others within their community have been neglected for so long, time and spatial constrictions make it impossible to consider the effects of social policies in all areas. Therefore, only the social policies and social and economic programs that emerged during the 1930s and again during the era of liberal social policy in the 1960s and 1970s are discussed later in this chapter. Specific attention is given to social welfare programs, affirmative action programs, job training and health and medical programs. A description is given of the various social and economic programs that were enacted, followed by their impact on the status of African American women in macrocultural and microcultural institutions. It is important to note that the lives and opportunities of African American women have been severely restricted by social policies, many of which were based on erroneous assumptions that attributed the social and economic problems facing African Americans to African American women; the absence of social policies for African Americans has also had a devastating effect on the functioning capacity of African American women and their communities.

Aside from a brief period from 1865 to 1872, about seven years, during Reconstruction, when the Freedmen's Bureau provided goods and services to African American women and their community, African American women received little support from the federal government until the 1960s.

SOCIAL WELFARE POLICIES AND PRACTICES AND AFRICAN AMERICAN WOMEN

It was not until 1935 that the federal government was forced to formulate a national social policy to relieve economic pressures resulting from the Depression. The passage of the Social Security Act in 1935 marked the federal government's first attempt since emancipation to respond to the needs of the economically disadvantaged on a large scale. By creating social insurance, public assistance, and health and welfare services under the Social Security Act, the federal government temporarily restored confidence and the productivity necessary for consumption. Not all members of society derived the same level of benefit from these initiatives. In fact, African American women, men and children received relatively few benefits from these efforts. For example, social security benefits were not extended to individuals employed in service industries and agricultural occupations; thereby excluding the majority of African American women and their spouses who were employed in these occupations. Since African American women have always played a major role as co-breadwinners, and because the rates of African American male unemployment and underemployment have had a significant effect on the economic well-being of the family, it is important to examine the impact that social policies and social welfare programs have had on African American families, including those headed by women.

Aid To Dependent Children, the first federally sponsored public assistance program, is a social welfare program that should have had a positive effect on African American families. In reality, African American women who headed families were not

105

significantly affected. Although African American families suffered immeasurably from poverty in the 1930s, only 18 per cent of Black family heads in 1933 and 15 per cent in 1935 were certified by the government to receive public relief.[3] These programs offered subsistence payments to the few African American children who were certified. Certainly, greater numbers of African American children were impoverished than those who received government financial assistance. In fact, during the Depression years the rate of African American unemployment was 50 per cent, while White unemployment was 25 per cent.[4] In addition, the early public assistance programs offered no financial support to children's guardians, who were usually women. By the mid-1940s federal allocations to the few existing social programs, created under the New Deal, had been reduced.[5] Several years later, in the 1950s, legislation was passed to expand social welfare programs further, to enable more of society's dependents, namely women and children, to improve their standard of living. Again, African American women who headed families or were married to spouses whose employment was adversely affected by economic downturns and institutional discrimination did not receive adequate financial support to care for their families.

The 1950s, while introducing legislation that increased the number of potential beneficiaries by liberalizing benefit payments through modifications in benefit formulas, was a period in which the conservative, and even reactionary, administration of these programs resulted in few benefits for African American women and their children. The Aid To Dependent Children Program was amended to include guardians and became known as Aid to Families with Dependent Children in 1950. However, African American women were frequently prohibited from being recipients of this program by discrimination in its administration. In addition, several regional policies and practices severely limited the number of African American women and children who were admitted to public assistance rolls. The stigma associated with these programs also began to increase as it was defined as a program for the needy. By contrast, social programs, like social security insurance, which would enhance the standard of living of the middle class, received considerable public support. Policies that prevented African American women and their children from qualifying for public monies to which they were entitled included the "man-in-the-house" rule, "substitute fathers," "suitable home" and residency policies. These policies were adopted by many states to prevent the addition of new recipients and to remove existing recipients from the welfare rolls.

According to Valentine, the Aid to Dependent Children Program contains the implicit assumption that men are supposed to provide for their families; if the government assumes this responsibility then the government becomes the father. Further she states ". . . and as a requirement for continued aid specifies that no other man may have a relationship with the mother or children."[6] These policies and practices had a devastating impact upon African American women and their families, who found themselves systematically excluded from the labor market, and from acquiring a quality education and marketable job skills. African American women and children were also at a disadvantage because of the inexorable social and economic conditions that were placed upon their African American husbands and fathers, such as the "man-in-the-house" rule and residence requirements that were enforced to prevent African Americans from receiving public assistance. The "man-in-the-house" policy clearly has its origins in early premisses regarding the causes of poverty. Colonial beliefs that poverty is a function of able-bodied men refusing to adopt American values of work, moderate consumption and frugality undergirded the US social welfare system's policies and practices. Added to the social and economic disadvantages imposed upon the African American woman and her family was the societal presupposition that people are poor because of laziness, a flawed moral character, and a disregard for the American values of work and moderate consumption. In addition to these assumptions regarding the poor were the philosophies retained from slavery that African Americans possessed many of the same qualities attributed to the poor – laziness, shiftlessness, dishonesty, and so forth. It was, therefore, believed that African Americans who were poor, like poor Whites, had but themselves to blame. When men could not adequately provide for their families blame was attributed to the individual and his community and not to an unjust society. Moreover, the "man-in-the-house" policy forced the man, who was thought to have shirked his familial responsibility because of his inability to provide for the economic needs of his wife and children, to leave his family. In so doing, they were able to qualify for public assistance. When husbands and fathers left their families to enable their wives and children to obtain meager, but essential, benefits from social welfare programs, they were labeled by society as deserters. In reality these men were forced out of their homes to ensure the survival of their wives and children.

Welfare administrators and practitioners, as well as the privileged in society, strongly believed that a family should not be impoverished if there was an able-bodied man residing in the house. Therefore, in order for children and, later, their guardians (a mother or other single female) to receive benefits no man was permitted to reside in the house. This type of reasoning had two adverse effects on African American families. First, this policy and its underlying assumptions has led to the cultural devaluation of African American men who are financially unable to care for the economic needs of their wives and children. Second, this policy has contributed to the existence of female single-parent families among African Americans, by forcing African American men to leave their families, thereby enabling their wives and children to qualify for needed social and economic social services.

Midnight raids to determine if welfare mothers were ineligible for aid, by virtue of living with a man, were frequent. The "man-in-the-house" policy precluded children and their adult female guardians from receiving aid if a man resided with them.

When these policies were revised during the 1970s they were replaced by practices that have had the same effect of disrupting African American families as the earlier policies. There is evidence that social welfare agencies and practitioners usurp and obviate the role of the African American father.

Hopkins states that social welfare agencies exclude African American fathers from decision-making and planning, and that this affects the stability and future socioeconomic status of fathers.[7] Bahr quotes Theodore Caplow as labeling social welfare programs as a "family smashing device."[8] Few can argue that the current and past social welfare system in the United States is designed to facilitate the maintenance of African American two-parent families. I am not suggesting that African American men and women dissolve their marriages for the purpose of qualifying for the social and economic services provided by the social welfare system, for such is not the case. Rather, it is fairly obvious that the social welfare system generates dissension between spouses and establishes a familial climate in which the father's role is devalued. When these factors are combined with the problems and complexities of occupying a socially and economically depressed status caused by poverty, it is no wonder that the US social welfare system is a destabilizing factor for two-parent poor families. In many instances fathers are not included in social welfare agencies' planning and programming involving mothers and children. Cash payments are usually endorsed to the mother, and training, educational programs, career counseling, housing, medical and other services are usually geared to the needs of the mother and children. And planning and the approval of such services generally occur between the social worker and the mother. Hill also reports that welfare payments tend to be lower in states that offer aid to dependent children with unemployed fathers. Therefore, in some states, social welfare policies and practices are more financially advantageous for single mothers with incomes below the poverty level than for two-parent families in need of welfare services.[9]

Another means of reducing welfare rolls was the determination of whether a home was "suitable." Clearly, these definitions were established by welfare administrators and are replete with cultural biases related to race, social class and custom. Even when African American women and their children lived in homes that met the conditions for suitability, the level of scrutiny to which single mothers and their families were subjected was unconscionable.

Of all the policies that were instituted, residency policies were among the most devastating, and were the most successful in keeping African American women and their children from ever being admitted to the public welfare rolls. Residency policies, adopted by many states, were employed most effectively to keep African American women and children from receiving public assistance. Residency policies required that a welfare recipient be a resident of the state in order to receive public assistance. By enforcing residency policies, states were able to prevent African American migrants who moved from the South to the North from receiving public assistance. And since large numbers of African Americans migrated from the North to the South between 1950 and 1960, a sizable percentage were affected by this policy. Many African American women and their families, including their spouses, who had limited job opportunities in the South, undoubtedly made decisions not to move North because they were in need of but ineligible for the emergency, albeit temporary, assistance that would have "tided them over" until they secured permanent employment. The AFDC program became known as a social welfare program for women and children. And because of the higher visibility of poor urban-dwelling African American families headed by women, the AFDC program became synonymous with a program for African American women and their children. All of the stereotypic images and belief systems associated with being poor and African American coalesced to create the image of the program as one that was a drain on the social fabric and economic coffers of American society. Continuous efforts to coerce men to leave their families through more sophisticated methods of intimidation had the desired results. States developed policies for administering public assistance to two-parent families, where the husband was unemployed, which sometimes resulted in lower benefits for two-parent families than for female-maintained families.[10] In addition, the social welfare practice of making decisions about African American families that excluded the male thereby usurped his authority as husband-father. Such practices are disruptive to African American families and contribute to female headship. The prevalence of these families, which are blamed for the dire social and economic conditions facing African Americans, is due in part to the US social welfare system. Thus, an overt form of pushing African American men out of the home, the "man-in-the-house" rule, was replaced with more subtle policies and practices that also contributed to female headship and its concomitants.

There is little doubt that social welfare programs that were designed to improve the standard of living for African American women and their families had a destabilizing effect on them. These programs have helped to foster African American single-parent families who are poor and for whom ascent from an impoverished class is highly improbable. The added role strain, and financial and social responsibility, that this places on African American women is tremendous.

The first real indication that a relationship existed between social welfare programs and the stability of African American families became apparent in the 1950s.[11] Gradually, observable changes in the structure of African American families became discernible. Amidst high rates of unemployment during the 1950s, the proportion of women and children who were welfare recipients began to increase. Previously, African American women and their families received considerable support by consolidating their economic and noneconomic resources with extended kin; however, new social programs that provided social security coverage

110

for the elderly resulted in a decline in extended families. The greater independence of the African American elderly, based on a value system embraced by the larger society, was interpreted as a positive accomplishment. Looking closer, such was not the case. The fact that the African American extended family began to decline meant added hardships for African American women, many of whom worked outside the home and benefited from the domestic duties and child care that older African American women, usually a relative, provided. This familial arrangement served to reduce role strain and financial pressures. Elderly African American women also experienced tremendous financial problems brought on by limited resources and independent living arrangements. In 1989, 30.8 per cent of all African Americans 65 years of age and over were poor compared to 9.6 per cent of Whites. Moreover, elderly African American females were three times as likely to be poor as elderly White females.[12] And when one considers the innumerable problems associated with female head-ship it is reasonable to believe that African American children raised, for myriad reasons, without a father in the home suffer even more being reared in a family without the benefit of an extended family.

Medicaid, another social welfare program instituted in 1965 as Title XIX of the Social Security Act, defrays medical and health costs primarily for individuals receiving public assistance. Clearly, Medicaid has had an impact on the availability of health and medical care for African American families with incomes below the poverty level. Nevertheless, Medicaid has not been available to numerous families with incomes slightly above the poverty level. In addition, there are large numbers of private health care providers who do not accept Medicaid as a form of payment. For example, 95 per cent of dentists in New York State refuse to accept Medicaid payments because of the low fee schedule. Therefore, although Medicaid is designed to increase access to health care, as Law points out, "it is limited in its ability to assure the availability of doctors in private practice".[13] An inordinate number of African American women and their children who reside in the inner city must use outpatient service, usually emergency rooms, of hospitals to receive medical attention.

Medicare was established in 1965 to ensure greater access to medical and health care for the elderly, but falls short of this goal. This is particularly true for inner-city women, many of whom are poor and elderly. Because African American women tend to out-live their spouses they usually reside alone in the inner city. And since private physicians prefer practicing in suburban communities and on the periphery of cities, where self-pay and private insurance carriers reside, African American elderly women, like their youthful counterparts, have limited access to private health care physicians. Law, and others, discuss the dilemma of the demand for quality health and medical care for the large number of African American women and their dependent children who live in the inner city and the relatively small number of physicians available to render these services.[14] Thus, while health care policy in the 1960s and 1970s has improved the overall health of African American women in terms of extending their life expectancy from 68.3 years in 1970 to 73.8 year in 1988, a number of problems remain for African American women and their dependents.

In the United States the infant mortality rate, 10 deaths per 1,000 live births, is extremely high compared to other industrialized countries. The lack of accessible and available prenatal care continues to contribute to an infant mortality rate for African American infants that is twice the rate of White infants. In 1981 there were approximately 20.0 African American infant deaths per 1,000 live births compared to 43.9 in 1950. In contrast, there were 10.5 White infant deaths per 1,000 live births in 1981 as opposed to 26.8 per 1,000 in 1950.[15] African American women also experienced a 76 per cent decrease in maternal deaths related to reproductive complications, which is reflected in 22.1 deaths per 100,000 live births in 1981 compared to 92.1 per 100,000 in 1960.[16] By 1987 the maternal death rate for African American women had declined to 14.2 per 100,000 live births. White women's maternal mortality rates decreased from 22.4 per 100,000 in 1960 to 6.5 per 100,000 in 1981. And by 1987 White women had an even lower maternal death rate of 5.1 per 100,000. Aside from issues of availability, accessibility and affordability of health care, Headen and Headen (1989) attribute the continuing high rate of maternal and infant mortality for African American women to the higher birthrate and frequency of age-related high-risk pregnancies for African American women.

Clearly, health policies have had a positive impact on the overall health status of African American women. However, it is still the case that while they will live longer they are still likely to experience illness and disability for a considerable period of their lives.

The chronic conditions that African American women are likely to have, some associated with a higher proportion that are overweight, include diabetes mellitus, hypertension, heart disease and cerebrovascular disease. Existing government-funded medical and health insurance is inadequate to ensure that these and other health problems of African American women are prevented or treated effectively.

The Foodstamp Program is a social welfare program administered by the US Department of Agriculture. In 1990 the government allocated $14 billion to the Foodstamp Program. Foodstamps are purchased by individuals for a portion of their face value, or are received without payment based on family size and income. They are generally used for the purchase of food products in grocery stores. Approximately one in every four African Americans is a recipient of foodstamps. Because foodstamps and cash outlays to poor families are generally insufficient to meet the nutritional needs of growing children, many states offer school lunch programs. In 1990, the federal government spent $3.8 billion on the National School Lunch Program. In 1982, 1.9 million African American households and 3.5 million White households relied on school lunch programs to supplement their children's diets. Women, Infants and Children (WIC) is another nutritional program for which the government allocated $2.2 billion in 1990. It is a program that is offered to families with incomes below the poverty level. Not only Children and their mothers, but also pregnant women, have participated in the WIC program. However, while the demand for such programs increases, federal budgetary allocations do not; thereby, limiting the availability of these much needed programs.

Job-training programs were expected to make a major change in the rate of unemployment and in poverty and its concomitants for African American women, especially those who head families. But while job-training programs have increased women's participation in the labor force, they have done little to effect a permanent and substantial improvement in the labor market participation rates of African American women. Contrary to popular belief, securing employment does not guarantee that women will not be poor. This is especially true of African American women, who are more likely to be trained for and employed in female-intensive labor. Since traditional female occupations generally provide entry level salaries, women who are trained for these jobs are seldom able to make significant improvements in their standard of living.

Job-training programs, including the Manpower Demonstration and Training Act (MDTA) in 1962, the Comprehensive Employment and Training Act (1973) and the Joint Training Partnership Act in 1982, have offered limited opportunities to African American women, particularly those who maintain families.

These programs, and other job-training programs, initiated in the 1960s during Johnson's war on poverty, were designed to reduce welfare rolls by providing work to women recipients of Aid to Families with Dependent Children. They included Job Opportunities in the Business Sector (JOBS), established in 1968; Job Corps and the Neighborhood Youth Corps (NYC), created by the 1964 Economic Opportunity Act (EOA); and the 1967 Work Incentive Program (WIN), created by Title IV of the Social Security Act.

The 1962 Manpower Demonstration and Training Act (MDTA), which paved the way for the first employment and training program, provided classroom and on-the-job training to occupationally disadvantaged workers. Unlike MDTA which, like other "Great Society" job-training programs, was nationally administered, the Comprehensive Employment and Training Act (CETA) required that state and local governments or local prime sponsors accept responsibility for administering employment and training programs.[17]

Burbridge cogently responds to the impact that employment and training programs have had on women by identifying the following four "facts" which, she states, characterize employment and training programs:

1 Women have been underrepresented in these programs.
2 Large proportions of female participants have been trained for female-intensive occupations.
3 Underrepresentation and occupational segmentation notwithstanding, women have experienced higher income gains compared to men which are attributable to these programs.
4 Postprogram earnings of women trainees are generally barely enough to keep them out of poverty.[18]

Although Burbridge applies these facts to both White and African American women, they have greater applicability to the latter, largely because 50 per cent of African American children are in families headed by a woman and because, even in two-parent African American families, wives contribute more to family income than in White families.[19]

In examining African American women's experiences in the Joint Training Partnership Act Title IIA programs, Harper (1989) was interested in determining to what extent JTPA provided economically disadvantaged African American women with employment and training services. She was also interested in determining whether African American women who had experienced occupational displacement and "employment setbacks" during the 1982 recession had gained assistance in reentering the labor market. She found that approximately 64 per cent of the female participants who completed this program secured employment. However, the majority of participants who entered employment were involved in on-the-job training as opposed to classroom training. Because so few African American participants were involved in on-the-job training during the period studied (6,700 or 11.8 per cent), Harper (1989) states that the data do not allow for any meaningful conclusions to be drawn. However, Harper maintains that the only significant activity for African American women was classroom training; and that slightly more than 50 per cent of those who participated in this activity (17,000 or 52.6 per cent of adult females 22 years and older, and 11,800 or 48.6 per cent of females under 22 years of age) secured employment.

Assignments had a significant impact on the program outcome. On-the-job training was superior to classroom training, yet African American women were significantly underrepresented in the former activity. Taggart's research revealed that women, Hispanics, single parents and those with limited English-speaking ability had a higher probability than males of being assigned to classroom training instead of receiving OJT assignments.[20]

Jeffries' assessment of placement outcomes is also revealing. He notes, as did Harper, that training assignments were correlated with employment placement. Since African American women were generally assigned to classroom training, they were often placed in the less desirable and less rewarding assignment of public service employment (PSE).[21] Thus, the most frequent placement for African American women was work experience (WE). Whether an individual was given a particular assignment was determined, according to Bloom, by participants' preprogram earnings and "relative employability."[22] Prospective participants with higher preprogram earnings were assigned to OJT. Therefore, African American women, who tended to have lower earnings, were assigned to classroom training and ultimately received work experience placements in traditionally female occupations, with accompanying low earnings. According to Jeffries, "there may have been some confusion over the extent to which pre-program earnings reflect an economically-disadvantaged person's potential employability as opposed to sex-differentiated wage systems."[23]

In view of impact studies, it is clear that greater percentages of African American women should be given training assignments in OJT and provided with ancillary supports that will ensure placement in jobs in non-occupationally segregated employment.

AFFIRMATIVE ACTION

Affirmative action was intended to bring about equality in education and employment. In effect, affirmative action was designed to increase the level of participation of African American men, women and children in societal institutions. Affirmative action was directed towards two major institutions which had systematically excluded African Americans, thus contributing significantly to their economically depressed status. Essentially, educational institutions and the economic system had excluded African American women and others in their community. Moreover, these institutions, because of race, gender and class discrimination had effectively consigned African American women to the lowest rung of the socioeconomic ladder, with the African American male positioned only slightly above the African American female. African American men, women and children had been systematically excluded from these and other societal institutions through laws, policies and practices predicated on a belief system that defined African Americans as deficient in the qualities essential for successful participation in societal institutions. Because these beliefs were largely perpetuated by the mass media it was essential that the mass media play a strategic role in eliminating these negative and stereotypic beliefs regarding African American men, women and children. Moreover, the media carried the responsibility of exposing the myths and contradictions inherent in these belief systems and of purveying accurate information and images of African American women that legitimized their ability and right to participate fully in institutions from which they had been historically excluded. In effect, the media's role in the Civil Rights Movement of the 1960s and 1970s was important. The ability of social movements to effect social change due to the integral role of the mainstream media has received considerable examination by Gitlin.[24]

Assessing the extent to which social and economic advances were made by African American men and women because of affirmative action policies and practices instituted during the 1960s and 1970s requires that gender and class be included in the analysis. Differential gains in education and employment were registered by African American women compared to African American men. In effect, African American women with a slightly higher level of educational achievement than African American males continued to experience slightly higher increases in their levels of educational achievement. Similarly, African American women experienced a higher rate of occupational mobility during the 1960s and 1970s, mainly because of affirmative action legislation. Still, gains that African American women made were being minuscule and were gradually attenuated by the 1980s.

Wilkerson notes that a cursory glance at college attendance rates fails to reveal the inordinate number of African American students enrolled in two-year community colleges. Stating that the dropout rate is higher at these institutions than at four-year colleges, she also asserts that the economic recession of 1975, along with a decrease in federal assistance to students, has meant that the two-year college, while representing a dead-end for many African American students, is the only "viable educational route for many African American single women with children."[25]

Considering the wide educational gap that once existed between African Americans and Whites, substantial strides were made in narrowing this gap. Still, when the dropout rate is considered it becomes clear that, while there was an increase in the number of African Americans attending and graduating from high school, the attrition rate was also high. According to Wilkerson, although African American female high school dropout rates had decreased by 7.2 per cent between 1971 and 1981, this rate was still 5.1 per cent higher than that of White females.[26] In 1988 the dropout rate for African American females remained higher at 15.9 per cent compared to White females whose dropout rate was

117

13 per cent.[27] Ostensibly, teenage pregnancy is a major factor that accounts for 50 per cent of African American females who drop out of high school. In 1990, 55 per cent of African American females had children out of wedlock and a disproportionate number of these children were born to African American teenage mothers. And while teenage pregnancy is, as Wilkerson states, responsible for teenage mothers entering into a cycle of poverty, unemployment and underemployment, these social dislocations also lead to teenage pregnancy. In other words, teenage females who live in families characterized by poverty, unemployment and underemployment, with mothers who also had teenage pregnancies, are likely to have daughters who continue, rather than initiate, this pattern. The high rate of teenage unemployment is also an important determinant of teenage pregnancy. It is therefore alarming to note that in 1988 African American female teenagers had an unemployment rate of 32.0 per cent compared to 12.3 per cent for White female teenagers.[28]

Financial difficulties confronting historically African American colleges have also had an adverse effect on the number of African Americans attending and graduating from institutions of higher education. Before the 1970s most African American college students attended historically Black colleges. However, affirmative action led to African Americans having greater access to and being better able to afford to attend predominantly White institutions of higher education because of their financial aid programs. Enrollment declines have been constant for Black colleges since 1980 and, today, only 20 per cent of African American college students are enrolled in historically Black colleges. This is true in spite of the fact that approximately 80 per cent of all students attending these schools graduate. By contrast, of the almost 80 per cent of African Americans enrolled in predominantly White colleges, a mere 20 per cent graduate.

The failure of colleges and universities to increase significantly the participation and graduation rates of African American women became apparent in the 1980s. The fact that enrollment has not increased substantially for African American women, especially in graduate and professional schools, has been attributed to cutbacks in federal dollars and an anti-affirmative action posture of colleges, due to the reverse discrimination complaints of Bakke and Defunis, both upheld by the Supreme Court.[29] Other factors that have contributed to the failure of colleges and universities to increase significantly the number of African American females earning graduate and professional degrees include the paucity of faculty mentors, a lack of African American feminist scholarship integrated into the collegiate literature, and a limited number of African American women in policy-making positions. Overall, the gains that African American women made in the area of education began to undergo erosion in the later 1970s and throughout the 1980s. And in view of the fact that the 1990s represents an era characterized by a reactionary posture, it is unlikely that additional gains in educational achievement are likely to be experienced by African American women. In order for such advances to occur, African American women and other disenfranchised groups will have to remobilize and pursue various forms of protest to make affirmative action policy, and enforcement, effective in the sphere of education.

Affirmative action has also provided minuscule rewards relative to occupational mobility and income for African American women. Because of the correlation between education and occupation it is no surprise that modest gains in education, after the peak of the Civil Rights Movement in the 1970s, would also characterize African American women's experiences in the economic arena. Affirmative action is usually cited as having given African Americans access to occupational areas that had been restricted to them prior to the 1960s. Occupational advances did take place between 1960 and 1980 after which a devolutionary trend became firmly entrenched again, eroding earlier advances made by African Americans, especially women. Between 1960 and 1980 African American women made greater advances regarding their occupational status than did African American men. During this period, many African Americans moved from service to semi-skilled occupations to white-collar jobs. In 1960, only 16 per cent of African Americans in the civilian labor force worked in white-collar jobs, compared to 47 per cent of employed whites. In 1980, 36.6 per cent of African Americans had risen to white-collar positions while 53.9 per cent of Whites were white-collar workers. By 1990, 43.5 per cent of African Americans were working in white-collar occupations compared to 55.6 per cent of all White workers.

Occupational shifts for African American women between 1960 and 1980 were apparent as the proportion of African American women working in technical, sales and administrative support jobs increased from 9 per cent in 1960 to 34 per cent in 1980 and 39.7 per cent in 1990. Like African American women, White women in 1990 were overrepresented in these female dominated occupations with 45.7 per cent. Nevertheless, when all service occupations are considered, such as nursing aides, attendants, cooks and so forth, the percentage of African American women in service-related occupations exceeded one-fourth in 1990 (27 per cent) compared to 16.1 per cent for White women workers. A sizable number of African American women remain in low-paying and entry-level jobs.

Hence, although there were more African American women in white-collar occupations, largely due to affirmative action policy, these women remained in occupationally segregated jobs. African American women did not move in appreciably large numbers into managerial and professional occupations. African American female managers and professionals increased from 10 per cent in 1970 to 11 per cent in 1980. By 1989 18.8 per cent of African American women were working in managerial and professional occupations. In the same year 27.4 per cent of White women were employed as managers and professionals.[30]

In general, occupational gains in professional areas were made by African Americans, particularly African American women, in female-intense occupations such as teaching, social work and nursing.

Unquestionably, the resistance to affirmative action was more apparent in the area of employment than in any other area. Efforts were made through various civil rights enforcement agencies to enforce affirmative action laws. Regulations required that public agencies and private firms holding federal contracts of prede-termined amounts had to establish affirmative action policies and practices. Typically, these measures were used reluctantly and resulted in only a modicum of token jobs.[31] Because of the resistance to affirmative action, and the inability of enforcement agencies to bring about compliance in employment, it is under-standable that the impact of this policy for effecting equity in the workplace generated little success for African Americans, including African American women. Hill sheds some light on the benefits that African Americans derived from affirmative action programs in the private sector. He states that, between 1974 and 1977, 53 per cent of all new jobs in the private sector went to White women. White males obtained 26 per cent of new jobs, Hispanics

12 per cent, and African Americans and Asians secured a mere 5 per cent.[32] While Hill's discussion has applicability to African American men and women collectively, it is possible to make some reasonable deductions regarding the extent to which African American women benefited from affirmative action programs in the private sector.

The corporate sector, seeking quasi-compliance with affirmative action, found catchall positions for African Americans, including women, in human resources. These positions, while vital to the recruitment and retention efforts of the corporation, usually result in the acquisition of job skills that have limited utility and marketability throughout the corporation and within other corporations. Therefore, promotion and policy-making opportunities for those who work in this area tend to be confined to this organizational unit. Accordingly, placing a disproportionate number of African American women in human resources ensures that they will remain isolated from, and outside, the mainstream of corporate decision-making. Certainly, the career ladder in human resources is considerably shorter and earnings are significantly limited relative to other occupations within the corporate environment.

The government has not been an exemplary role model, in spite of the fact that it has the ultimate responsibility for establishing and enforcing the nation's affirmative action policy. The percentage of African Americans in federal employment *is* higher than their proportion in the population. This trend, established during the Depression, continues today as one of every four federal employees is either African American or a member of another non-European racial or ethnic group. But African Americans do not hold policy-making positions throughout the government. Rather, they tend to be employed in such enclaves as the departments of human services and human resources.

Critics of the federal government's role in enforcing affirmative action in both the public and private sector cite the inability of the enforcement entities, the Equal Employment Opportunity Commission and the Civil Rights Commission, to eliminate occupational segmentation, to effect pay equity for protected groups, and to ensure that African Americans have the same employment opportunities as do Whites. The federal government has not been able to enact or enforce an affirmative action policy that has the capacity to overcome the societal barriers, including policies, practices and laws, that prevent African American women from reaching educational, occupational and economic parity with others within society. Before the federal government could establish effective enforcement policies and procedures, efforts were under way to challenge existing affirmative action policy in educational and employment milieux. Legal challenges to affirmative action, along with the conservative position of the Nixon–Ford administrations in the 1970s and the reactionary posture of the Reagan–Bush administrations in the 1980s and 1990s, are responsible for the failure of affirmative action to increase significantly opportunities for African American women and other disenfranchised groups. Various strategies and approaches are proposed in Chapter 9 for the purpose of strengthening affirmative action policy and reducing the effects of laws, policies and practices that perpetuate race, gender and class discrimination within the United States.

7

THE US LEGAL SYSTEM
Protecting the rights of the privileged

Despite appearances to the contrary, the extent to which women in the United States enjoy legal rights is determined by the power and privilege of the men to whom they are socially, politically and economically aligned.

The US legal system represents a codification of laws, procedures and enforcers, all with the express purpose of representing the interests of the privileged. It is a system that is enshrouded in the belief that purports to offer fair and just treatment in all cases based on the merits of each. In sum, the American legal system is predicated on the belief that purportedly guarantees that all individuals will receive justice in the resolution of civil, criminal and constitutional matters. There is evidence that this ideology has been challenged by academicians, legal experts and others. However, there has never been a collective social movement which has successfully instituted meaningful legal reforms resulting in a fairer and more equitable system of justice for African American women and others, whose race, gender and class mitigate against their ability to receive justice in the United States.

Theoretically, the legal system provides the mechanism for the enforcement of social and economic policies, and imposes sanctions for the violations of these policies.

It is through policies and practices that societal resources are allocated to individuals based on their position on the social hierarchy of discrimination. The rights of groups of individuals are also protected by the legal system in accordance with their location on the social hierarchy of discrimination. The rights of women, in general, and African American women in particular, are less likely to be protected than those of any other group in society, because African American women occupy the lowest position on this hierarchy. Although the legal system has the primary mission of protecting the rights of the privileged this does not mean that others within society do not receive justice within the legal system. In some instances the legal system does provide legal remedies for African American women and other women of color when their civil rights have been violated. However, this occurs when these women are aligned with men whose political, social and economic standing permit them to enjoy the same privileges as the males. In other words, African American women, and women in general, are likely to receive justice within the American legal system whenever their needs and interests coincide, rather than conflict, with the needs and interests of those in power.

The mass media have always played a salient role in contributing to the ineffectiveness of the legal system in protecting the civil rights of African American women. It is the media who define and purvey to the masses the legitimacy of individual and class action legal claims of civil rights violations. Interestingly, it was the mass media that exposed the many social injustices committed against African Americans prior to and during the Civil Rights era in the South. Again, Gitlin convincingly argues that the media have a powerful impact on social movements.[1] In addition, Tuchman and Gitlin are among those who contend that the news media are dependent upon ideologies established by social institutions. Moreover, they suggest that media news organizations accept these ideologies and information as legitimate and reject ideologies and information from other sources.[2] Although African Americans were also the victims of *de facto* racial segregation as well as class and gender discrimination, in regions outside the South, the mass media focused on the enormous civil and constitutional rights violations that occurred in egregious forms in the South.

Shortly after African Americans began to benefit from affirmative action and the various social and economic initiatives instituted during the 1960s and 1970s, the mass media began to transmit the message that African Americans and White women were gaining admission into institutions of higher education and were being hired for positions for which they were less qualified than White male applicants. The media were explicit in conveying the information that affirmative action was a concession to African Americans at the expense of Whites. Included in this message was the premiss that affirmative action universally resulted in tokenism, whereby members of racial and ethnic groups and

124

women were being hired in positions exclusively because of their race and gender, with little regard for qualifications. In addition, the mass media have systematically portrayed affirmative action as a mechanism that undermines meritocracy, one of the most championed virtues in America. After all, one of the most widely held beliefs in Western culture is that individuals who succeed do so because of merit. Moreover, the privileged have successfully inculcated the masses with the belief that race, gender and class are factors that determine an individual's ability to compete. They concede that there are exceptional individuals who belong to certain groups of underachievers but, none the less, they are able to achieve because their efforts are meritorious. These individuals are considered rare, but are examples to others who are members of these marginal groups, that there is hope for them if they change their values and behaviors. These success stories are held up as role models because they suggest that with proper values and hard work all people, even those who belong to what are called subcultures, can succeed. These contradictions are seldom addressed by those who proffer such ideologies.

The mass media also made African American women the recipients of greater hostility and contempt from Americans who believe media images that African American women, more than any other disenfranchised group are the greatest beneficiaries of affirmative action. The mass media erroneously informed the larger society that African American women represent a group known as "two-fers."[3] According to this myth, African American women, because of their race and gender, enable employers to meet two sets of affirmative action goals fulfilling the requirements for gender and race. Epstein refuted this widely circulated and accepted myth, which, like others, has resulted in considerable media-inspired disaffection with affirmative action.[4] The harsh reality that confronts African American women clearly indicates that their race and gender place them in double jeopardy rather than offering them dual benefits. And when class is taken into consideration, African American females are likely to experience a multiplicity of adverse consequences due to the interactive effects of race, gender and class discrimination.

AFRICAN AMERICAN WOMEN AND CIVIL RIGHTS

Regrettably, the legal system has done little to provide remedies for African American women for race and gender discrimination, which are prohibited by law. One of the reasons that African American women continue to face the most egregious forms of race and gender discrimination, without protection from the legal system, is that the long-awaited 1964 Civil Rights Act, like social policies of that era, is highly ineffective as a remedy for civil rights violations of African American women and other disenfranchised groups. There are many problems with the 1964 Civil Rights Act and the legal system that prevent women in general and African American women, in particular, from receiving fair and equitable treatment within all societal institutions including the legal system.

First, assumptions regarding the legal rights of African American women suggest that because of their gender they are not entitled to the same rights as men. Next, by virtue of their race, it is assumed that African American women are not entitled to the same rights as Whites. The assumption that African American women, and all women, do not enjoy the same rights as men is deeply entrenched in American society. Accordingly, these same assumptions are responsible for the socially and economically depressed status of African American women in all institutions within the United States.

There is a surfeit of evidence that slavery elevated the status of White women in the United States, freeing them from the lowest social status and from performing menial jobs, within and outside the home. It is also the case that White women continue to receive privileges and rights not available to African American women. They do so not because men with power believe that their value and worth is equal to that of men. On the contrary, White women indirectly and vicariously enjoy the privileges guaranteed to the men with whom they have established liaisons, and in most cases such liaisons exist within the legal confines of marriage, an institution over which virtually all men have unchallengeable control.

Ideologies regarding the rights of women, like most social conventions, originated in the United States from privileged males. Maintaining supremacy on the basis of gender has enabled men in power to create and maintain a permanent divisive force between males and females within American society. Creating artificial systems of domination based on superficial qualities, such as gender and race, detracts attention from the real factors and conditions that contribute to inequities among various groups in society.[5] In our society, since gender is used as a basis for

126

domination, men who subscribe to male superiority as an ideology believe that the rights of women are subordinate to those of men. Proponents of this view expect the legal system to offer greater protection to men than to women.

Similarly, because race is also employed as a system of domination, the legal system is designed to enforce the rights of Whites at the expense of the rights of African Americans and other non-European ethnic groups. The legal system is not the only institution in society that was established on the myth that race, gender and class are determinants of one's entitlement to societal resources and institutions. All societal institutions were founded upon this and other myths; yet it is the legal system that has the ultimate authority and responsibility for enforcing the rights of one group of individuals over those of another. Clearly, those in power perceive the maintenance of their monopoly of power and wealth as a winner-take-all proposition; thus, they designed the legal system as an adversarial zero sum game.

It is within the legal system that ideological hegemony is nurtured and promulgated to convince the masses that when decisions are rendered in this milieu justice has been unfailingly served. Another fallacy of the legal system is that judges and juries are capable of making fair and impartial determinations regarding legal matters facing individuals and collectives. To corroborate and further prove the accuracy and integrity of the judicial system's capacity to protect the rights of the innocent, the masses are educated to believe that if an error is made at one level there are other levels, such as appellate courts, that provide checks and balances to correct any errors or deficiencies that occurred at previous levels in the judicial system. This hegemonic ideology fails to explain that biases based on race, gender, class and many other factors are firmly entrenched in the legal system at all levels of the judiciary, as well as in the attitudes of those (judges and jurors) who are placed in a position to render adjudications.

The legal rights of African American women were initially established during slavery. The institution of slavery in the United States failed to recognize slaves as having any legal rights, to show preferential treatment to female slaves because of their gender, or to permit slaves legal recourse for the frequently harsh and cruel treatment they received. In addition, African American freewomen, like White women, had few legal rights that were recognized.

Throughout the colonial period, single women enjoyed greater legal rights than married women. This was true of free African American women and White women, who were not indentured servants. "Married women and widows, particularly those living in urban areas, were declared 'femme-sole traders', a title that gave them the right to sue, conduct business, be sued, enter into contracts, sell property and have power of attorney in the absence of their husbands."[6] Wilson states that, whether they were married or single, women in the seventeenth and eighteenth centuries could not act as attorneys-at-law even though they were attorneys-in-fact.[7]

Women suffered major legal losses following the American Revolution. The fact that they had more rights in the American colonies prior to the American Revolution was due in part to the shortage of women for labor, both economic and reproductive. When their numbers increased, their legal rights decreased. Wilson notes that the absence of a professional class of lawyers in the colonies contributed to more liberal laws for women, especially married women. This climate had changed by the middle of the eighteenth century, as law practices increased when "secular law practices supplanted theological ones."[8]

In spite of liberal laws for White women prior to the American Revolution, it was an unequivocal fact that legal sanctions were more severe for free African American women, native American women and White women who were indentured servants than for White women who were free of bondage.

Historians, theologians, and advocates of slavery and the subordination of women set forth treatises and commentaries on the rights of women during the eighteenth and nineteenth centuries. Responding to women's agitation in the North for women's rights, greater independence and freedom from subordination to males, George Fitzhugh (1965) succinctly expounds upon the rights of women in American society, including female slaves. This widely accepted ideological position on women's rights is the presupposition upon which the American legal system bases its differential treatment of women, including African American women compared to men. Fitzhugh stated that:

the agitation for women's rights in the North offered incontrovertible evidence of society's dissolution. In the North, woman found herself in a false position. In the South, be she

128

White, or be she Black, she is treated with kindness and humanity. Women, like children, have only one right – the right to protection. The right to protection involves the obligation to obey. A husband, a lord and master, whom she should love, honor and obey, nature designed for every woman. If she accepts her obligation to obey, she runs little risk of ill treatment, but if she stands upon presumed rights, she will become coarse and masculine. Man will loathe, despise, and in the end abuse her. Law can do nothing on her behalf, but true womanly art will give her an empire and a sway far greater than she deserves.[9]

This position, advanced by champions of slavery, subscribed to the belief that the rights of women were predicated upon their willingness and ability to use their feminine charms to meet the needs of men. Certainly, the expectation of how those charms were to be manifested to guarantee the right of women to protection was defined differently if the woman was a slave or the wife of a slave owner. In either case women's rights were inextricably tied to their willingness to fulfill their womanly responsibilities as defined by men, especially those who had immediate and direct control over their lives. That paternalism is an integral feature of this cultural perception of the rights of women is indeed an understatement. What is most revealing is the acknowledgement that even the legal system, with its ultimate authority, could not offer a woman any remedies for the violation of her rights, because after all her only right is one of protection which, according to this position, was guaranteed if she but obeyed by submitting to the demands of men. These warnings to women, that they will experience the most inexorable forms of retribution if they choose to assume roles outside of those prescribed to them by men in power, are evident throughout various institutions, but are most pronounced in the treatment of women who seek protection of their civil rights through the legal system. In seeking legal redress for violations of their civil rights, African American women are refusing to accept that women do not enjoy the same legal rights as men unless they are aligned with men who have social, economic and political privileges comparable to or greater than those of the individuals who have violated their civil rights. This is true regardless of the meritorious nature of her complaint.

African American women have not fared well in terms of the

legal system in the United States during and subsequent to slavery. Patricia Williams states that "Blacks and women are the objects of a constitutional omission that has been incorporated into a theory of neutrality. It is here that omission becomes a form of expression, as oxymoronic as that sounds: racial omission is a literal part of original intent; it is the fixed, reiterated prophesy of the Founding Fathers."[10] Not only have African American women had their civil rights violated, they have been subjected to whimsical forms of punishment that have resulted in harsh penalties, in the form of physical and emotional abuse. In spite of the legal system's denial of their legal rights, in spite of systematic denigration and inexorable social and economic hardships, African American women have refused to submit to culturally established male domination. Pauli Murray quotes E. Franklin Frazier's discussion of African American women's determination to reject a culturally imposed subordinate status due to their gender. Frazier states, "Neither economic necessity nor tradition has instilled in her the spirit of subordination to masculine authority. Emancipation only tended to confirm in many cases the spirit of self-sufficiency which slavery had taught."[11]

The case of Eliza Gallie characterizes the systematic violations of African American women's legal rights that have occurred throughout history. And while the methods by which African American women's rights escape legal protection continue to occur, in a subtle institutionalized form since the 1960s, the outcome is almost as cruel and indicative of the violent nature of those who influence, as well as administer, justice in the American legal system as during the antebellum period.

Lebsock gives the following account:

In November 1853, Eliza Gallie, a free black woman of Petersburg, was arrested and charged with stealing cabbages from the patch of Alexander Stevens, a white man. She was tried in mayor's court and sentenced to thirty-nine lashes. There was nothing unusual in this; free black women were frequently accused of petty crimes, and for free blacks as for slaves, whipping was the punishment prescribed for by law. What made the case a spectacle was that Eliza Gallie had resources, and she fought back. She filed an appeal immediately, and two weeks later she hired three of Petersburg's most eminent attorneys and one from Richmond as well. If the Commonwealth, God Bless her, has not met her match in Miss Liza, a local newspaper commented, it won't be for lack of lawyers. The case came up in hustings court in March 1854.

Despite the brilliant arguments of Miss Gallie's lawyers, she "was pronounced guilty and sentenced to twenty lashes on her bare back at the public whipping post . . . At first, she set another appeal in motion, but deciding that the case was hopeless, Eliza Gallie dismissed her lawyers and took her punishment."[12]

Lebsock notes that, while this case was unusual, it reflects the contradiction inherent in the "historic" cultural image of the African American woman. She further states:

Eliza Gallie was relatively speaking, a powerful woman, propertied, autonomous (divorced actually), and assertive. But she was helpless in the end, the victim of the kind of deliberate humiliation that for most of us is past imagining. So it is with our perception of the history of Black women as a group. On the one hand, we have been told that Black women, in slavery and afterward, were a formidable people, "matriarchs," in fact. And yet we know that all along Black women were dreadfully exploited. Rarely has so much power been attributed to so vulnerable a group.[13]

It is clear that the term "matriarch" and cultural images of the Aunt Jemima, mammy, Sapphire and the bad-black-girl have been applied to African American women because their use of power and display of independence represent a threat to men who are determined to marshal societal resources and control institutions. Moreover, the legal system is the vehicle that those in power use to squash challenges to masculine authority and prerogative. In so doing, the privileged class has accomplished two goals. First, the privileged use the legal system to maintain control over all other institutions and resources in the United States. Second, African American women's attempt to seek protection of their civil rights through the legal system is generally futile, because they are challenging race and gender conventions which deny that the same rights exist for females and African Americans as for males and Whites. Therefore, the privileged class sends an explicit message to all African American women, women belonging to other racial and ethnic groups, and African American males that nothing has

changed. Further, the harsh treatment, debasement and humiliation to which African American women are subjected by the legal
system sends a clear and concise signal to the African American
population that African American men have no means available to
protect members of their community since they cannot even
prevent or control the violation of their women by men in power.
During slavery and following emancipation, African American
female slaves and free women were violated, sexually and
physically, by males in power. In so doing, the privileged class
conveyed a message to African American males and females,
reminding them of their social, political, economic and legal
impotence.

When the legal system denies African American women protection of their legal rights, whether civil or constitutional, African
American males are emasculated because they are precluded from
performing one of the primary functions associated with
masculinity, that of a protector. Considering that social barriers,
particularly institutional forms of racial discrimination, limit
economic opportunities and mobility for the African American
male and prevent him from being a provider, the other key function that our culture identifies with masculinity, it is obvious that
the frustration, alienation and anger experienced by African
American males is system-precipitated. In addition, structural
barriers that deny African American males the opportunity to
fulfill the culturally prescribed roles of provider and protector
create dissension between African American males and females
who have fallen prey to cultural definitions and images of
masculinity.

African American males who are able to ensure protection for
the legal rights of African American females (daughters, wives,
mothers, etc.) with whom they are aligned are able to do so
because of their own alliances with White males with power and
privilege. In these situations a trickle-down effect is operative,
whereby the African American male passes the benefits that he
derives from his relationship with more privileged White males to
the African American female. In the case of the African American
female, system-created barriers make alliances such as these
between African American males and White males with power
highly unlikely. It is also rare for African American males to be in
a position to establish such relationships. Consequently, as greater
numbers of African American males and females accept cultural

definitions of masculinity, in which the male is expected to be the chief provider and offer protection to his mate and other members of his community, this contentious issue will continue to contribute to the disintegration of married-couple families and other salient microcultural institutions.

Legal rights were established for African American women largely through citizenship and voting rights for women; yet African American women who have sought legal avenues to secure civil rights protection learn of the hypocrisy of American society; they discover that civil rights guarantees and indeed constitutional rights are not extended to them if they conflict with the civil rights and constitutional guarantees of the privileged class or the rights of those who occupy higher positions on the social hierarchy of discrimination. Again, the only mitigating factor which African American women may employ to supersede this condition, thereby guaranteeing their rights, is to align themselves with men whose power is as great as or greater than that of those who have violated their civil or constitutional rights. However, because of the marginality and history of African American women, as well as the myths and stereotypes that separate African American women from privileged men it is highly improbable, and frequently undesirable, for African American women to forge such alliances.

African Americans looked forward to the protection of their civil rights for the second time in the history of this country. The 1964 Civil Rights Act was considered a legislative mandate that would restore the legal rights to African Americans that had been rescinded after the brief guarantees of civil liberties during the first reconstruction following emancipation.

One reason for the renewed faith in the American legal system, and in the plethora of laws designed to guarantee the rights of African Americans, were the landmark civil rights cases that were won in courtrooms across the country, and upheld by the United States Supreme Court. In particular, the 1954 *Brown* v. *the Board of Education* case, ruling separate but equal in educational institutions, was unconstitutional. A myriad other legal decisions dismantling Jim Crow laws in the South and *de facto* segregation in the North made the African American activists who challenged the legal system, along with all institutions in the United States in the 1960s and 1970s, believe that these legal victories would significantly reduce the discriminatory treatment perpetrated by institutions and individuals against African Americans. Civil liberties denied to African Americans in the areas of education, employment, housing, public facilities, the legal system, the political arena and even religion were challenged by African Americans and Whites through a variety of protests, from sit-ins to urban riots.

THE AFRICAN AMERICAN WOMAN AS LITIGANT: IMPEDIMENTS TO JUSTICE

Individual legal successes and even class action litigation did not in themselves result in permanent or complete social, economic or political parity for African Americans and similarly situated Whites. Thus, while many prevailed in securing protection of civil liberties, for many people significant changes in the status of African Americans did not occur in the most salient institutions in the United States. That is, both the private and public sector at best complied with the letter, but not the spirit, of the law. And in far too many institutions resistance was so great that, while on the surface, policies were amended to conform to legal mandates, discriminatory practices and practitioners became more covert and more difficult to prove using legal imperatives.

Chief among complaints that the legal system supports the violators of civil liberties, and not the victims of social injustice, is the fact that litigating civil rights violations requires inordinate amounts of time and money. And because the burden of proof is on the litigant, civil rights violations are extraordinarily difficult to litigate successfully. Moreover, with the mood of ultraconservatism that swept the country in the late 1970s, becoming fully entrenched in the 1980s and 1990s, it is now almost impossible for the victims of civil rights violations to obtain legal redress.

Because of the overwhelming number of cases being tried and the shortage of judges, referees and magistrates, a civil rights case may take from two to seven years to come to trial. During this period there is likely to be considerable stress, financial and emotional, on the litigant. This is especially true in employment cases where individuals who are victims of civil rights violations in the workplace are likely to lose considerable monies while they pay attorneys to represent them. In many employment cases, attorneys attempt to reduce their clients' financial expenses by taking cases on contingency, whereby they collect a percentage, frequently one-third, of the settlement. Witnesses for the litigant in civil rights cases are also affected by the lengthy time periods that elapse before a civil rights case goes to trial. Because there are rules regarding the distance that a witness lives from the county, witnesses cannot be subpoenaed if they move outside of the court's jurisdiction. In addition, it is quite common to hear of employers harassing and intimidating employees who serve as witnesses for litigants in employment discrimination cases. In certain age discrimination cases, the Equal Opportunity Commission took so long to hear the cases that the statute of limitation ran out, making the litigants ineligible for seeking legal redress from their respective employers. Supreme Court Justice Clarence Thomas, then Director of the EEOC, was severely criticized for the slow response time. The fact that Thomas took an excessive amount of time to hear these cases was cited as a major point of contention among critics who opposed his nomination to the United States Supreme Court to replace Justice Thurgood Marshall.[14] When an individual has had her civil rights violated it is preposterous to expect that redress (if it occurs) will be equitable if she must wait for a considerable period of time to receive restoration or remuneration for such abuse.

Possessing and having access to adequate resources is a major problem for individuals who file complaints of civil rights violations in court. The sheer imbalance whereby organizations, firms and government agencies have access to unlimited monies, while individual litigants have only meager resources, increases the likelihood that employers who perpetrate race and gender discrimination will prevail. The availability of unlimited resources becomes pronounced in the case of large public and private firms and agencies. The situation becomes more complex and of dubious ethics when the discriminatory conduct is perpetrated by a large governmental agency. When governmental agencies, regardless of size, are charged with discrimination they are free to use large sums of taxpayers' dollars to retain legal counsel, including taxes paid by the litigant. On the other hand, the litigant has limited resources but must either pay extremely high legal fees or agree to a contingency-fee arrangement, whereby the attorney will receive a percentage of the settlement or court award if the employee prevails. What is even more disturbing is that an individual who sues a large organization or firm usually does not have access to attorneys who are affiliated with law firms that have the capability, including personnel, resources and expertise, to litigate a discrimination case effectively against an organization or firm

135

that can use its vast resources to retain the most reputable and heavily staffed law firms in the community. There is another problem that commonly occurs when individuals file discrimination lawsuits against large employers: large firms frequently retain the majority of capable law firms in the local community, thereby reducing the number of able law firms that individuals can use to file discrimination lawsuits against organizations.

The problems facing individuals receiving legal redress when they are victims of race or gender discrimination in employment are compounded when discrimination occurs in institutions of higher education that are considered major research institutions. The availability of a lawyer who is affiliated with a law firm that can successfully litigate a race or gender discrimination case against a major university is extremely difficult to identify. In addition to a major educational institution having a tremendous financial impact on most segments of the community, by providing jobs, business contracts and other forms of economic development that enhance the cultural, economic and social spheres of a community, various conflicts of interest and ethical questions arise. For example, when the author filed a sex discrimination lawsuit against her employer, a major research university, she discovered that several local law firms were unable to litigate a discrimination lawsuit against the university because of a conflict of interest. Such conflicts may take the following form: first, there is a conflict of interest when law firms have been retained by major employers, thereby excluding these highly qualified, resourceful and politically connected law firms from offering their services to individuals or those interested in class action civil rights lawsuits. Second, when the discrimination occurs at a major university, there may be attorneys at various law firms who hold adjunct faculty positions in the university. This can be a major problem since law firms rely on the unique and sometimes specialized skills and knowledge of various practicing attorneys on their staff.

There are other problems that severely reduce the effectiveness of affirmative action and the 1964 Civil Rights Act. The appointment of judges, frequently labeled conservative, by the Reagan and Bush administrations in the 1980s and 1990s has radically impacted upon the successful litigation of civil rights cases for individuals whose civil rights have been violated. These judges, representing the views of the "new right," exhibit behaviors that prior to and during the Civil Rights era would have garnered them the labels of racist, bigot and sexist. However, the media's new posture enables the euphemistic appellation of "conservative," "insensitive to race and gender issues" or a "representative of management" to be assigned to judges. Even Bork, the unsuccessful Reagan Supreme Court nominee noted for the his judicial history of total disregard for civil rights of protected classes, states that judges have a tendency, on occasion, to abuse their discretionary powers and the authority vested in them.[15] For example, in the author's sex discrimination lawsuit against her employer, a major research institution,the federal judge who heard her case was a graduate of the university that was one of the defendants, received all of his degrees from this university and was a member of the university's alumni association. One must question the integrity and motivation of judges and a judicial system that permits these, and other, kinds of conflicts of interest.

There is an unspoken, but real, interrelationship between major institutions of higher education, large law firms and judges who try civil rights cases. This relationship is economically based and cyclical in nature. In effect, institutions of higher education that are major research universities have inordinate budgets which enable them to retain the largest and best qualified law firms. These law firms receive retainers and a certain number of adjunct faculty positions for attorneys practicing with their firm. In some instances, the law firms retained by universities make monetary contributions to the University affiliated programs and services; which means that the exchange of monies between law firms and their clients is bilateral. There are other ways in which judges, law firms and universities enjoy a mutual dependent and beneficial relationship. Before federal and state judges are appointed to the bench, a political appointment, they were once attorneys practicing with a law firm. Hence, some attorneys who litigate civil rights cases are former colleagues of judges. And clearly there exists an exclusive fraternal relationship between attorneys and judges. Finally, when judges retire they may choose to return to practicing at a law firm or opt to teach at a university. Therefore previous, existing and prospective relationships of those involved in civil rights lawsuits can have a significant impact upon the ability of women whose civil rights have been violated to receive a fair hearing in gender and race discrimination lawsuits. When the legal system's flaws, and other nuances of litigating gender and race discrimination cases, are taken into consideration it becomes apparent that affirmative action as a social policy, along with the 1964 Civil Rights Act, may have been well intended but is inherently highly ineffective in ensuring that protection for African American women's civil rights. Thus, the legal system has done more to raise false hopes than to eradicate social injustices or to provide remedies for victims of race and gender discrimination.

Understandably, when African American women faculty experience race and gender discrimination, it is fairly obvious why they have a proclivity for choosing flight over fight. They realize that the legal system continues to fulfill the mission for which it was established in the seventeenth and eighteenth centuries, namely, to represent the will of the privileged. That is, when the legal system became more developed after the American Revolution and the number of professional lawyers increased, it began unswervingly to represent the interests of those with a monopoly on power and wealth.[16] According to many historians, in their analyses of the various forms of revolt that were used by slaves, the most efficacious form of revolt against this oppressive system was "flight and not fight." Therefore, African American women who choose the former method to escape the injustices that they experience in the academy do so recognizing that affirmative action, and the 1964 Civil Rights Act, is more a myth than a reality. Frequently, when African American women faculty choose flight or fight they become involved in college-hopping, going from one institution of higher education to another. And all too often, they are forced to accept trade-offs, ultimately being employed at a second- or third-tier university or college. In some instances, African American women faculty find themselves, compelled by discrimination, accepting an environment that affords greater comfort and emotional support in lieu of the high salaries, research leaves, abundant clerical support and other amenities that many White male faculty members take for granted. Civil rights legislation to replace the existing ineffective law is long overdue. The fact that President Bush signed the 1991 Civil Rights Bill is considerd by some to be a positive sign. According to the language of this bill, for the first time women who are victims of sex discrimination are entitled to receive punitive damages up to $300,000. However, such a law is only a rudimentary imperative in view of the monumental obstacles legitimized by a legal system designed by, and for, those who, either directly or indirectly, will experience monetary and political losses if individual litigants seeking redress for civil rights violations are successful. Thus, African American women seeking justice in the legal system for the violation of civil rights are subjecting themselves to further victimization, as there is a partnership between the legal system and major institutions, and large public and private employers, who violate the civil rights of African American women. To be sure, the legal system is an appendage of the privileged, like, other societal institutions over which they have control.

Many gender and race discrimination complaints never reach the courts. Some are resolved through an employer's internal grievance process. Still others are thwarted due to the prospective litigant's unfamiliarity with statutes of limitation and other preliminary requirements which must be followed, such as filing complaints with the Civil Rights Commission or the Equal Employment Opportunity Commission before filing a complaint of discrimination in a state or federal court. When cases are settled out of court the records are sealed, preventing the public from knowing whether the decision was favorable for the litigant or prospective litigant. There are far too many cases, as Handler reports in his exhaustive studies of the legal system, that are never filed in a court.[17] In fact, there are numerous legitimate discrimination claims that, because of prospective litigants' lack of information regarding the rules of civil litigation, are not permitted to be filed in court. It is no coincidence that the public is uninformed regarding the procedures and rules that govern filing and litigating discrimination complaints. In addition, sealing court documents and forbidding litigants to discuss certain aspects of their cases, as well as the terms of settlement, deny other women information regarding successful strategies to use in litigating and negotiating discrimination cases.

In the case where an African American woman or another member of a protected class is successful in litigating a civil rights case against a major employer, the jubilation, while well deserved, is solely an individual victory; for, as Derrick Bell notes, a civil rights victory in a court of law is not generalized beyond the individual, as each subsequent case must start anew.[18] This alone is disturbing, considering the enormity of civil rights violations and the major obstacles that make it highly improbable that an individual will prevail in civil rights cases, whether the organization or firm is small, moderate or large.

139

Those who construct images and myths in our society have effectively perpetuated the belief that African Americans, particularly African American women, benefit immeasurably from affirmative action policy and protection from the 1964 Civil Rights Act. African Americans who have tested the legal system and learned either directly or vicariously that the American judicial system will not fairly represent their interests frequently experience disillusionment, frustration, alienation and anger. Members of the larger society also experience frustration and anger, believing that affirmative action policy and supporting legislation gives African Americans, especially African American women, an unfair advantage. These falsehoods and misinformation are channeled through the mass media. The dissension, and overall poor race relations, between Whites and African Americans is further fueled by the myth that the legal system is designed to represent the interests of African Americans who, after being permitted to participate in institutions for which they are believed to be unqualified, can receive further protection from the legal system for civil rights violations, while Whites are denied the same opportunities. Such myths create and sustain divisiveness between African Americans and Whites.

Since African American women and other protected classes are really offered fewer protections of their civil rights than Whites, it is clear that the most effective recourse is collective action. In any case, the most favorable outcomes are likely to occur when individuals who have experienced civil rights violations expose the inconsistencies and contradictions inherent in the legal system and the institution, or firm, in which the discrimination occurred. In so doing, the myths and hypocrisies that constitute ideological hegemonic belief systems will be dispelled. This is by no means an easy task, as African American women and other marginal groups have limited access to the mass media, which are needed to legitimize their claims. Combining a legal and political strategy to ensure that an individual secures relief for civil rights violations is an approach that is supported by Supreme Court Justice Thurgood Marshall, who stated that, in order to obtain effective relief for civil rights violations, political and legal avenues must be pursued simultaneously.[19]

In effect, African American women must collectively develop strategies to resist and challenge the American legal system's proclivity for protecting the rights of the privileged, while compounding the victimization of African American women. This effort must challenge the image of institutional innocence and of the legal system as a fair, impartial and legitimate institution for remedying social injustice for African American women, and other groups, for whom institutional discrimination is normative.

8

DETERMINING ENTITLEMENTS

The exclusionary nature of cultural imagery

PREEMPTIVE MYTHOLOGY AND RECIPIENCY

There is an ideological tug-of-war that places African American women who head poor families in a cyclical process that is virtually inescapable. They are forced to assume a status that is considered contemptible by most segments of the population. The materially privileged class has established a forced choice, a dichotomy that requires Americans to decide whether they prefer their tax dollars to be allocated to improve the lives of single mothers and their children, or for defense to ensure the security of the country.

Inherent in this mythology is the implication that the African American woman and her children are the primary recipients of welfare. Associated with the media-born conceptualization that welfare is synonymous with African American women is the contention that the African American male, whom the media portray as lazy, shiftless and economically and socially dependent on the African American woman, is also an undeserving beneficiary of social welfare services. The fact that social policy is constructed as an either–or proposition, whereby the taxpayers are compelled to support defense or social welfare, is a strategy contrived by those with a monopoly on economic wealth and political power. Furthermore, perpetuating the belief that welfare is a system designed to make public funds available to able-bodied African American women, their mates and dependent children, all of whom are portrayed as consumers and not producers, guarantees the stigmatization of the welfare system and its recipients. Building upon fears of racism, sexism, classism and patriotism, the materially privileged have carefully constructed an image and ideology of social welfare that results in the devaluation of such programs and their participants. These and other myths associated with social welfare programs make it extremely difficult to develop and propose effective methods that will result in an equitable reallocation of societal resources.[1]

Through the mass media, those with economic wealth and social power have convincingly established an inferential link that eventuates in the following myths: that welfare recipients have extremely large families, are reluctant to work, have a propensity to increase family size to increase welfare benefits, lack moral character, refuse to engage in moderate living, have abandoned the traditional American values of work, family and frugality and are the major cause of the country's social and economic problems. This inferential chain suggests the following: individuals who are poor are poor because they are unwilling to work; these able-bodied undeserving poor must rely on welfare to assume the responsibility for their families that they are shirking; the welfare system and its recipients are a drain on the US economy; and the majority of taxpayers are denied services and resources commensurate with their production and commitment to the nation, solely because they must assume financial responsibility for the needs of the poor. Added to this logic is the inference that the majority of welfare recipients belong to a racial group that is outside of mainstream American society. In conjunction with this stereotypical image of welfare-dependent poor families is the belief that these families belong to a culture of poverty and constitute a culture of violence.[2]

Proponents of these theories receive media support as the media focus their attention on covering criminal activity in inner-city low-income communities. Seldom do drug raids occur in the opulent surroundings of those who are purported to be the financiers of large cachets of drugs. Instead, lower-income inner-city communities that fall prey to drug wars and related acts of criminality continue to be the focus of media attention.

The public are unwilling to lend their support to a social welfare system that they believe exists to support individuals who are willing to be consumers and not producers. The mass media are successful in constructing the image that supports this ideology by systematically depicting African American women and children as the primary recipients of social welfare services. The mass media, particularly television news programs, focus on African American poor women and their children when they report on services to the poor. Whether waiting in foodstamp lines or seeking assistance from social welfare offices, the message that is proliferated by the media is that welfare is for African American women and children. It has been argued that the reason the media include African American women in almost all stories or reports on poverty programs is due in part to their accessibility.[3] That is, since larger numbers of African American poor families, as well as those headed by women, live in the inner city they represent a captive market for reporters, cameramen and others who are interested in reporting on poverty and social welfare programs. Ignoring poor families who live in rural areas and on the periphery of American cities reinforces stereotypes regarding welfare recipiency in the United States. The fact that an inordinate number of poor families are White and reside in areas outside major metropolitan areas means that they are seldom included in media reports of poverty and welfare or attendant problems that such families encounter. The argument that the media systematically use African American women and their children to represent the nation's poor and welfare recipients because they are more visible is untenable. Given that the news media exhibit phenomenal mobility, that they travel to remote areas within the United States and throughout the world, that news bureaux exist in virtually every continent, and that they have the capacity to establish satellites to transmit news throughout the world, it is an unacceptable proposition that the mass media cannot accurately and fairly dispatch reporters, journalists and cameramen to cover reports on the nation's poor and welfare recipients to areas outside the inner city. Further evidence of the media's insistence on constructing the image that African American women and children comprise the largest group of individuals with incomes below the poverty level, and in receipt of welfare, can be observed when the media focus on rural poverty. One would suspect that, when rural poor families are the focus of poverty and social welfare reports, White families would also be visible. This is usually not the case. To the contrary, reports that examine rural poverty, like those that concentrate on inner cities, include visual imagery of African American poor female-headed or two-parent families. The rare occasions when White poor families, female-maintained or married-couple families, are depicted by the media are limited to coverage of Appalachian poverty. Hence, the public are led to believe that only a small segment of the White population, living in remote mountain regions, are poor and receive social welfare benefits. It is also suggested in such media

144

coverage that these are proud, hard-working families who make up the "new poor" due to the decline of the mining industry, and that such families would have to undergo catastrophic changes in their lifestyles if they are to elevate their socioeconomic status. Generally, the media suggest that these families must move many miles away from their homes and communities, leaving families and friends and a tradition of intergenerations that have valued family, hard work and other virtues that characterize the All American ethos.

By contrast, since the media systematically focus on African American poor women and children in reports on welfare, fraud, poverty and related topics, the outcome is that welfare and poverty are perceived as synonymous with African American women and children.

The welfare versus warfare debate is fraught with still other misconceptions. Consistent with the belief that the country's social and economic problems are directly related to the absence of morals, goals and motivation among poor families in America is the belief that a disproportionate amount of the federal budget is allocated to care for this segment of the population. Related to this belief is the contention that, because of this relatively high expenditure to care for the poor, other needs such as education, repairing the infrastructure of the country (building roads, repairing bridges, etc.) and national defense must suffer.

In 1990, the federal budget exceeded $1 trillion. In the same year, $100 billion or a mere 10 per cent of the national budget was allocated for social welfare services or programs for the poor.[4] Excluded from this figure are monies for services to the nonpoor such as Medicare, social security and unemployment benefits. In contrast $226 billion was allocated for defense. However, when salaries and benefits for military personnel, including veterans, are added, it is estimated that over 50 per cent of the nation's budget is allotted to defense and defense-related expenditures. In addition, considerable wealth is amassed by select groups of individuals who control major corporations through their investments. These corporations and their investors are dependent upon defense contracts. The military–industrial complex that Eisenhower referred to is responsible for the corporate dependence of industrial concerns on government dollars. According to Cook, the top 100 corporations in this country have a monopoly on three-fourths of all defense contracts, and 85 per cent of these contracts are awarded without competition.[5] Interestingly, this form of government dependency is seldom defined as such by policy-makers; nor do the media define such an entrenched monetary exchange system as a method that allows those who have a monopoly on wealth and power to maintain their advantage.

This elite group of individuals shares a commonality of interests with society's *petite bourgeoisie* who receive their federal entitlements through stocks, bonds, subsidies and various forms of tax shelters and tax abatements. While space prevents an exhaustive enumeration of the firms who have received federal dollars to enable them to survive and expand, some of the more notable and larger beneficiaries of US tax dollars include Chrysler, Amtrak and the Concorde. In addition to the billions of dollars that these and other corporations have received in the form of bailouts, there are numerous monetary benefits that corporations and wealthy American families receive from various tax shelters and abatements. Generally, the rationale for providing such monetary benefits to this small, but powerful elite is the belief in the trickle-down theory. That is, when business owners enjoy prosperity they are able to pass the benefits of their wealth and auspiciousness down to their employees and consumers. This group conforms nicely to a rarely discussed segment of the population whose dependence upon the government is intergenerational. Accordingly, this form of government assistance is known as ADC, which should not be confused with the social welfare program of Aid to Dependent Children. Rather, this form of government dependence is more appropriately called Aid to Dependent Corporations. Because those who are in power are generally the recipients of large amounts of government monies it is understandable that they justify such government dependence as being good for the economy, and therefore good for the nation. Obviously, the media, while reporting on such expenditures, are careful not to define the dependence of corporations on government grants and contracts as dependency or as an unfair distribution of taxpayers' monies.

There are still other beneficiaries of government subsidies, apart from those who are recipients of the corporate welfare system, who are dependent upon the social welfare system. According to a commentary on poverty written by the economist Walter Williams, entitled "Do You Know Why We Need Poverty?",[6] in 1983 there were at least 5 million workers out of a labor force of over 100 million people who benefited from the social welfare system. These individuals and companies do not benefit equally from the social welfare system. Rather there are different degrees of dependence. Those who derive the greatest benefits are private sector service providers. Beneficiaries such as supermarket owners, dentists, physicians and pharmacists, and owners of apartment buildings and single-family houses for low-income families are among the many entrepreneurs who are guaranteed benefits from the existing social welfare system. The provision of medical cards, foodstamps, housing subsidies and so forth, instead of a total cash payment that would cover the costs of these goods and services, ensures that those who own or operate such businesses will receive a projected income from poverty programs on an annual basis. These monetary guarantees also create a form of welfare dependence among the middle and upper classes, who depend on monies from poverty programs for their livelihood. These goods and services are guaranteed by the US welfare system, which provides cash in-kind services rather than a total cash allotment. Critics of this system argue that recipients of public assistance should receive a cash allotment only. This would permit them to determine how much would be spent on medical or health care, food, housing and so forth. Instead, the current welfare system establishes a cash amount and then issues in-kind services to cover other basic human needs. As a consequence, various industries are guaranteed income by providing services to welfare recipients. Walter Williams once commented that this group of individuals, more than others in the country, really care about the poor. The reason for their compassion, he suggests, is that they benefit directly or indirectly from programs that are designed to provide goods and services to the poor. Looking again at Williams's esti-mation that in 1983 there was a workforce of over 100 million workers, with almost 5 million workers with jobs that were either directly or indirectly related to poverty programs, his analysis is still applicable. Williams's assessment of the costs of maintaining poverty programs, including the payroll of workers whose jobs are related to providing services to the poor, indicates that it is far less costly to lay off these mainly white-collar workers and provide them and the nation's poor with a guaranteed minimum income, even considerably above the poverty level. Such an income maintenance program would cost substantially less than paying the costs of maintaining the existing social welfare system.[7]

Edna Bonacich addresses the issue of the role of the middle class as benefactors and mediators of our existing system of inequality. She states:

> In my view, middle class people (including myself) are essentially the sergeants of the system. We professionals and managers are paid by the wealthy and powerful, by the corporations and the state, to keep things in order. Our role is one of maintaining the system of inequality. Our role is essentially that of controlling the poor. We are a semi-elite. We are given higher salaries, social status, better jobs and better life chances as payment for our service to the system. If we were not useful to the power elite, they would not reward us. Our rewards prove that we serve their interests. Look at who pays us. That will give you a sense of whom we are serving.[8]

Again, the media have never defined these groups of individuals as welfare-dependent. Instead, they are perceived as providing goods and services in exchange for monetary remuneration. On the other hand, critics of poverty programs argue that welfare recipients, unlike social service providers and corporations, have no legitimate right to receive welfare benefits because they are consumers and not producers. Still, it can be argued that if the poor were recipients of a sufficiently high guaranteed income, adequate training and ancillary supports they, too, would be able to establish and maintain themselves in viable occupations or businesses. This argument is also vitiated by the fact that the federal government has an established policy of providing subsidies to farmers to encourage them *not* to grow certain crops. The idea is to contain market prices by maintaining control over the availability of certain crops in the marketplace. Although subsidies may avoid creating surplus commodities, thereby driving market prices down, those who benefit from such government subsidies are not only failing to produce but may also be reducing the availability and affordability of products that are essential to Americans' diets. Furthermore, they are doing so with the federal government's blessing, which in this case is monetary.

IMAGERY AND THE ADMINISTRATION OF SOCIAL WELFARE PROGRAMS

One of the most damaging media portrayals of African American females who head families, and are recipients of public welfare, appeared in a documentary produced and narrated by Bill Moyers in January 1986.[9] In this two-hour documentary, entitled "The Vanishing Family – Crisis in Black America", Bill Moyers focused exclusively on African American young mothers with out-of-wedlock children, who were recipients of public assistance. Some of these young females had never established paternity and had children fathered by different males. When the fathers of these children were interviewed they, as well as the teenage welfare mothers, showed little concern over their status, nor did these young males express much interest in parenting or assuming financial responsibility for the children they had sired. Intergenerational teenage pregnancies were normative for the non-representative sample of African American female single parents who were depicted in this program. The males and females reacted casually to the prospect that their sons and daughters may choose to pattern or model their behaviors on their parents, thereby continuing the trend of teenage pregnancies and welfare recipiency. When images such as these are systematically portrayed by the mass media, they represent irrefutable evidence to many that African American women and men are deriving benefits from the social welfare system at the expense of the American taxpayer. Bill Moyers attributed this phenomenon of out-of-wedlock births to male sexual recklessness. The fact that this belief is generalized to the African American population reinforces stereotypes of African Americans. One of the most adverse consequences of these images, and the messages they contain, is their effect on the expectations that members of society have of African American women and their community. Studies reveal that teachers tend to have low expectations of African American male and female students. A 1990 survey conducted by the National Opinion Research Center revealed that 57 per cent of White Americans believe that African Americans are less intelligent than Whites.[10] Still others believe that African Americans also have lower morals than Whites. Clearly, these and related beliefs are reinforced by media-transmitted imagery and information.

Images such as these lend credence to the culture of poverty theory and its proponents.[11] Summarily, African American women who head such families are categorically believed to contribute to their own inexorable social and economic status because of sexual irresponsibility. It would be more accurate to describe the African American women and their families depicted in documentaries, such as the one produced by Bill Moyers, as individuals who developed survival mechanisms in response to inumerable social, political and economic obstacles that are overwhelmingly system-precipitated. Rather than defining these women as a problem to society, it is more accurate to describe the state of helplessness that they reflect. Davis provides insight into the role that the media play in perpetuating the belief that African American women are responsible for poverty in the African American community.

She states: "Media propagandists continue to attribute a significant portion of the blame for poverty in the Black community to unmarried mothers – particularly to pregnant teens". Davis adds: "Media mystifications should not obfuscate a simple, perceivable fact: Black teenage girls do not create poverty by having children. Quite the contrary, they have babies at an early age because they are poor – because they do not have an opportunity to acquire an education, because meaningful, well-paying jobs and creative forms of recreation are not available to them."[12]

Clearly, it is easier to attribute the depressed socioeconomic status of African American women to the victims themselves. It would be more revealing, however, and even novel if policy-makers and academicians would begin to seek answers to the uneven allocation of society's resources through the laws, policies and practices that are employed within the public and private sectors. In some ways such an effort is already under way – the media have uncovered the Savings and Loan debacle in which numerous savings and loan executives mishandled large sums of taxpayers' monies, many with total impunity. The drain on the public coffers is inestimable, yet the public continues to be inundated with information that attributes culpability for the country's dire economic problems to the poor, especially social welfare recipients. Nevertheless, conservative academicians such as George Gilder, Lawrence Mead and Charles Murray are proponents of the view that African American women disrupt marriages, avoid marriage and intentionally conceive children for the sole purpose of receiving welfare services, which is detrimental to the country.[13]

Gilder in his book, *Wealth and Poverty*, argues that Black women are largely to blame for the poverty in the Black community. He also states that Black women become pregnant in order to live on welfare payments. Moreover, Gilder argues that there is collusion on the part of African American men who he contends, live off the benefits that African American women receive.[14] Despite the fact that Johnson and others refute this myth, claiming that there are no economic advantages associated with welfare recipiency, the mass media continue to support the view that African American women value welfare dependency and transmit this value to their children.[15]

On the contrary, the range of welfare benefits, while variable depending on the region in which a woman and her children reside, do not enable women to escape overcrowded housing, inadequate health care, illness, crime and other concomitants of poverty, not to mention the stigma and ignominy associated with welfare recipiency. The disparity in cash benefits is evident across the United States. In 1987 the average AFDC family of three received $4,400, yet in California the benefit level exceeded $7,000 while a similarly situated family in Mississippi received less than $4,500 per month.[16] It is also the case that not all single African American women who head families are welfare recipients. In 1987, two out of five African American single mothers worked outside the home. This in no way reflects countless others who work part time, or those for whom employment is not available due to the lack of child care and transportation to the suburbs and the periphery of cities where many new industries are located. Further, this does not take into account McGhee's findings that health care problems preclude a large number of African American women who head families from working. He states that 43 per cent of African American single mothers suffer from hypertension and 13 per cent are victims of diabetes.[17]

While the total number of African American women and their children who live in abject poverty in the United States has diminished since the late nineteenth century, their relative numbers are high. The consequences of their impoverished socioeconomic status remain harsh; and the avenues of escape continue to be limited. In 1989, 46.5 per cent of African American women who headed families had incomes below the poverty level.[18] The power elite has used the mass media as a primary vehicle for perpetuating these myths that attribute poverty and the social and economic plight of African Americans to African American women. In effect, the privileged class has used the media to inculcate Americans with stereotypical images that suggest that single African American mothers constitute the undeserving poor. The fact that the materially privileged have successfully proliferated these myths over a period of more than 100 years has enabled them to maintain a monopoly on power and wealth. Equally important, these media-created images facilitate the efforts of policy-makers, who represent the interests of the nation's elite, to formulate policy and pass legislation which is in the interest of those in power and to the detriment of the country's poor, many of whom are African American women and children.

In effect, the US social welfare system is stigmatized and administered in a manner that degrades its recipients. The ultimate purpose of the structure and functioning of the social welfare system, that is designed to make recipiency unpleasant, is to dissuade individuals from receiving goods and services from the social welfare delivery system, and to discourage taxpayer support for the social welfare system. At best, taxpayers have no choice but to finance social welfare programs with their tax dollars. And because of the imagery surrounding the recipients of these services, the support that taxpayers provide is generally begrudging. The ultimate beneficiaries of the negative images and myths that pervade the US social welfare system are the nation's power elite. This is not to suggest that those who mediate societal resources influence the construction of negative imagery that characterizes the social welfare system for the purpose of eliminating it. Such is not the case. It is recognized by many that the social welfare system represents a program that siphons off monies from the federal budget that those who are in power would rather garner for themselves. However, it is important, as Piven and Cloward suggest, that the government demonstrate some effort to care for the needs of the poor in order to maintain social control. The presence of a social welfare system that provides, albeit minimally, for the needs of the country's poor staves off the hostilities, overt forms of aggression and mass protests that would unquestionably be directed at those whose extraordinary wealth is the real source of discontent and enragement.[19] What the US social welfare system does is permit the nation's elite to cut their losses. They are able to ensure fewer social protests and minimize social criticism from the poor and the middle class by maintaining a social welfare system that provides relative benefits to both the poor and the middle classes.

The working poor either earn too much or are victims of the elite's successful efforts to inculcate the masses with the belief that it is un-American or unpatriotic to be recipients of welfare. There-fore, the working poor displace their frustration by attributing their misfortune and economically depressed status to individuals who rely on social welfare programs for their survival. One of the social consequences of a stigmatized welfare system is that it creates a false sense of status and personal worth for the majority of Americans who are not welfare recipients. Social distance separates all groups of individuals who are not recipients of social welfare from those who are on the welfare rolls. Thus, the social welfare system is responsible for an informal stratification system that differentiates the status, and presumably the worth, of indi-viduals based on recipiency or non-recipiency. The system thus denotes a quality of inferiority to its recipients. They become tainted and are therefore encouraged, through a variety of social pressures, emanating from the structure and functioning of the system itself and from a cultural perception of ignominy, social ostracism and humiliation, to vacate the welfare rolls with the greatest degree of rapidity. Under these conditions recipients are pressured to identify other sources of private transfer payments, for the purpose of limiting their involvement in social welfare programs. The other consequence of stigmatizing the social wel-fare system is to prevent its expansion. And, finally, the wrath and contempt that are aroused in the masses by myths carefully con-structed about the social welfare system and its recipients are designed to ensure that no public pleas for welfare reform will be directed toward those who influence the allocation of resources and the formulation of social policy. The tragedy of doling out societal resources, which are an entitlement in a country with the wealth and ideological promises of equality that exist in the United States, is that in many cases the nation's poor, overrepresented by African American women and their children, must bear the brunt of public contempt in conjunction with a plethora of problems caused by discrimination and their economically depressed status.

It is clear that cultural imagery depicting African American women as the chief, and most undeserving, group of welfare reci-pients is as untenable as the myth that African American women who constitute the impoverished class are responsible for

153

numerous social anomalies. It defies reality to explain how African American women, who represent a group that is economically, educationally, politically and socially disenfranchised, could be responsible for a country's major social and economic problems. It is inexplicable how those who possess a monopoly on inordinate resources are able to escape responsibility for the systems they have so carefully crafted. Imagery that attributes culpability to African American women is carefully constructed and systematically purveyed by the mass media. In addition functionaries such as socializing agents, teachers, social service practitioners and representatives of salient societal institutions play an invaluable role in the transmission of such implausible information and imagery to successive generations.

The real issue is the extent to which African American women benefit from social policies in general and social welfare policies in particular. This is a question that cannot be answered exclusively by examining African American women's levels of participation in social programs and rates of social welfare recipiency.

While African Americans have never been the exclusive or primary recipients (34 per cent overall and 54 per cent on AFDC in 1990) of the social welfare system, they, like other recipients, are adversely affected by the policies, practices and programs. In many ways, African Americans feel the inequities of the social welfare system in the most inexorable manner. Given that African American men and women are often excluded from earning incomes that will enable them to establish and maintain socially and economically independent lives, the social welfare system represents an added system-created impediment which undermines confidence and reinforces the stereotypes that African American women and their mates are welfare-dependent. Many believe that African Americans do not possess or value the traditional virtues which, purportedly, guarantee social and economic stability and independence.

One of the most disturbing features of becoming a welfare recipient is qualifying for recipiency. To become a welfare recipient requires passing a means test. In effect, qualifying for welfare is not determined by simply being without a job or not having money. Individuals must demonstrate that they are without adequate economic and material resources. Generally, to qualify for welfare requires that a family possess no more than $1,000 in personal property, excluding a home and car.[20] Thus, any property that exceeds this amount must be disposed of before a family can qualify for public assistance. This raises an important question. Why should an individual who has little or no income be subjected to this demeaning process in order to obtain goods and services that will provide a subsistence living?

Because of the inequities in pay for African American women and others in society, it is understandable how securing employment may offer the substandard living similar to and in some cases lower than that afforded through welfare recipiency. Consequently, pay equity is extremely important to African American women who, in 1989, earned only 52 per cent of the median earnings of White men and 75 per cent of the annual median income of African American males.[21] The 1963 Pay Equity Act has had a minimal impact on the earnings of all women, including African American women. Because of the high rates of unemployment and underemployment of African American men, African American women must contribute more to the family income. Thus, the earnings of African American women are of considerable importance to the economic well-being of their families. In addition, the large number of African American families headed by single mothers also places demands on African American women to generate incomes to meet the needs of their families. In addition, African American women, like other women, receive only a paucity of child support payments. Weitzman indicates that one year following divorce the divorced mother's standard of living has decreased by 73 per cent. She also found that during the same period the divorced father, who is usually the non-custodial parent, realizes a 43 per cent increase in his standard of living.[22] In addition, African American women remain single for a longer period of time than white women. Therefore, African American divorced women are likely to experience a depressed economic status for a longer period of time than their White counterparts. Given that African American women are over-represented in clerical jobs that offer entry-level salaries, pay equity is essential to increasing their income. Although pay equity is a policy that exists in the United States, it is one that is rarely enforced. Disparities continue to exist between the pay of men and women in similarly situated employment. The critical question which has yet to be answered is why women, including African American women, are paid less than their male counterparts in spite of the enactment of pay equity legislation. Answers to this question can be found in the value system that continues to place a higher value on men's work than on women's work, even when men and women are performing the same tasks. Another factor that contributes to pay inequity for women is the failure of the American legal system to provide relief for women who receive lower pay for performing the same work as their male counterparts. It is the legal system that continues to support pay differentials for men and women. Until the legal system provides relief for women receiving lower salaries and imposes sanctions on employers who violate the 1963 Pay Equity Act, women will continue to earn incomes that are less than those of men.

Comparable worth policies have been slow to become recognized by employers and the government. Undoubtedly, comparable worth legislation will be beneficial to African American women. In view of their overrepresentation in female-dominated positions that generate low to moderate pay, African American women will benefit from a comparable worth model that guarantees that women who work in low-paying female-intensive occupations receive salaries comparable to males employed in male-predominated occupations whose jobs are similar in value. Clearly, this is an area with a great deal of ambiguity. Developing formulas and rationales for equating female-dominated employment with comparable male-intensive occupations is more than merely a definitional and economic issue. The political and social implications cannot be ignored. When occupational groups that are gender-related are ranked and assigned the same values irrespective of gender, the result is that the status of women and their income will be increased. Because income is the primary condition for maintaining patriarchy, the entire system of male dominance will face an enormous challenge when women's work and the resultant incomes are elevated to a level comparable to that of men in America.

There are other social services that African American women receive in limited amounts. For example, despite the fact that African American women have always had high civilian labor force participation rates, they also have high rates of unemployment. In 1990, African American women had an unemployment rate of 10.8 per cent compared to 4.6 per cent for White women. In comparison, in 1990, African American men and White men had unemployment rates of 11.8 per cent and 4.8 per cent respectively.[23] In 1986, of all recipients of unemployment benefits, only

13.5 per cent were African Americans while 67.3 per cent were White. The proportion of African American women receiving unemployment benefits was even smaller. Further, in 1986, of all social security benefits received, 11.7 per cent of recipients were African Americans and 86.3 per cent were White. Again, an even smaller proportion of African American women received social security benefits. Thus, African Americans, including women, are underrepresented as recipients of social security and unemployment benefits. In view of these data, it is understandable why African American women and men are overrepresented among the poor.[24]

Child support laws and the enforcement of child support payments by the courts have been of limited utility to African American women. In 1985, the courts awarded child support to 61.3 per cent of all women with children. Of this number, only 38.3 per cent of African American women with children were awarded child support by the courts, compared to 70.6 per cent of White women with children. Compliance with child support awards is nearly the same regardless of the absent parent's race. In 1985, 72 per cent of African American mothers received child support compared to 74.6 per cent of White women. Child support payments paid to the custodial parent, who is usually the child's mother, are depressingly low. When one considers that in 1985 the average child support payment annually per child was only $2,215, and that African American mothers received a mere $1,754 per child annually, it is little wonder that an inordinate proportion of single mothers and their children are victimized by poverty and its concomitants.[25] Certainly, the courts must bear the brunt of responsibility for their failure to award child support to a disproportionate number of African American women and for not vigorously enforcing child support payments. In addition, the federal government must share in this culpability because of its failure to subsidize adequately the incomes of all single parents to ensure an adequate rather than subsistence standard of living for these families. In effect, single mothers, particularly African American women, are faced almost exclusively with the financial responsibility for meeting the basic needs of their children.

The fact that the single mother is faced with large expenses on a diminishing income is evidence of the tremendous economic pressures sustained by single women heading families. African American women who maintain families encounter even more inexorable social and economic conditions due to the higher levels of unemployment and underemployment of both African American women and men. Because African American men earn less than White men the former's capacity to provide adequate economic support for their children is reduced, even when the courts award child support to single mothers.

Other social policies that have not been beneficial to African American women are policies such as the Stepparent Budgeting Methodology, that require women to lose their welfare payments when they remarry. Under the Reagan administration's Omnibus Budget Reconciliation Act, states adopted this policy initiated by the federal government. It requires welfare agencies to remove recipients from the AFDC rolls when a woman remarries. In such cases the new spouse must assume financial responsibility for his new step-children. In effect, the income of the step-parent is usually considered as part of the means test. This policy makes it mandatory for women and their families who receive welfare to undergo requalification upon remarriage to determine if they are eligible to remain on the welfare rolls. Thus, private transfer payments are mandated by the government to supplant public transfer payments. The assumption that underlies this policy is advocated by the New Right. They argue that women who are poor have two options: receiving public assistance or private transfer payments from a spouse. This same argument is addressed by Burnham and Higginbotham in their criticism of the feminization of poverty thesis, which, its merits notwithstanding, presupposes that if a woman has an employed spouse the family will be able to avoid poverty and provide sufficiently for their needs.[26] According to Duncan and Hoffman, African American divorced women have a low probability of remarrying a spouse with a moderate to high income. By contrast, these researchers found that when a White woman remarries, her second husband's income usually is higher than that of her first spouse.[27] Specifically, they discovered in their sample of divorced women that five years after divorce new husbands of remarried African American women earned $8,813 a year compared to $15,125 for new husbands of remarried White women. Therefore, this policy is clearly a marriage disincentive for single African American women with children who receive public assistance.

Under the Reagan administration, the federal government established a policy to withhold federal dollars for abortions to poor women through the Medicaid program. In addition, the federal government expanded its position of non-support for abortions by withholding federal dollars from federally funded family planning clinics if they provided abortion counseling. Because the Planned Parenthood program was unwilling to discontinue presenting abortion, in its counseling, as an option for women clients its federal funds were cut. It was and continues to be federal policy that federally funded programs are mandated not to explore abortion as an alternative to unwanted pregnancies. These policies have received support from various segments of society who oppose abortion and the use of taxpayer dollars to finance abortions and programs that support a woman's freedom to decide how to handle unwanted pregnancies. Supporters of government funding for abortions believe that this policy places poor women in a disadvantaged position unlike that of middle and upper class women who can afford to pay for abortions should they opt to do so. In addition, opponents of the federal government's position not to fund federally funded family planning clinics that offer abortion as an option for unplanned pregnancies state that poor women are frequently unaware of the various methods of contraception and are therefore likely to conceive and give birth to unwanted children at a rate considerably higher than that of more knowledgeable middle and upper class women. Another argument held by opponents to the federal policy of non-support for family planning clinics that include abortions as a choice for unwanted pregnancies, is that the federal government, under the conservative administration of Reagan and his successor George Bush, has not been willing to support social programs and poverty programs which will enable the poor including their children to live quality lives and to increase their chances of ascending out of poverty. In effect, these critics believe that the government and conservatives who support these policies are attempting to cast more children and their families into poverty by preventing the termination of unplanned pregnancies. Because the correlation between family size and poverty is irrefutable, those who oppose such federal policies find scientific corroboration for their position.

Social policies (with the exception of a few, namely Headstart, WIC, youth training programs and Medicaid) and educational grants have been of little effectiveness in elevating the socio-economic status of African American women. In addition, the lack of social policies have had a noticeable adverse effect on African American women and their communities. Perhaps the largest void is in the area of health care, with catastrophic consequences for African American and poor women. The shortage of medical doctors in the inner city, where a disproportionate number of poor African American women and their families reside, makes it even more difficult for this population to receive adequate medical care. The result of a large proportion of African American women receiving no medical care or poor quality care is that they tend to wait until their medical problem becomes severe before they seek treatment. When this occurs, treatment is likely to be more costly and, in the case of serious illness, prognosis is generally not as good as when treatment is sought during the onset of the disease or disorder.

In the case of young African American women the inability to obtain prenatal care has a definite effect on the infant mortality rate. In many cases, the high infant mortality rate for African Americans is directly related to the lack of prenatal care for African American females residing in the inner city. This is particularly true for African American teens who have out-of-wedlock births. Many of these young females live in poor female-maintained families and, therefore, neither they nor their mothers are financially able to afford medical care.

Often, the issue of receiving medical care is not simply a matter of whether the medical service provider is willing to accept Medicaid as payment for services provided to families who receive Medicaid benefits. It is not uncommon for African American women and White women to make up the working poor, who do not qualify for Medicaid. In 1990 there were approximately 11 million working poor individuals in the United States. This group of individuals is usually in a marginal status relative to health care. They usually work in occupations where employers do not provide health insurance benefits, or their incomes are slightly above the poverty level, which means that they are ineligible to receive health care benefits paid by Medicaid. Johnson contends that many poor families which fall into this category are able to function on a daily basis, until a medical emergency arises.[28] When this occurs it is not uncommon for such families to descend into poverty; many already at a financial disadvantage may occupy this position permanently, becoming a part of what Glasgow calls the permanent underclass.[29]

A close examination of social policy, particularly social welfare policies and practices, clearly reveals that African American women have benefited little from these efforts. What becomes increasingly obvious is that policies, practices and laws are responsible for the systematic inclusion in major societal institutions of some members of American society and the exclusion of African American women.

9

A MICROCULTURAL RESPONSE

Alternatives to macrocultural institutional support

MICRO-LEVEL INSTITUTIONAL SUPPORT SYSTEMS

Historically African American women have been unable to access institutions within the larger society to fulfill their basic needs and the fundamental necessities of their families. They have had to rely on institutional and noninstitutional support systems within the African American community. For example, the legal system, educational institutions, adoption agencies, employment agencies and so forth within the larger society have generally not responded effectively to the needs of African American women and their community. Consequently, institutions within the African American community have attempted to meet these needs. The microcultural institutions that have supported and contributed to the survival of African American women and their communities are the African American family; the Black church; African American administered educational institutions, including historically Black colleges and universities; and African American owned businesses.

THE AFRICAN AMERICAN FAMILY

The African American family, with its willingness to adapt its structure to meet the social and economic needs of African American relatives and non-relatives, has enabled African American women to withstand the various forms of institutional discrimination, exploitation and oppression that have characterized their existence in the United States. In spite of the structural barriers that have confronted African American women they have been able to rely on the African American family as a buffer.

African American women themselves have also contributed significantly to the survival of the institution of the family. It is within the confines of the African American family that African American women have transmitted the necessary skills and strategies for combating and deflecting systematic forms of social inequality. Invaluable information on the history and experiences of African American men and women has been transmitted from one generation to the next. Specifically, African American women have maintained an oral history that has enabled each generation of women to learn the most effective methods of interacting with groups of individuals in diverse milieux. Information on child-rearing, employer–employee relations, and male–female relationships has been passed down from one generation to the next, largely by older adult African American females. Whether there is a consanguine or nonconsanguine relationship, African American women who socialize young female children within their household or communities usually consider them kin. McAdoo refers to such familial ties as "fictive kin."[1] Frequently, African American women, like the African American adult women in Shay Youngblood's play *Shakin the Mess Outa Misery*, advise and assist the biological mother in socializing young African American females.[2] These surrogate mothers are called "mama" or "aunt." Specific information is transmitted from one generation of adult women to younger females regarding gender role expectations, child-rearing, social skills, macrocultural and microcultural values, norms and belief systems. This practice, like many others, reflects an African retention, one that the institution of slavery was unable to destroy.

Unlike the traditional idealized nuclear family, African Americans adopted a nuclear-type family that had the capacity to incorporate sub-families of adults and children, relatives and non-relatives, whenever necessary. This practice of absorbing individuals into the family became extremely important following emancipation. When African American men and women traveled from the South to the North it was common for the African American family in the North to act as a host family, enabling the newcomer and his or her family to become socially integrated into the new urban environment. In addition, the African American family has also embraced individuals and families experiencing hardships and displacement due to unemployment, lay-offs and other conditions causing economic exigencies. After all, employment for African American men and women has always been tenuous. In view of the effects of race and gender discrimination as well as economic downturns, African American men and women have not been afforded economic security. Therefore, it has been necessary for African Americans to maintain nuclear-type families or family structures that extended their composition beyond the narrow scope of the husband, wife and children, a constellation that conforms to the ideal nuclear family. Aside from its socializing function, the idealized nuclear family is chiefly an economic unit designed to ensure that the chief breadwinner, the husband/ father, has the support necessary to provide for the economic needs of its members. This familial arrangement has not been adequate for meeting the economic needs of African Americans, whose ability to produce tends to be affected by numerous extraneous factors, including equity in the labor market. The fact that employment practices result in lower pay and higher rates of unemployment and underemployment for African American men means that the income of African American women is also important to the maintenance of the family. In addition, African Americans have frequently constructed extended families, augmented families and sub-families for the purpose of consolidating resources. Moreover, when individuals other than the immediate family resided in the same household, family members could provide important functions that traditional nuclear families would receive from societal institutions. For instance, since the husband–wife incomes were needed, adult relatives and non-relatives residing in the same household could ease the burden of domestic duties by cooking, cleaning and providing child care, thereby reducing role strain for African American women, who like other women are primarily responsible for tasks of domesticity and serve as a primary socializing agent.

African American families made decisions regarding the education that their daughters would receive, to afford them greater occupational choices. Such practical decisions meant that African American women were frequently encouraged to pursue higher education because of limited career choices prior to the 1960s. They had two primary occupational choices, either to become a school teacher or a domestic. The latter option was fraught with considerably more problems than low pay and long hours. There were also the job hazards of potential molestation by men in houses in which domestics worked. In addition, African American women domestics became viewed as permanent household members and were expected to perform extra duties, such as babysitting. In effect, the African American female domestic was consigned to perform as many tasks as she was assigned by the woman of the house.

Added to the enormity of daily responsibilities, African American women domestics received little respect, as the relationship was not an employee–employer relationship; instead emphasis was on servitude rather than employment. While husbands earned the money by which the domestics' wages were paid, their wives assumed primary responsibility for assigning tasks and supervising domestics' work – the domestic's responsibilities were defined by the woman of the house. In many instances the African American domestic, although a symbol confirming the status of upper middle and upper class families, was relegated to a position similar to that of a subentry level employee. The typical reference that was made to the African American domestic was "girl."[3] She was rarely accorded respect as an adult. This was true despite the fact that domestics had families of their own, and frequently also worked for multiple generations of the same family. That is, the African American domestic was sometimes in the employ of a child's parents and later would work as a domestic for the children when they reached adulthood. Despite the fact that the female domestic was expected to impart advice and wisdom to family members, she was never accorded equal status. Therefore, African American families, recognizing the limited career options for their daughters, attempted to send them to four-year colleges or to teacher's colleges. One of the consequences of this pattern among African American families is that significantly more African American females have attended and graduated from institutions of higher education than African American males.

Preparing African American women for motherhood and the problems of socializing their children into dual cultures is a task that African American mothers and other adult female women have assumed throughout their history in the United States. African American females learn through their childhood and adult life how to access societal institutions and how to function effectively in their own microcultural environment. Historically, much of this information was acquired by African American domestics through their daily contacts with Whites. African American mothers have demonstrated their ability to socialize their children, male and female, to function effectively in both

African American and European American cultures. It has also been necessary for African American mothers to ensure their daughters' awareness of how the interactive effects of gender, race and class result in societal perceptions and expectations that are unique to African American women. For example, African American women, unlike their White counterparts, are not socialized to expect their husbands to assume the sole responsibility for being a provider and protector.

Before the Civil Rights Movement in the 1960s, segregation and overt forms of discrimination contributed to the maintenance of two separate and distinct cultures with conflicting sets of norms, values and belief systems. African American mothers emphasized the importance of their daughters' subscribing to African American values of cooperation, collective responsibility, an extended family structure and the like. However, one of the conditions imposed by the larger society, when greater opportunities arose out of the demands of the Civil Rights Movement, was that African Americans embrace the values inherent in the larger society. Added to this requirement was the belief that the lives of African Americans, because of increased opportunities, would begin to parallel those of White Americans. Therefore, the values that appeared to make the lives of White Americans more functional were frequently adopted by African Americans who anticipated and experienced upward mobility. African American women, aware that larger numbers of African American males were pursuing college degrees, believed that they, like White women, would have more men with educational and occupational statuses equal to or higher than their own. Prior to the 1950s it was not uncommon for the middle class African American wife to have a higher occupational status than her husband; yet her husband's income, frequently as a factory worker, was higher than his wife's.[4]

Because of affirmative action policies and expanded social and economic programs, it was reasonable for African American women to expect that their future husbands would be better able to perform the role of the provider. In so doing, the African American woman, like her White counterpart, would be afforded greater opportunities to nurture and rear her children and provide the emotional support that would further catapult her husband's career and earnings. The fact that White middle class women were beginning to reject their assigned roles and dependence had not gained considerable attention. Besides, it was

166

difficult for African American women, who had labored intensely and suffered various forms of physical and emotional exploitation, to reject or scoff at an opportunity to avoid the labor force with its inexorable stress. At this time White women, still outside the labor market in large numbers, were just beginning their new forms of protest against paternalism and patriarchy whereby their husbands kept them in the homes, reducing labor market competition. Since this new wave of feminim had not yet collectively crystallized and become proliferated throughout the mainstream, African American women anticipating dropping out of the labor market and depending on their spouses to be the sole economic providers had not yet learned of the inordinate social and psychological costs associated with this traditional gender role. The major problem that has emerged since the sixties and seventies is that most economic opportunities for African American men and women did not come to fruition; yet, the expectations of African American women were raised. African American women who accept the European American value that the husband/father should be the chief breadwinner and have an occupational and educational status equal to or greater than his spouse are faced with a genuine paradox. The conflict is not one that is borne exclusively by African American women, but is one that has contributed to the societal devaluation of the African American male. Today, when African American mothers socialize their daughters they are faced with resolving conflicts that exist between traditional African American values and those that prevail in the larger society. The resurgence of racial pride and an acknowledgement of Africentricity, that favorably valuates values, beliefs and norms inherent in African American culture, is one method by which African Americans can combat discrimination and conflicting mainstream values. When messages are transmitted to African American female youth regarding dating, courtship and marriage they must be encouraged to place emphasis on marrying a husband with integrity, a strong work ethic and sensitivity to women's issues.

According to Hooks, the socialization of African American females is quite unique. Hooks contends that African American females, unlike African American males, White males and White females, are not socialized to exploit, discriminate against or to oppress others.[5] Further, Hooks states that the African American woman has no "institutionalized other" to perceive, and treat, as subordinates. The irony is that, although African American women are not socialized to discriminate against others on the basis of gender and race, they are more likely than other groups of individuals to experience the inexorable effects of various forms of discrimination. Even more disheartening is the fact that, when African American women experience diverse forms of social inequities, the injustices are likely to occur simultaneously as their effects are interactive rather than independent. It is astounding that African American women who challenge various forms of injustice demonstrate remarkable perseverance and determination. Interestingly, African American women are neither inculcated with a belief system that places them in a superordinate position, relative to another group of individuals in society, nor are they imbued with the premiss that they are subordinate to others. Accordingly, African American women are socialized to believe in the precepts of social equality and to reject the idea of submitting to any system of domination. This does not mean that African American women, like other groups, do not discriminate against others, but when this occurs it is likely to occur against individuals and not a group of individuals.

While the African American woman and other adult females, both kin and non-kin, assume a key role in socializing African American females, it is also the case that African American fathers and other males, usually relatives such as grandfathers and uncles, contribute to their socialization as well. And because a sizable proportion of African American families are headed by women, the role of the minister in assisting African American women in socializing their children, including their daughters, cannot be understated. In this regard, the minister in the Black church has played, and continues to play, an instrumental role in providing advice and direction and serving as a positive adult male role model for African American male and female children in homes where the father is not in residence. To some, the African American minister is actually a surrogate father. There is also evidence that African American women rely on their ministers to provide more than advice regarding child-rearing. I conducted a study that revealed that divorced African American women rely on their ministers to provide a variety of forms of counseling, whereas their White counterparts depend on formal institutions for similar forms of counseling and support.[6]

The Black church has also played a significant role in

168

socializing, supporting and sustaining African American females and their families. The role of the Black church as an agent of social change, as an entity that establishes moral precepts for the African American community and family, is well documented. The Black church's support of African American women is generally considered a primary reason for the ability of African American women and their communities to survive and progress in spite of limited opportunities and minuscule social and economic gains since emancipation.

In the pre-Civil Rights era, the Black church had a tremendous influence on African American women and their communities. African American families, whether nuclear-type, female-headed, or one of many other structures, were directed by the church to use certain strategies to access macrocultural and microcultural systems. The law of reciprocity governed the lives of African American men and women. In fact, the interdependence of members of the African American community encouraged by the Black church, accounted for the viability of self-help networks, formed by African American women. The Black church did more than provide directives and principles for cooperative living. Because of the historic importance of spirituality among Africans and later African American women, the Black church has been perceived as the foundation for the spiritual, physical and emotional well-being of African American women and their community.

African American educational institutions have also helped to shape African American women's lives and their capacity to resist and challenge institutional discrimination. Prior to the government's efforts to desegregate public schools, African American women received more than education in segregated schools. Teachers, generally African American females, were integral to the socialization of African American females. Serving as role models, African American school teachers were evidence that young African American girls could successfully challenge race, gender and class occupational inequality. Clearly, segregated schools that were predominantly African American represented enormous difficulties for African American female students, because of inadequate resources and inferior facilities due to low levels of government funding compared to predominantly White schools. Aside from constructive role models, segregated schools reinforced African American values that produced interdependence,

169

unity and mutual sharing and caring; all values that are essential for the survival and progress of African American women and their communities. In addition, segregated schools, while devalued by the larger society, like all entities that are exclusively operated, administered or managed by African Americans, significantly reduced the probability that African American female students would be subjected to pejorative statements regarding their race. Equally important, Black schools provided opportunities for the development of friendships and feelings of social approval from adults as well as children. M.L. Clark discusses how forming and maintaining friendships has a positive influence on the psychosocial development of African American youth.[7] When African American females attend racially desegregated schools, friendships are not as easy to establish, because most individuals develop friendships with individuals whose race and social class are like their own. Developing a strong race consciousness and positive self-esteem are considered necessary prerequisites for effective functioning within African American culture and throughout the larger society. African American schools have always placed considerable emphasis on teaching African American history and the contributions that African Americans have made to this country and have systematically stressed the importance of racial pride. As well as the environment, teacher expectations of students in African American schools create an atmosphere which facilitates learning. The problems that resulted in inferior education were a function of material deprivation rather than the existence of a social climate that was not conducive to learning. Racially balanced schools, in which the teaching staff includes only a small number of teachers with social and racial consciousness, have adequate resources yet offer a social milieu that precludes high levels of academic achievement for African American females. That is, such learning environments tend to thwart academic achievements for African American female students. According to Weinberg, Dubois expressed concern over this dilemma of segregated and desegregated schools; each has severe limitations that result in low levels of academic achievement for African American youth.[8] The disparities between inner city schools and suburban schools, both usually segregated today, are monumental. The provisions made available to urban schools, disproportionately comprised of African American students, are generally far more inferior and inadequate compared to suburban schools in which White students are overrepresented.[9]

Historically, Black institutions of higher education have also been assets to African American women. Prior to affirmative action legislation the majority of African American men and women, excluded from predominantly White colleges and universities, attended predominantly Black institutions of higher education. However, affirmative action laws resulted in a reversal in the percentage of African American women attending institutions of higher education. Because of the desegregation of colleges and universities throughout the country, 80 per cent of African Americans attend predominantly White colleges and universities while only 20 per cent of African Americans attend historically Black colleges and universities.[10] There continues to be more African American women attending and graduating from colleges and universities than African American males. It is likely that the continued pattern of more African American females than males attending institutions of higher education is a function of the former having more experience in pursuing college degrees; they are better able to access these institutions through information obtained from adult female role models, who are college graduates.

Despite the fact that, throughout the 1980s, 66 per cent of all African American college graduates were female, the number of African American females attending graduate and professional schools continued to decline. And those who are pursuing graduate and professional degrees in predominantly White institutions of higher education have difficulty securing faculty mentors, who are necessary for academic and professional career development. The majority of faculty at predominantly White institutions of higher education are White males, so it is largely this group who must be mentors to students, irrespective of their race or gender. Cultural images of African American women as hypersexual individuals (bad-black-girl) impact significantly upon the inability of many African American female students to find a mentor. According to one study, White male faculty members reported that they believed that African American female students were interested in seducing them; and, therefore, they avoided contact with this group of students.[11] In the same study, the respondents stated that they maintained distance from African American male

171

students because of their fear of intimidation. In this case, the image of the African American male as "the buck" continues to have serious repercussions and represents an impediment to African American male students.

In spite of the fact that a disproportionate number of African American women attend predominantly White colleges and universities it is still the case that historically Black colleges and universities, offer greater opportunities for African American male and female students. Studies reveal that historically Black schools create an environment that is perceived by Black students as inclusive, caring and supportive. By contrast, African American students attending predominantly White institutions of higher education commonly experience alienation, isolation and a lack of support.[12] These different experiences contribute to differential rates of graduation. Again, of the 80 per cent of African American students attending predominantly White colleges and universities, only 20 per cent graduate, while 80 per cent of those attending historically Black colleges and universities graduate. Fiscal problems in higher education due to cuts in the allocation of federal dollars to education have had an impact on colleges and universities throughout the country. The ongoing reduction in government funds for education has had an even more dramatic effect on historically Black colleges and universities.

Historically, African American owned businesses have represented an opportunity for African American women to acquire, refine and utilize various skills by providing valuable services, mainly to the African American community. These businesses have provided economic development to the African American community while enabling many to join the African American middle class.[13] The determination and initiative of African American women have been demonstrated in business ownership. African American women recognized that they possessed skills which could fill service voids for the African American and White communities. Some of these services were provided exclusively by African American females to the African American community. Segregation meant that African American women who needed the services of beauticians and midwives relied exclusively upon other African American women to provide these services. It is also the case that many African American women were able to provide for their families by establishing businesses which offered the services of caterers, seamstresses and laundresses to members of the White community as well.

Unquestionably, African American women have not remained passive while a number of factors have worked in an interlocking fashion to contribute to the low socioeconomic status of this population. On the contrary, aware that societal institutions have rarely been available to them, African American women have designed complex systems for the purpose of survival and progress. Specifically, they have established self-help networks known as mutual aid networks.

A surfeit of evidence reveals that these networks have their origin in Africa and can also be traced to slavery in the United States. In their most dramatic form, mutual aid networks, comprised largely of women, provided invaluable goods and services for slaves living on plantations. Sudarkasa provides convincing evidence that there existed a transresidential self-help system that enabled African American women to provide basic goods and services from one plantation to another.[14] The sisterhood that existed prior to European slavery was transported along with African slaves to America. Immediately following the abolition of slavery, African American women assumed an integral role in establishing and expanding mutual aid networks.[15] These self-help groups, comprised largely of women, related and non-related, continue to represent a noninstitutional support system that has assured the survival and progress of African American women and their community. Concern over the ability of mutual aid networks to maintain their positive influence over the lives of African American women and their community with increasing government participation in funding, administering and monitoring social and economic programs was expressed by McCray.[16] The warning that government bureaucracy could lead to the disruption of mutual aid networks within the African American community was a sagacious projection that came to fruition. There is overwhelming evidence that informal self-help networks were adversely affected by expanded government involvement in the African American community.

The decline of mutual aid networks occurred largely because of an increased demand for goods and services due to the growth of an urban population that could not rely on farming to meet their needs. Moreover, a diminishing supply of resources due to the decline in old line industries such as steel, mining and railroads also resulted in a permanent loss of employment for many African American men and women. There has been a change in values;

whereby African Americans have been encouraged by the larger society to embrace individualism, competitiveness and independence. The fact that a growing number of African Americans began to internalize these values meant they became reluctant to seek assistance from each other. To do so, according to the larger society, means that individuals are unable to function effectively. Moreover, this new set of values means that individuals who depend on each other for survival are considered a burden rather than an integral component of a social exchange system. This proclivity for individualism, associated with the impersonal nature of urban dwelling, gives the appearance that others, who do not rely on individuals within their communities for support, are better equipped to function effectively. By contrast, those who systematically rely on an exchange system are perceived as lacking the necessary skills for survival. This type of reasoning is antithetical to traditional African American values where all individuals were considered essential and in possession of valuable skills, knowledge, goods and services. These resources were considered important to the survival of the individual who possessed them, and also to the family, the community and the entire race of African Americans.

The 1980s brought a period known as retrenchment in which many of the social and economic gains registered by African Americans were not maintained. One of the consequences of this period of ultraconservatism is that the mutual aid network, frequently out of necessity, began to be revitalized. In 1981, when the Reagan administration initiated severe budget cuts in social and economic programs, African Americans had to rely more on mutual aid networks. In doing so, African American women, particularly single females who headed households, had to reevaluate mutual aid networks. Thus, negative definitions associated with informal self-help networks had to be replaced with positive definitions that considered these exchange systems as valuable and essential mechanisms for the survival of the African American family, particularly those maintained by women. The resilience demonstrated by African American women who have been able to withstand the oppressive and exploitative institution of slavery and the subsequent inexorable social and economic conditions brought on by race, gender and class inequalities can be attributed largely to the effectiveness of these networks.

Prior to the Civil Rights Movement and the acquisition of more mainstream values by African American women and their communities, mutual aid networks were useful to married-couple families as well as to African American families headed by single women. Support for mutual aid networks was provided by the Black church and inextricably woven into the fabric of African American culture. In addition, institutions within the African American community reinforced and perpetuated informal self-help networks. For example, predominantly Black schools and Black owned businesses stressed the importance of self-help efforts. There are essentially two reasons why self-help efforts governed the lives of African American women and their communities before the Civil Rights Movement. First, there was an African tradition of extended families living within the same geographical area. The goods and services of these familial structures were augmented by a strong sisterhood, whereby women exchanged information and worked and lived in a cooperative environment. Second, societal institutions, with basic goods and services, were not available or accessible to African American women and their communities. Therefore, African American women were in the vanguard of establishing and maintaining mutual aid networks to meet the needs of individual women and members of their communities. One of the primary services exchanged by mutual aid networks formed after emancipation was child care. There were no formal child care facilities so, because African American women generally had to work outside the home, mainly as domestics in the homes of White families, they exchanged child care services with each other. These forms of noneconomic exchanges of in-kind services did not occur solely because African American women had only limited economic resources to pay for these services. Rather, African American women and men believed firmly in the values of cooperation, helping those in need and collective living. These same values were culturally transmitted by African American women, as the primary socializing agents, from one generation to another.

The Civil Rights Movement brought about two major changes that affected the viability of mutual aid networks in the African American community. First, social and economic programs were developed and expanded, thereby increasing their availability to African Americans. Second, because of higher levels of participation of African American women, men and children in these programs, along with increased educational and employment opportunities, African Americans were encouraged to accept values such as individualism and competitiveness, values that are diametrically opposed to the existence and use of mutual aid networks. In effect, African Americans were expected to shift their dependence on each other and those involved in mutual aid networks to societal institutions and organizations. To do otherwise was purported to thwart the career mobility of African Americans and to sustain them in a position of marginality. In total, all traditional African American values were challenged by educational and economic institutions.

In the past, African Americans had attended Black schools with Black teachers who reinforced traditional cultural values that supported reliance on mutual aid networks. As a result of efforts to desegregate public schools attended by African American children, the values of the teaching staff were those of the White middle class. These values did not support, and often conflicted with, traditional African American values. Accordingly, schools became competitive socializing agents. The adherence to White middle class values distinguished African American students who achieved in and conformed to their new environment from those who experienced academic underachievement, and were unable to conform to the new educational climate.

Employers, particularly corporations, expected African American women to modify their value orientations. Corporations deemed it a necessity for African American women to adopt new values, norms and belief systems for career mobility. For example, if Corporation A offers a promotion to an employee and requires the employee to relocate to a city 2,000 miles away, the employer is operating from the assumption that the employee is autonomous and relies on societal institutions and organizations to fulfill her needs. In the case of African American women, accepting this career opportunity may create conflicting emotions. Obviously, a promotion that would lead to additional career growth would be rewarding; yet, leaving one's family, friends and community may present a set of problems that would lead to an approach-avoidance situation regarding the new position. In the first place, even if the African American woman is in the middle class, there is still likely to be an involvement in a mutual aid network where valuable resources are exchanged. Studies reveal that African American women across socioeconomic lines are involved in self-help networks.[17] The chief difference between middle-class and lower-income African American women is in the amount of commodities that are exchanged and the frequency of exchange. In the case of African American middle class women, advice, emotional support and social approval are the primary commodities exchanged. While exchange also involves these items in the case of lower-income African American women, it is more likely to include an exchange of financial resources. Thus, if the African American female employee accepts the promotion and moves to a distant city she and her family and friends are more likely to experience separation anxiety than individuals who subscribe to mainstream values that promote individualism, competition and social isolation. On the surface it appears that the African American woman would further her career by accepting a promotion 2,000 miles away and that African American women who adhere to traditional African American values of mutual dependence, collective responsibility and strong kinship bonds are limiting their professional careers. Those who subscribe to mainstream values would erroneously consider the African American woman's thwarted career mobility to be an individual rather than an institutional problem. This logic ignores the fact that social exchange is not unilateral but bilateral. Thus, while the African American woman proffers valuable goods and services, she also receives from her informal social support system valuable goods and services. The network is likely to provide social approval, emotional support and advice. Thus, in relocating to accept a promotion, she may lose valuable resources that have contributed to the career success that she has achieved as an employee of Corporation A. This is an extremely important situation that reflects the increased marginality and value conflicts that extant members of the Black middle class encounter.

Resolving such conflicts in macrocultural and microcultural value orientations is no simple task. On the one hand are the European American values that stress economic factors and material possessions over noneconomic factors and nonmaterial resources. The middle class African American woman realizes that she is likely to be the ongoing victim of discrimination and that her informal social support system will help to counter the negative effects of overt, and covert, forms of institutional race and gender discrimination. In fact, many African American women who accept what appears to be a promising job opportunity report that their experiences with social isolation and other forms of alienation produced by overt and subtle race and gender discrimination in the new employment situation necessitate the resources of a mutual aid network more than ever. And while individuals can establish new informal social support systems, the same values – individualism, competition and social isolation – that enable a woman to accept a promotion in a distant city militate against her establishing a strong social support network. Clearly, while new social networks can be established this requires time and familiarity with one's new environment. And because these networks tend to be localized and not regionalized, unlike in the pre-Civil Rights era, it is highly improbable that African American women can move from one region to another and be given a "letter of introduction" as was the case prior to the 1960s when African Americans migrated from the South to the North. During the periods of ongoing and mass migrations of African Americans from the rural South to the urban North, there was a greater likelihood that individuals new to a community would be accepted or absorbed as a member of the family merely because a relative or friend from the South requested that the family do so. In effect, African Americans assumed responsibility for each other, maintaining a norm of reciprocity. The norm of reciprocity, discussed by Gouldner, was universal throughout African American culture and was largely responsible for the survival of African American women and their communities.[18] Such mutual sharing also served to strengthen the sisterhood and to unify the entire African American community.

When the Civil Rights Movement resulted in the increased participation of African American women in societal institutions, it created more than intrapersonal and interpersonal conflicts between traditional African American values and European American values. It has also created an ongoing debate over the extent to which mutual aid networks and strong kinship bonds are beneficial or detrimental to African American women, men and children. Those who support the premiss that mutual aid networks are important to the survival of African Americans argue that African Americans, unlike Whites, are excluded from networks such as the old boy network, that exchange information about acquiring property, securing employment, accessing educational and financial institutions and so forth. And because African Americans are excluded from these mainstream networks, they must rely on self-help networks to provide some of the same goods and services. McAdoo contends that, because African Americans have been excluded from societal institutions, they have not acquired and amassed resources that can be passed down from one generation to another.[19] Thus, each generation of African Americans must start anew. It is essential that critical information and resources be exchanged and transmitted by each generation to successive generations.

Alternatively, those who criticize mutual aid networks believe that if African Americans assume responsibility for their relatives and friends who comprise these networks, they will thwart their own individual professional growth. In effect, critics argue that mutual aid networks drain the resources of a member who is more economically solvent and has a higher income potential than other members. This kind of reasoning, predicated on traditional European American values, is offered as an indicator that African American cultural values, not institutional discrimination, account for limited career mobility among African Americans. What this logic fails to take into account is that ongoing discrimination does not stop with job promotions and other career opportunities. Consequently, African Americans who accept career opportunities by relocating need the continued interdependent relationships with members of a mutual aid network.

In addition, one cannot ignore the important role that middle class African American women play as role models to young African Americans who reside in their communities. After all, there is the expectation in the African American community that when African Americans achieve success they should return, and contribute, to their communities, which are believed to be responsible for the individuals' success. This paradox is one which has yet to be satisfactorily resolved. To some extent it affects all middle class African American women, especially those reared in the inner city. They are expected by employers and co-workers to confirm their status by acquiring specific status symbols such as designer clothing, foreign automobiles and suburban houses. On the other hand, they are expected to reside in the inner city to contribute the benefits of their accomplishments, that is, information, knowledge and skills.

Some believe that middle class African American men and women comprise what Dubois called the talented tenth, who have a responsibility to lead the African American masses.[20] This notion of collective responsibility is also reflected in the saying "lift as we climb", a goal espoused by African American social activists in the pre-Civil Rights Movement era. The question which this paradox

179

poses is whether the African American woman can offer more to her community by placing her own interests above those of her reference group. While this is a dilemma that is relatively new for middle class African American women, who had fewer career choices before the 1960s, it is still the case that the success of African American men and women occurs largely as a result of the support which they receive from the mutual aid network. Therefore, their responsibility to the community should take priority over their own individual interests. In fact, individual and collective interests should coincide if they have attained a level of awareness of African American values along with their academic and career success.

While mutual aid networks have historically offered invaluable goods and services to all types of African American families, Stack found in her research that these self-help networks adversely affected the stability of African American married-couple families.[21] However, her study revealed that informal self-help networks were beneficial to African American female single-parent families. One plausible explanation is that the acceptance of a European American value system has resulted in African American two-parent families being unable to continue a mutual dependent relationship with family and friends who make up the mutual aid network. When a growing number of African Americans embrace mainstream gender definitions of masculinity, establishing that husbands/fathers must be providers and protectors and maintain a socially isolated autonomous familial unit, then mutual aid networks are viewed as usurping the husband/father role. Basically, when African American two-parent families accept this European American mainstream definition of masculinity, they believe that depending on self-help networks indicates that the husband/father is unable to provide adequately for his family. Thus, ongoing dependence on the mutual aid network leads to the devaluation of the husband/father, as he is considered a failure. To a large extent, the developments of the 1960s and 1970s influenced many African Americans to reexamine and replace traditional African American values with those embraced by European Americans, who had greater access to and participation in social, economic and political systems. This transition has contributed to the decline of salient African American institutions and informal survival mechanisms such as mutual aid networks.

One of the consequences of the period of retrenchment in the

1980s, whereby the government began to rescind social policies that were designed to elevate the status of African Americans, was a revitalization of mutual aid networks. It should be noted that to a large extent economic necessity influenced the revival of these networks. There has also been a resurgence of race consciousness which is consistent with the peaks and lulls that Lincoln states characterize social movements.[22] Thus, as mutual aid networks are increasing in their importance and viability for African American women, the sisterhood that served to undergird mutual aid networks has also begun to regain its significance and capacity to restore unity among African American women and members of their community.

Criticisms of African American women and men who are striving to revitalize mutual aid networks and other self-help efforts have been proffered by many within the larger society, who viewed them as detrimental to the upward mobility of individual African Americans. However, the fact that some African American scholars are critical of those who propose self-help strategies within the African American community is alarming. Butler discusses the fact that some academicians define self-help as a negative strategy for elevating the socioeconomic status of African Americans. He states that these critics tend to label African American scholars who are proponents of this approach as neoconservatives. Moreover, Butler contends that academic opponents of self-help strategies are critical of this approach because they fear that self-help strategies will absolve the government of its responsibility for improving the social and economic conditions affecting the African American population.[23]

It is clearly the case that, during the decade of the eighties that brought about the revitalization of mutual aid networks and the strengthening of the sisterhood among African American women, the cultural images of African American women began to undergo redefinition. This period, that was marked by economic deterioration and the continued rescission of the social and economic advances that African American women made in the areas of income, education and occupation, also included a significant modification in the cultural imagery of African American women. It was during this decade that the image of Clara Huxtable emerged, a middle class college-educated African American woman attorney with a professional husband, a medical doctor played by comedian, educator and philanthropist, Bill Cosby. The audience receptivity to this image, which approximates the real life African American middle class female who manages family and profession well, was significant. This positive cultural image and the audience's favorable response negated producers' statements that audiences liked the traditional distorted imagery of African American women. The onset of a new decade proved the mainstream media that had vilified one African American woman, Vanessa Williams, unsuccessful. In 1990 the first African American female, Vanessa Williams, to be crowned Miss America overcame the mainstream media's vilification when the African American-owned *Ebony* Magazine's article entitled "Vanessa Williams: Success Is the Best" described her triumphs after her beauty pageant problems.[24] Another article appeared in the mainstream media's *McCall's* Magazine, entitled "Vanessa Williams's Extraordinary Comeback."[25] Moreover, the third African American female to be crowned Miss America, following Suzette Charles, reigned uneventfully in spite of media attempts to initiate a character assassination campaign against her. The ability of African American women to overcome negative cultural imagery is indicative of their strength and their resolve to overcome individual and societal barriers to success, but also reflects how such triumph is achieved through the support, confidence and understanding embodied in the African American sisterhood upon which the mutual aid network is grounded.

10

REDEFINING IMAGES OF AFRICAN AMERICAN WOMANHOOD AND RESHAPING SOCIAL POLICY

REDEFINING AFRICAN AMERICAN WOMANHOOD: A CONTINUING PROCESS

The effort of African American academicians to redefine African American womanhood, by challenging nonrepresentative images as inaccurate portrayals of African American women, is ongoing. It is a component of the continuing struggle for liberation that African American women and social activists have undertaken. As is the case with the inequities overcome by African Americans in social, political, economic, educational and legal arenas, images of African American women based on myths and stereotypes continue to resurface, only to be challenged, modified and temporarily eliminated.

Unquestionably, there have been changes in the traditional images of mammy, Aunt Jemima, the bad-black-girl, and Sapphire. The major changes that were made in the mammy image affected her physical characteristics more than her emotional make-up. The same was true for the visual image of Aunt Jemima. In the 1970s the African American female portrayal of Aunt Jemima that appeared on the Quaker Oats Company's Aunt Jemima pancake mix underwent noticeable changes. Her complexion was lightened, her head rag was replaced with a head band, she was reduced in size, and her grin was replaced with a smile. Aunt Jemima's image underwent another modernization in the late 1980s when the head band was removed and she donned a contemporary moderate length hair style. These changes were publicized by the Quaker Oats Company in newspapers throughout the country. Traditional portrayals of the tragic mulatto, mammy, Aunt Jemima and Sapphire began to diminish in the 1970s in all media. That is not to say that these images disappeared entirely. Such is certainly not the case. One image which was infrequently portrayed was the bad-black-girl. Other images, such as mammy and Sapphire, were depicted with great regularity with certain modifications. They were frequently synthesized, resulting in an African American woman domestic whose comedic ability was displayed as she issued verbal put-downs in her relationship with the leading African American male character. The "sitcom" became the vehicle in which the contemporary mammy was portrayed. Jean Carey Bond notes that the media's response to demands for better representation on television was to increase the visibility of traditional stereotypes.[1]

Television, more than any other medium, is responsible for portraying and perpetuating these symbols of Black womanhood. Throughout the 1980s the most popular television sitcoms with African American female actors were "Amen," "Gimme A Break," "What's Happening," "That's My Momma" and "Family Matters." Each of these shows contained contemporary versions of mammy and Sapphire characters. The program "227" was another popular television sitcom that featured several African American working class families residing in one apartment building. This sitcom introduced American television audiences to the bad-black-girl image in the character Sandra Clark, portrayed by actress Jackee Harry. "The Cosby Show" and its offshoot, "A Different World," represented the only sitcoms in the 1980s that departed from the traditional and contemporary versions of cultural images that symbolize Black womanhood.

Other contemporary mammies were portrayed by individuals on television. In these programs, specifically the talk show, the mammy image was not portrayed by an actress but by a real African American professional female, who, like many other African American professional women, did not perform domestic tasks but assumed the nurturing role, one of the other key affective roles attributed to the traditional mammy.[2]

Oprah Winfrey became America's most popular daytime talk show host. Demonstrating concern, compassion and under-standing regarding a variety of issues, Oprah Winfrey's ratings surpassed those of the Phil Donahue, the veteran talk show host. She also revealed her own human frailties and challenges of growing up as she shared personal experiences and interpersonal

184

relationships with television audiences throughout the country. She, like mammy, was able to transcend the color line, winning the hearts of White Americans as well as African Americans. Critics of Oprah did surface, however, from members of the African American intelligentsia, who complained that she displayed little race consciousness as she downplayed the significance of race and racism in her television talk show.[3] Others believed that she attempted to increase the comfort of Whites by speaking in the Black English vernacular and sharing bits of enlightening information about African American culture. Oprah's large size was consistent with the mammy image. And when she successfully lost weight, she received plaudits as well as complaints about the liquid diet method by which she shed over sixty pounds within a brief period of time. In reality, it is probable that the dissatisfaction registered by many of Oprah Winfrey's viewers was related to the drastic change that she made in her appearance. Oprah's reduced size after dieting was consistent with the image of White womanhood; yet she was visually unsatisfying to White Americans who associate obesity in the African American woman with wisdom, caring, understanding and the capacity to be emotionally soothing and nurturing. Thus, it came as little surprise when Oprah Winfrey regained her weight, and vowed never to diet again. After regaining weight, she expressed her satisfaction with her large stature and it is likely that her acceptance of being overweight, a state that she underwent deprivation to abandon, was due in part to the positive reinforcement of millions of viewers. Many of these viewers were unaware of the subconscious correlation between the large stature of an African American woman, her credibility and capacity to provide comfort to adults and children. Despite the fact that Oprah Winfrey has demonstrated her proficiency as a talk show host and actress, it is still the case that cultural images that symbolize African American womanhood continue to impact upon her and other African American female high achievers. This is true because African American female professionals continue to be evaluated and rewarded, not merely for their ability to perform the instrumental functions inherent in their position; they are also expected to conform to the physical and affective qualities symbolized by cultural images constructed by those in power and propagated by the media.

The positive imagery portrayed in "The Cosby Show" and "A Different World" was not able to counterbalance the traditional cultural imagery of African American women that the media continued to purvey. The preponderance of the latter clearly obscured the former. Nevertheless, there were also some rudimentary signs that African American women were gaining greater acceptance as models, movie actresses and as Miss America, America's ultimate symbol of beauty and womanhood. By 1990 the United States could boast a record three African American women had been awarded the Miss America title. Some would question whether this occurrence symbolized that African American women were being accepted for the beauty and physical characteristics that are unique to their culture or whether the larger society was more willing to accept African American women who approximate the American image of beauty and womanhood. In all likelihood it is the latter which is the basis for the acceptance of African American women as Miss America. In addition, waning interest in the pageant was certainly curbed by selecting African American women to hold what was once a highly coveted position.

This process of redefining the African American woman's cultural image will continue until this imagery is empirically verifiable. In addition to the ongoing efforts of African American women to redefine cultural images that symbolize them, there is also a parallel movement that is gaining momentum. The Civil Rights Movement of the 1960s and 1970s is being revived. And while African American women were involved, and played a critical role, in the Civil Rights Movement during the 1960s and 1970s, their role in the social movement which became reinvigorated during the latter part of the 1980s is increasing. In many ways the Civil Rights Movement in the 1960s and 1970s, while sustained by African American men and women, was perceived largely as a movement led by African American males. Unlike the earlier Civil Rights Movement, African American women are assuming more prominent roles along with African American males in the revived effort for social change. One reason for the greater assumption of leadership among African American women is the recognition that a collaborative effort is essential if African Americans are to experience substantial social and economic gains. Relying on the dynamics and gains of the 1960s and 1970s, African American women recognize that, despite opposition, they must contribute to social change by functioning in instrumental and affective roles.

Another reason that African American women are assuming greater leadership in challenging institutions to eliminate

186

inequality is the increased percentage of African American women who are forced, by a variety of circumstances, to maintain families independent of a husband/father. That is not to say that African American women who are the heads of households do not have input, or receive assistance, from African American males, such as fathers, brothers and grandfathers, but for a growing number of African American women heading a family is a function for which they must assume greater responsibility.

Because of the increased percentage of African American males outside the civilian labor force, the increasing number of African American males who are victims of homicides, the growing proportion of African American males who are institutionalized and the fact that more African American males are voluntarily enlisting in the military due to the limited availability of other employment opportunities, fewer African American males are present in African American families.

It is also important for African American women to play an integral role in establishing goals, objectives and strategies for achieving social change. Because African American women experience gender discrimination along with the race and class inequality that confront African American men, they are well equipped to engage in social, political and economic struggles that address all forms of social inequality. Clearly, it is easier for African American women to articulate their experiences as victims of the interlocking forms of oppression than for others who, while sensitive to these issues, may not have strategies and methods for successfully addressing social inequality in the different forms in which it manifests itself.

In the past, some believed that African American women did a great disservice to the struggle for race equality by pursuing the elimination of all forms of discrimination, including gender, class and race. Those critical of African American women's participation in the feminist movement expressed the view that African American women who pursued the elimination of gender discrimination diffused the efforts of the Civil Rights Movement. These critics also argued that, while there was legitimacy to African American women's concerns regarding sex discrimination, race discrimination was more prevalent, limiting and debilitating. In the evolution of the African American feminist agenda, race, gender and class discrimination are forms of oppression that are being equally weighted and concurrently challenged.

187

African American women play a vital role in the elimination of social inequality, as they have a tradition of achieving through individual and collective efforts. That is, irrespective of the strategy or method that activists employ to bring about social change, at the very minimum there must be a unified effort between African American men and women. Coalitions must also be explored, and formed, as a strategy to broaden African American women's power, information and resource base: such coalitions are imperative to ensure that meaningful changes will occur within social, economic and political systems. The ability of African American women to establish and maintain complex self-help exchange networks is an invaluable skill that has been effective in bringing about positive change for African Americans. It is inconceivable that there can be an effective social movement, designed to bring about legal remedies for past and present social injustices, without the use of a unified and collective effort of African Americans. It is imperative that African American women strengthen their own collective efforts before forming coalitions with other groups of individuals committed to social change.

EMERGENT POSITIVE IMAGES OF BLACK WOMEN

The efforts to effect positive cultural images symbolic of African American women have resulted in modest success, if one considers the appearance of Vanessa Williams, the first African American Miss America, as a precedent-setting occurrence that presented a positive cultural image of African American women, and the period thereafter as one in which there was a return to traditional images of African American women, along with the fact that a fourth African American woman, Marjorie Vincent was awarded the title of Miss America, in 1990. From the perspective of the larger society and also from some members of the African American community, these occurrences represent a gradual modification in the cultural imagery of African American womanhood. This is particularly true since, as many have observed, Marjorie Vincent's physical characteristics, complexion, hair color and facial features, are more African than European. Equally important is the small, but increased, number of positive cultural images of African American women. The introduction of "The Cosby Show" and "A Different World" represent a first in television for introducing and maintaining positive imagery of African

188

American women without any of the traditional negative images that were portrayed in previous television sitcoms. This does not mean that these images are representative of the African American women, but they are indicative of a beginning of accurate and positive representations of various segments of the African American female population.

Another television sitcom, "Roc," presents positive imagery of an African American working class family. Roc, the main character, played by Charles Dutton, along with his wife Eleanor, portrayed by Ella Joyce, his father and an adult freeloading brother, constitute an extended family. While extended families for African Americans is not novel for television, including two adult male relatives as members of this familial arrangement is unique. Eleanor and Roc both work outside the home and cooperate as they experience challenges and opportunities that confront African American working and middle class families throughout the United States. One of the advantages of Roc's father residing in the home is that his father's wisdom facilitates problem-solving for both Roc and his wife. The parallel benefits of extended families for African Americans in real life are similar.

When accurate and representative imagery of African American women is portrayed in television sitcoms, these images are generally accompanied by traditional stereotypical images. Thus, the media will portray an African American middle-income mother and in the same sitcom include an African American female character who conforms to the mammy, Aunt Jemima, Sapphire or bad-black-girl image. The film industry has been slower to replace traditional images of African American women. In general, the print media's cultural images of African American women more accurately represent African American women and their experiences in the United States. Again, the influence of African American writers, particularly female writers, has contributed significantly to the prevalence of cultural images of African American women that have empirical validation by the print media.

While there are many factors that influence the traditional cultural imagery of African American women and the reluctance of the mass media to modify images that are challenged by African Americans as being unrepresentative, the most recent advances in presenting positive images are related to the advances that African Americans made during the Civil Rights Movement. Positive images of African American women as portrayed in Cosby-produced sitcoms, "The Cosby Show" and "A Different World," are largely a function of the efforts of African Americans such as Bill Cosby (producer/actor), Debbie Allen (director/actress) and Alvin Poussaint (psychiatrist/consultant to "The Cosby Show"). What this demonstrates is that any substantial changes in the status of African Americans in social, economic, political and educational institutions must be initiated by African Americans themselves. However, in order to do so, individual African Americans must develop strategies and vehicles that will enable them to acquire information and to gain access to key networks that facilitate their own achievements. This is not to suggest that African Americans should not work together collectively to bring about change, but it must be recognized that individual successes must serve as the basis for collective action. It should also be noted that while African Americans must assume primary responsibility for challenging institutions they must also include others in key positions in their efforts. White Americans must also play a critical role in insuring greater participation of African Americans in mainstream institutions. The same is true of portraying positive and representative cultural images of African American women. It would be untenable to expect that African Americans alone can ensure that the mass media portray African American women and all African Americans using positive and empirically accurate cultural images without the cooperation and involvement of Whites. Clearly, it is not only important but essential that African Americans enlist the support of Whites to bring about empirically representative cultural images of African American women. After all, it is Whites who own and control the mass media, and who produce and direct media-transmitted productions that contain images of African American women.

A great deal can be learned from the modicum of success in bringing about changes in the media's portrayal of cultural images of African American women. It is clear that changes in these images are predicated in large measure on the critiques and criticisms and redefinitions of African Americans within the academy. It is this group of individuals who have historically argued that cultural imagery which is unrepresentative, distorted and negative has an adverse effect on all of society's members, particularly those portrayed by such imagery. An example of the influence of African American academicians on the portrayal of cultural images of African American women can be found in Bill Cosby. Cosby, while an actor, is also an academician whose academic preparation includes graduate work in the area of media-produced images of African American males. The reemergence of cultural images that are more representative of African American womanhood can also be attributed to actresses who have a genuine commitment to the portrayal of imagery that reflects the positive and constructive experiences and qualities of African American women. Assuming such a position and remaining guided by a set of principles that emphasize a commitment to positive and constructive imagery of African American people in general and African American women in particular certainly places constraints and limitations on the careers of actresses. It is this level of race and gender consciousness that contributes to positive and representative imagery of African American women.

In the vanguard of actresses who have assumed a position of selectivity in accepting or rejecting roles that either support or suppress positive images of African American women is Cicely Tyson. Having starred in numerous productions in stage, film and television, Cicely Tyson has been nominated for and received many awards for her outstanding performances in roles portraying African American women. Brian Lanker, noted photographer and author of *I Dream a World*, states that "Cicely Tyson, throughout her career, has portrayed many heroic women on stage, screen and television and her courageous choice of roles has had an impact far beyond her individual career."[4] Only rarely have actresses demonstrated Cicely Tyson's resolve in remaining committed to portraying positive and constructive images, reflecting the strengths, challenges and triumphs of African American women. She has had a dramatic influence on the emergence of positive cultural imagery of African American women. Cicely Tyson states:

> I did not set out to become a role model. I did set out to become the best possible actress I could be. My careful choice of roles came as a direct result of the type of negative images that were being projected of Black people through-out the world, particularly Black women. I knew deep within me that I could not afford the luxury of just being an actress – I had something to say as a member of the human race, Black and female.[5]

Clearly, by selecting roles that reflect the strengths rather than weaknesses and stereotypes of African American women, and refusing to compromise their principles, African American actresses limit their income and career opportunities. However, the long-term effect is a greater collective effort on the part of African American activists to challenge the mass media to make permanent changes in the images that are generalized to African American women. It is the persistence of those who, along with African American feminists, challenge the mass media to redefine the images of African American women that is responsible for the gains that have occurred. Nevertheless, changes in the cultural imagery of African American women have been slow and marked by retrogression as well as progress. When positive images of African American women have surfaced, they were usually temporary and certainly not evident in all media simultaneously. Because of the minuscule changes in the cultural imagery of African American women, the continued negativism and emphasis on weaknesses rather than strengths continue to have a significant effect on members of the larger society and those who are authorized to control major societal institutions.

The role of the Black press is key to effecting positive and constructive imagery of all African Americans, including African American women. Historically, it has been the print medium that has provided some balance and greater representativeness in portraying imagery of African American women. The higher percentage of African Americans with access to these media has had an influence on the print media's greater propensity to portray the strengths of African American women. Publishing and distributing newspapers, magazines and journals entails lower costs than owning electronic media, and producing programs and transmitting information on them. Therefore, African Americans in general, as well as African American women, have been responsible in large measure for developing and disseminating more positive and representative cultural images through the print media that they own and to which they have greater access. There are two specific means by which the print media have offered positive and representative cultural images of African American women. First, African American writers and artists whose works have generally found a venue in African American-owned print media rather than in mainstream print media have developed imagery that African Americans define as more positive and representative. Second, the owners of print media have also assumed responsibility for proliferating positive images of African

192

Americans, including African American women. However, not all individuals who fall into these categories develop and disseminate positive and representative cultural images of African American men, women and children. In both the electronic and print media there have been African Americans who have portrayed imagery of African American men and women that has been consistent with the stereotypical images systematically portrayed by the mass media. In both instances those who have a commitment to the development and perpetuation of positive cultural images of African American men and women have challenged individuals of all racial and ethnic backgrounds to purvey positive cultural images. In spite of the relatively few exceptions where African Americans themselves have demonstrated a lack of racial identification and consciousness by perpetuating stereotypical and non-representative images of African American men and women, it is still the case that African Americans have been in the forefront of challenging those who own the mass media, as well as individuals such as writers and artists, to develop positive imagery irrespective of gender, race or ethnicity.

African American writers and artists who have a commitment to portraying African American women using positive and representative imagery have been involved in various waves of the social movement with its highs and lows. It is particularly effective when the efforts of these individuals culminate into a visible momentous movement as in the 1960s and 1970s that brings about significant positive changes in imagery of African American women. While cultural images appear to change at certain points in time, usually during a period when the movement has reached its peak, what really occurs is that the ongoing and relentless efforts of artists, writers and other activists contribute to the emergence and re-emergence of positive imagery of African American women. It is therefore incumbent upon those who are interested in improving the images of African American women to undertake this effort with the knowledge that it is ongoing and requires persistence and an understanding that change, when it does occur, will be minuscule and painstakingly slow. Certainly, those who seek to effect changes in the portrayal and redefinition of the cultural imagery of African American women are not likely to consider this goal as their only or major objective. Instead, individuals who are determined to bring about changes in the cultural images of African American women are also concerned with policies, practices and laws by which African American women are exploited and precluded from acquiring and maintaining valuable societal resources. That is, when individuals reach a level of social consciousness which serves as the impetus for seeking positive cultural portrayals of African American women, they also possess, or are seeking to acquire, higher levels of social consciousness, which means that they understand that improving the cultural imagery of African American women is but one of many changes which must occur if the lives of African American women are to be substantially improved. Individuals have been able relentlessly to seek changes in cultural images because of their understanding of how images serve as the basis for societal perceptions; thereby providing the basis for policies, practices and laws that justify ensuring certain groups greater access to societal institutions and resources, while denying other groups of individuals the same opportunities. It is this understanding of how cultural imagery operates as an essential component of ideological hegemony that propels and serves as a catalyst for changing cultural images, policies, laws and practices that benefit some and adversely affect others.

RECURRENT NON-COMPLIMENTARY IMAGES

Changes in cultural images, because they are significant and impact upon the extent to which individuals are the beneficiaries of various policies and have access to societal resources, are slow to occur. Understandably, institutional resistance to redefining positive images of African American women and other disenfranchised groups is difficult to overcome. Positive changes in images of African American women that have occurred over the past twenty-five years have not been uniform, permanent or complete. Imagery modification is the most accurate description of changes that have taken place in the cultural imagery of African American women. As mentioned earlier, it was not until Bill Cosby produced sitcoms that other television shows changed the physical features of characters who reflected images of African American women. For the first time in any of the electronic media the African American woman was permitted to relate in a non-confrontational, non-emasculating fashion with her mate. In fact, allowing the African American mother to establish and maintain a constructive relationship with her husband was novel. Verbal put-downs, in which an African American woman was debasing an African American male, were absent. In addition, the four traditional cultural images of African American women were absent from the Cosby-produced television shows.

"The Cosby Show" with its unparalleled success and consistently high television ratings did not thwart the well-ingrained pattern of portraying African American women from a stereotypical perspective. What did occur is that several family-oriented sitcoms emerged. With the exception of "Roc" they all attempted to replicate "The Cosby Show" and its success, but only in part. That is, each of these sitcoms maintained the basic theme of the intact family, with a husband in residence; they all contained the usual features of such shows, with the mother issuing verbal put-downs to her mate or with at least one of the stereotypical traditional images of African American women. And generally the traditional image was the bad-black-girl (Jezebel) image. For example, the sitcom "Family Matters" is one which, while containing a clever and popular child character Steve Urkel, has a wife Harriet whose verbosity is akin to the Sapphire image. By contrast, the sitcom "227" contains several familial arrangements, single parent, adult singles and the primary family, a husband, wife and daughter, played by Hal Williams, Marla Gibbs and Regina King respectively. The main attraction which buttressed the show's popularity was the character Sandra Clark, played by Jackee Harry. Interestingly, the character Sandra was a hot sexpot whose behavior, gestures and expressions conformed unequivocally to the bad-black-girl image.

One of the most unfortunate but recurrent problems in the effort to improve cultural images of African American men and women is the role that African American producers, directors and writers play. It is clear that living in America and claiming American citizenship theoretically entitles individuals to certain freedoms irrespective of certain prescribed qualities. And while the focus of this book brings into question the extent to which some of these constitutional guarantees are invalidated by virtue of race, gender, class and several other ascribed characteristics, it is the case that first amendment rights to free speech and free press appear to be enjoyed by many who fail to recognize that these constitutional rights like all others should be used to enhance and not adversely affect the lives of others. In the case of imagery, which has an impact far beyond its superficial visual effect, individuals systematically violate the rights of African American women by purveying imagery which is unrepresentative, distorted and reflective of stereotypes that support perceptions and beliefs regarding African American women.

Understandably, individuals have different levels of social consciousness and diverse degrees of awareness of the harmful effects of images and stereotypes inherent in these images; yet, it is incomprehensible why African American artists, writers and producers, who themselves have been denied constitutional guarantees, would portray negative imagery of African American women and other disenfranchised groups. Success defined by material and monetary gain should not be considered a justification for transmitting negative images. Nevertheless, in the 1970s and again in the 1990s it is possible to identify African Americans who portray negative and stereotypical imagery of African American men and women. Keannan Ivory Wayans and Damon Wayans, African American producers of the movie *I'm Gonna Get You Sucka* and the television comedy show "In Living Color," have perpetuated what was labeled in the 1970s "blaxploitation productions" in both the film and television show that they produced. Grounded in stereotypical images and lexicon, both the movie and the weekly comedy show represent throwbacks to the 1950s Amos and Andy show. The disaffection with inaccurate and nonrepresentative cultural imagery expressed by African Americans and other disenfranchised groups during the 1970s has been ineffective in preventing the recurrence of blaxploitation by African American artists, writers and producers in the 1990s. However, this is not to suggest that the Civil Rights Movement, of the 1960s and 1970s, and other forms of activism during and subsequent to this era of visible social change, did not have any positive impact on African Americans and others who produce and create cultural images.

While it is unlikely that there is a reliable measure of the extent to which the level of social consciousness, particularly race and gender consciousness, increased over the past twenty-five years there is an indication that images of African American women are being redeveloped and redefined. It is therefore fair to assume that these changes may not be solely a direct result of increased social responsibility on the part of their creators and producers, but are likely to be correlated with the demands of African Americans and others for images that these groups believe to be more accurate and representative. One issue that cannot be ignored is that the race and gender of producers, artists and writers are often expected to influence the cultural images that they develop and purvey. It is difficult to separate these qualities, race and gender, from the individuals who create and produce cultural images. Whether it is an unreasonable expectation is arguable; yet, there are many who maintain a higher set of standards for individuals who create and produce images that are reflective of their own race, gender and ethnic group. Undoubtedly, there is an expectation among social activists that these writers, artists and producers will feel and manifest a greater level of sensitivity to accurate and generalizable cultural images. They reason that African American artists, writers and producers who have achieved a level of success that affords them a national audience should have achieved a level of social consciousness that would result in the development and portrayal of images that are empirically valid and more reflective of the strengths than the weaknesses of members of their race. This is perhaps one of the most contentious issues among activists who desire social change and those who are in positions to effect social change. Frequently, these are not the same individuals. Whether one is examining cultural images or the labor market, African Americans who are advocates of social change, and have achieved a higher level of social consciousness, frequently find themselves in positions that enable advocacy rather than action. Many African Americans who hold positions that afford them opportunities to implement social change are not only in a tenuous position but may be selected for these key positions only if they demonstrate to other institutional gatekeepers either that they do not possess this affinity for social change and equity or that they are willing to sublimate or suppress their desire to improve the participation of African Americans in societal institutions. Maintaining control over ideology, rates of participation and societal resources ensures the perpetuation of the status quo. Therefore, it is not happenstance that African Americans and other dispossessed groups, employed in strategic decision-making positions, must hold certain academic requirements but must also express their belief in traditional values and ideologies, which support little or no social change. That is not to say that all African Americans or other disenfranchised individuals subscribe to traditional belief systems and values that reflect an insensitivity to others like themselves who have a history of systematic exclusion, but there is sufficient evidence that individuals with

197

a strong sense of race, gender and class consciousness may not adjust or function as well in societal institutions as individuals who have less sensitivity to, and identification with, issues related to race, gender and class. The question which must still be answered is: Should African Americans in positions to influence social change, including those who produce and create cultural images of African American women, be held to higher standards than others who generate and disseminate such images? To hold African American artists, writers and producers of cultural images of African American women to a higher standard that requires empirical validation and race, gender and class consciousness is the same as requiring a litmus test for Blackness and femaleness. Such criteria, frequently alluded to but seldom if ever codified, would imply, if developed, that African Americans have an obligation to demonstrate their race and gender identification before they are supported by the masses of African Americans. It is the case that African American writers, artists and producers should be held to higher standards than others who are not members of a disenfranchised group. If one understands that all African Americans regardless of relative freedoms, material possessions and social privilege are the victims of discrimination, it is fairly obvious that the entire cultural group, irrespective of gender, will either benefit or be adversely affected by imagery that is characterized by stereotypes. This contentious issue is decidedly different than the question of whether it is reasonable to assume that individuals who hold positions that enable them to create and produce images of African American men and women will possess race and gender consciousness which will result in more empirically valid and representative images? The answer to this question is extremely important as it directs the efforts of activists interested in improving the development and dissemination of images of African American women. Moreover, it establishes a broad set of parameters for the producers and creators of cultural images, especially African Americans, to initiate self-evaluation. These individuals must examine their values and the motivations which guide and influence their productions. If such individuals, motivated by self-interest and placing individual gain over the advancement of the community, produce works that are devoid of empirical validity, knowing how such images impact upon the life chances of African American women, then activists or those who have attained higher levels of race, gender and class consciousness are obliged to assist the creators and producers of cultural images in elevating their (i.e. the producers') levels of social consciousness. Thus, rather than criticizing African American creators and producers of cultural images, as well as African Americans who are in positions to influence positively the lives of significant numbers of African Americans and others who are outside of mainstream America, those who have achieved higher levels of social consciousness should enlighten them. One of the major problems with recurrent non-complimentary images, and retrogression in other areas in which social and economic gains have been eroded, is that generally the advances that took place were minor and lacked permanence. Moreover, the uneven pattern of change that marks social progress results in a paradox in that individuals who benefit from social movements become the gatekeepers themselves during periods of conservatism when social movements are characterized by lulls. There is an expectation that African Americans who create and produce cultural images, and others who are placed in critical positions in which they can increase the level of participation of African Americans in salient institutions, live up to what many consider an obligation to do so. However, whether these potential agents of social change accept this responsibility is not determined by social status or material possessions. Instead, it is the acquisition of knowledge, experiential and didactic, not wealth or position, that results in race, gender and class consciousness. The importance of acquiring race, gender and class consciousness cannot be overemphasized as they are requisites for social advocacy and activism. The fact that African American artists, entertainers, producers, administrators, managers and so forth are in positions to effect positive cultural images, with their inherent ideologies and other social and economic changes, does not mean that they will feel obliged to do so. It is erroneous to assume that all individuals who have attained higher levels of education (undergraduate, graduate and professional degrees), if placed in key positions where they could improve cultural images and African Americans' access to societal resources and participation in institutions, will effect such occurrences. Education alone is no guarantee that an individual has achieved a level of race, gender and class consciousness that will lead to gains for African Americans, in general, and women in particular. While education is an integral and essential prerequisite for achieving social consciousness, it is not the sole

determinant. Different levels of race, gender and class consciousness evolve when didactic instruction is combined with
experiential knowledge that includes an awareness of the history
and contributions of one's race to African American culture, the
larger society and to the world community. Thus, African
Americans who create and produce cultural images and enhance
social and economic opportunities for members of their race, and
others, must be learned and not merely lettered.

One cannot ignore the role that the mass media played in
reporting news in which African American women were central to
the news reported. Aside from day-to-day reports in which African
American women are vilified using the stereotypical imagery of
Jezebel, there were three major news reports in which African
American females were exploited, castigated and reviled by the
mass media. Specifically, Tawana Brawley, Robin Givens and Anita
Hill were subjected to the mass media's and, more generally,
society's negative and hostile perception of African American
women. The images of these women which the mainstream media
purveyed and the assumptions and interpretations derived from
these images were consistent with traditional stereotypical cultural
images and ideologies of African American women. They contained the same levels of denigration, contempt and human depre-
cation that American society has historically and systematically
assigned to African American women.

Tawana Brawley, a fifteen-year-old African American female,
was found in a vacant lot in 1987, after being missing for four days.
She was found in a plastic garbage bag, clothed in only a shirt,
dazed, smeared with feces, and with the words Nigger and KKK
written on her body. She stated that she had been raped by six
White males, including a highway patrolman, a district attorney
and a local police officer. The mass media's handling of this case,
involving a minor, was similar to that of Child Protective Services,
in that the identity of this juvenile was never protected, nor were
her emotions considered as she became further victimized by
innuendo and characterizations of her morality. In the end, the
mass media became an important instrument of the state as the
grand jury denied all of Tawana Brawley's allegations, saying that
she had fabricated the entire story and was not a rape victim but a
victim of self-mutilation. Whether the legal system had sufficient
evidence to corroborate Tawana Brawley's report of her victimi-

zation in no way justifies the mass media's treatment of this case during or subsequent to the investigation.

In the case of Robin Givens, who was married to heavyweight boxing champion Mike Tyson, the mass media relegated her claims of being the victim of physical abuse by portraying her as a woman whose sole interest in her husband was to derive monetary and material benefits from the wealth he had acquired through boxing. Seldom was Robin Givens's own success as an actress mentioned. To do so would have conflicted with the media's image of her as a woman who, along with her mother, was attempting to dupe her husband of his wealth. When the couple finally separated with a divorce pending, the media portrayed Tyson as a caring and vulnerable person, while the tabloids characterized Robin Givens as the most despised woman in America.

The news media's *coup de grâce* in perpetuating all of the myths and stereotypes of African American women surfaced in the Anita Hill–Clarence Thomas situation. When the Senate confirmation hearings of Judge Clarence Thomas, President George Bush's nominee for the United States Supreme Court, were almost completed, Nina Totenberg, with National Public Radio, reported a leaked confidential FBI report in which Professor Anita Hill had privately revealed that 10 years earlier Clarence Thomas, her former employer, then Chairman of the Equal Employment Opportunity Commission, had sexually harassed her. The mass media once again became a powerful tool which the privileged employed to control the assignment of one of the the the country's most significant, influential and prestigious positions – an honorific position on the US Supreme Court. Those in power used traditional stereotypes about the African American male's preoccupation with sex. Clearly, Professor Anita Hill became the victim and pawn of the country's privileged class when Senate staffers systematically sought and ultimately successfully solicited information from Professor Hill regarding her previous professional relationship with her former employer Clarence Thomas. And although Professor Anita Hill presented a credible account of the sexual abuse that had transpired when she worked for Clarence Thomas, the mass media were used to purvey an image of her as a fantasizing liar, who had spent time scouring legal briefs to identify lurid sexual language and discourse for the purpose of attributing such conduct to then Supreme Court nominee Clarence Thomas.

In spite of the use of the mass media to define and perpetuate negative images of African American women, African American women are generally able to overcome such negativism and barriers to their professional and personal growth. Clearly, mutual dependence among African American women, strong kinship bonds, spirituality, and other dynamics within the African American community serve as buffers and reinforcers, and help to insulate African American women from the ongoing institutional assaults with which they are faced. Since the mass media have been used by the privileged class to wage horrendous and unrelenting assaults, like the foregoing, African American women must challenge both the privileged and the mass media until such imagery and ideology is eliminated.

CHANGING IMAGERY, SOCIAL POLICY AND THE STATUS OF AFRICAN AMERICAN WOMEN

The changes that have occurred in cultural images of African American woman have been too limited and temporary to permanently replace traditional stereotypical imagery and societal perceptions and expectations of African American women. Social policies continue to be formulated which do not meet the needs and do not have the capacity to increase the resources that are available to African American women. Moreover, cultural images continue to influence the societal perception of African American women as matriarchs or sexually loose and irresponsible women who substitute welfare for work and marriage and cannot be taken seriously. These stereotypes continue to support reactionary and punitive social policies and practices that exclude African American women from societal resources and institutions. Therefore, welfare continues in the 1990s to be identified as a stigmatized program for African American women and their children. And welfare cutbacks are interpreted as being necessary since there is an erroneous societal perception that African American women are the only ones benefiting from public transfer payments.

The conservative opposition to social welfare programs, to a national health care policy, educational grants and loans, programs to eliminate homelessness, job-training programs, child care and government involvement in the development, funding and delivery of social welfare services is reflective of the pervading

202

mood of the country. Each of these programs is essential to elevating the social and economic status of African American women and their community. Further, the government's lack of interest in redeveloping the infrastructure of this country is also a matter of vital concern. The necessity for rebuilding and repairing bridges, roads, houses for the homeless, government buildings and so forth would provide publicly funded employment for numbers of young males and females who have been occupationally displaced as well as those who do not possess the technical skills that are marketable in the United States. Directing national attention to these matters and allocating monies from the federal budget in these areas would provide jobs, which are a prerequisite for establishing and stabilizing marriages and families. Ensuring that men and women have jobs in a society that correlates employment and materialism with self-worth is critical to reducing the suicide and homicide rates; and would lessen the tremendous tax burden for funding prisons and paying the economic and noneconomic costs associated with personal and property crimes. The effect of greater employment opportunities would certainly improve educational achievement and reduce social dislocations throughout the African American community and the larger society.

The failure of the Bush administration to support the 1990 Civil Rights Bill is also an indication of the extent to which social policy that considers the interest of African American women and men is not being formulated. The 1964 Civil Rights Act was considered a significant accomplishment at the time; yet, it was unable to overcome institutional barriers that had been erected and inextricably woven into the fabric of American society. Many express cautious optimism that the new 1991 Civil Rights Act will offer more relief than its predecessor.

Affirmative action policies that were integral to civil rights legislation also had major limitations in that the burden of proof for discrimination complaints was on the victim. In addition, time constrictions, or statutes of limitations, require that claims of gender discrimination must be filed within 180 days of when the discriminatory incident or action occurred. Other shortcomings of affirmative action include the lack of authority of the Civil Rights Commission and the Equal Employment Opportunity Commission, both regulatory agencies with no real enforcement powers; the failure to require employers to establish and meet time-specific goals for employing, retaining and promoting African American women and other disenfranchised groups in all occupational groups and organizational sectors; the absence of timely reviews for allegations of race and gender discrimination; the absence of intermediate remedies that preclude and obviate expensive legal court battles; and the failure of federal administrations to consistently establish reasonable monetary limits requiring employers with federal contracts to establish affirmative action policies.

If the 1991 Civil Rights Act is to be effective it will have to eliminate the inherent weaknesses in the 1964 Civil Rights Act. Proponents of the compromise 1991 Civil Rights Act feel that this Act more than the earlier one does shift the burden of proof more from the employee to the employer. Moreover, it now permits those filing sexual harassment lawsuits to receive compensatory damages; yet, it places a $300,000 maximum on the damages that individuals can recover from sexual harassment lawsuits. Therefore, the enforcement of the 1991 Civil Rights Act and tests for its constitutionality will be the determinants of its effectiveness as a remedy for discrimination. In 1990 the Bush administration's refusal to pass a civil rights bill was viewed by many as an unwillingness to reduce institutional resistance to educational, economic and social inequality for African American women and members of their community and other marginal groups. Arguing that the 1990 Civil Rights Bill would require employers to maintain a racial quota system, the Bush administration adamantly refused to support another much needed and long awaited replacement for the earlier civil rights act. If African American women and their community were defined favorably by those who control societal resources, influence the formulation of social policy and develop images that define the extent to which African American women and members of their community are entitled to societal resources, then the Bush administration and all other federal administrations would have felt compelled to pass and rigorously enforce new civil rights legislation. If the new 1991 Civil Rights Act is not rigorously enforced, then African American women, across all socioeconomic levels, will continue to wage individual and collective struggles for parity for themselves and other members of their community. In view of the reactionary period which characterizes the current social climate of the United States, African American women can continue to anticipate that, in the absence of a catastrophic phenomenon, the privileged who mediate their own private resources as well as public tax dollars will continue to use imagery, social policy and the legal system to maintain the existing inequitable distribution of resources in the United States.

It is extremely important that African American women acquire an understanding of how images serve as the basis for ideological hegemony, which defines the relative value and worth of various groups of individuals based on race, gender, class as well as a plethora of other ascribed and achieved qualities. The fact that Americans and others throughout the world accept these well developed assessments of groups of individuals and justify their status and personal worth based on these images must first be understood by African American women and others who are committed to effect changes which will bring about social and economic equity. When larger numbers of African American women recognize the powerful impact of how images transmit ideological hegemony, which along with force and the threat of force enable the privileged to maintain a monopoly on power while keeping African American women in the most economically and socially depressed status, then the mass media will be perceived, like other forms of oppression, as a major system of domination that must be challenged to bring about significant change.

It is imperative that all social structures and systems of domination be recognized for their own contributions to maintaining African American women and their communities in a position of marginality. Simmel cogently described the method by which subsystems that make up social systems work together to maintain an organism in a functional state, when faced with an external threat, thereby supporting the status quo.[6] Simmel posited that when a system is under attack, or in this case challenged, all subsystems will sound a red alert. In effect, red flags go up to alert the system of impending danger. Therefore, as African American feminist scholars and other activists set out to effect major changes we must anticipate the resistance that each subsystem will mount. We must also strategically plan methods of overcoming institutional resistance. African American women and other disenfranchised groups must challenge the rationale of the privileged class that resources are distributed differentially not because of an unjust system but because of a fair and equitable system of meritocracy. The fallacies inherent in this logic must be identified and the inconsistencies that undergird societal institutions and systems of domination must be exposed. In so doing, the image of innocence of the privileged is challenged while the guilt of the poor is found to be unsubstantiated.

Efforts to effect significant changes in the socioeconomic status of African American women must be based on the successes and failures of other social movements. Therefore, African American women must begin by defining and redefining their values, belief systems and life experiences. They must also establish time-specific and measurable goals that are both short-term and long-term. In addition, African American women must embrace precepts and strategies that are likely to effect meaningful changes. There must be an appreciation that equity in all spheres will be obtained only by acknowledging that African American women, like other segments of the population, are not monolithic but are stratified on the basis of ideology, religion, political persuasion, education, occupation, class and skill-level. Moreover, a resurgence and re-strengthening of mutual aid networks is imperative. Sister-helping-sister informal systems must be revitalized. These networks must redefine the commodities of exchange so that African American women with limited monetary resources are perceived as possessing valuable noneconomic resources, such as advice, child care and emotional support, to exchange for economic and non-economic goods and services. Developing coalitions with others and collaborating with African American men, who must be viewed as invaluable and integral to the survival and progress of African American women, can only evolve after African American women reestablish mechanisms and dynamics that will enable them to redefine themselves and attribute a higher value to their own contributions and role in the African American community and the larger society. African American women should undertake this challenge by soliciting support from the government, the private sector and the entire African American community.

While African American women must seek to involve women and men of other political persuasions and racial backgrounds in their efforts to effect social justice for all, one cannot over-emphasize the importance of being unified themselves. The fact that there is stratification among African American women should be perceived as an asset to collective action rather than a liability. Hence, African American women must develop meaningful and viable approaches to utilize their disparate ideologies and method-ologies, so long as they are committed to the same goal of social equality for all, regardless of race, gender or class. To this end, African American women are likely to make greater strides in their quest for social justice by reaching out to those within and outside the African American community. Ultimately, African American women must increase their access to societal resources by challenging policies, laws and practices that are based on ideological hegemony. In addition, there must be ongoing efforts to counter the effects of the mainstream media and the nonrepresentative images, and distorted ideologies, of African American women that they purvey. The accomplishment of these feats is no easy task. To do so, African American women must mobilize an effective social movement which has the capacity to overcome institutional resistance, preempt fragmentation and achieve a long-range goal of social equality. Such a movement must be eclectic in composition, comprised of individuals from diverse backgrounds. It is of paramount importance, if this social movement is to be effective, that it rejects culturally divisive ideologies that equate diversity with deviance. Instead, African American women, along with others who seek race, gender and class equality, must embrace the precept that unity does not require uniformity.

Poster by Jon Onye Lockard, 1972

NOTES

1 THE STATUS OF AFRICAN AMERICAN WOMEN: THE ROLE OF IDEOLOGY AND MYTHOLOGY

1 C.W. Mills, *The Power Elite*, New York, Oxford University Press, 1956, pp. 3–13.
2 J.B. Thompson, 'Language and Power: A Critical Review of Studies in the Theory of Ideology', *Media, Culture and Society*, 8, 1986, p.41.
3 M. Weber, *Economy and Society*, Berkeley, California: University of California Press, Vol.2, 1978, p.927; also see T.D. Boston, *Race, Class and Conservatism*, Winchester, Massachusetts: Unwin Hyman, 1988, pp. 10–11.
4 C.W. Mills, op.cit., p.4.
5 M.B. Wilkerson, 'A Report on the Educational Status of Black Women during the UN Decade of Women, 1976–85', in M.C. Sims and J.C. Malveaux (eds) *Slipping through the Cracks: The Status of Black Women*, New Brunswick, New Jersey, 1989, p.90.
6 C.W. Mills, op.cit., p.281.
7 D. Gersh, 'The Corporate Elite and the Introduction of IQ Testing in American Public Schools', in M. Schwartz (ed.) *The Structure of Power in America*, New York: Holmes and Meier Publishers, 1987, pp. 163–164.
8 Ibid., pp.170–180.
9 M.K. Asante, *Kemet, Afrocentricity and Knowledge*, Trenton, New Jersey: Africa World Press, 1990, p.21.
10 A. Gramsci, *Selections from the Prison Notebooks*, New York: International Publishers, 1971.
11 T. Gitlin, *The Whole World is Watching*, Berkeley, California: University of California Press, 1980, p.253.
12 H. Becker, *Art Worlds*, Berkeley, California: University of California Press, 1982.
13 S. Steele, *The Content of our Character: A Vision of Race in America*, New York: St Martin Press, 1990, pp.1–120.
14 Ibid., pp.1–20.

2 THE SOCIAL SIGNIFICANCE OF CULTURAL IMAGERY

1 K.S. Jewell, *Survival of the Black Family: The Institutional Impact of U.S. Social Policy*, New York, Praeger, 1988, pp.6–8.

2 J. Westergaard, 'Power, Class and the Media', in J. Curran, M. Gurevitch and J. Woollacott (eds) *Mass Communication and Society*, London: Edward Arnold Publishers, 1977, p.100.

3 A. Gramsci, *Selections from the Prison Notebooks*, New York, International Publishers, 1971.

4 D. Gersh, 'The Corporate Elite and The Introduction of IQ Testing in American Public Schools, in M. Schwartz (ed.) *The Structure of Power in America*, New York: Holmes and Meier Publishers, 1987, pp.163–164.

5 G. Gilder, *Wealth and Poverty*, New York, Basic Books, 1981, p.68; L. Mead, *Beyond Entitlement*, New York: Free Press, 1986, p.1; W.B. Miller, 'Lower Class Culture as a Generating Milieu of Gang Delinquency', in R. Giallombardo (ed.) *Juvenile Delinquency*, New York: John Wiley, 1976, pp.144–154.

6 Ibid.

7 K. Marx and F. Engels, *The German Ideology*, Lawrence and Wishart, 1970.

8 A. Gramsci, op.cit.

9 Ibid.

10 G. Gerbner and L. Gross, 'The Scary World of TV's Heavy Viewer', *Psychology Today*, April 1976; H. Marcuse, *One Dimension Man*, Routledge, 1964; and R. Milbrand, *The State in Capitalist Society*, Weidenfeld and Nicolson, 1969.

11 K.S. Jewell, 'Black Male/Female Conflict: Internalization of Negative Images Transmitted through Imagery', *The Western Journal of Black Studies* 7:1, Spring 1983, pp.43–48.

12 M. Karenga, *Introduction to Black Studies*, Los Angeles, California: Kawaida Publications, p.264.

13 F. Beale, 'Double Je%wardy: To Be Black and Female', in T. Cade (ed.) *The Black Woman*, New York: Signet, 1970; P.H. Collins, 'Learning from the Outsider Within: The Sociological Significance of Black Feminist Thought', *Social Problems* 33:6, December 1986,pp. S14–S31; *Black Feminist Thought: Knowledge, Consciousness and the Politics of Empowerment*, Boston, Massachusetts: Unwin Hyman, 1990, p.44; A. Davis, *Women, Race and Class*, New York: Random House, 1981; B.T. Dill, 'Race, Class and Gender: Prospects for an All-Inclusive Sisterhood', *Feminist Studies* 9, 1983: 131–150; B. Hooks, *Ain't I a Woman: Black Women and Feminism*, Boston, Massachusetts: South End Press, 1981; D.K. Lewis, 'A Response to Inequality: Black Women, Racism and Sexism', *Signs* 3, 1977: 339–361; and P. Murray, 'The Liberation of Black Women', in M.L. Thompson (ed.) *Voices of the New Feminism*, Boston, Massachusetts: Beacon Press, 1970, pp.87–102.

14 T. Sowell, *The Economics and Politics of Race*, New York: William Morrow and Company, 1983, pp.209–210.

15 D. Bogel, *Toms, Coons, Mulattoes, Mammies and Bucks: An Interpretation of Blacks in American Films*, New York: Viking Press, 1973; J.C. Bond,

'The Media Image of Black Women', *Freedomways*, First Quarter, 1975: 34–37; K.S. Jewell, An Analysis of the Visual Development of a Stereotype: The Media's Portrayal of Mammy and Aunt Jemima as Symbols of Black Womanhood, Dissertation, Columbus, Ohio: The Ohio State University, 1976; K. S. Jewell, 1983, pp.43–48; Verta Mae, *Thursday and Every Other Sunday Off: A Domestic Rap*, New York: Doubleday and Co., 1972; J.S. Wood, 'The Black Female: Mammy, Jemima, Sapphire and other Images', in J.C. Smith (ed.) *Images of Blacks in American Culture*, Westport, Connecticut: Greenwood Press, 1988, pp.235–256.

16 C. Alexander and D. Weber, 'Social Welfare: Historical Dates', *Encyclopedia of Social Work*, 17, 1977: 1497–1503.

17 D. Hebdige, *Subculture: The Meaning of Style*, London: Methuen and Co., 1979, pp.57–89.

18 P.H. Collins, op. cit., 1986, pp.S14–S31.

19 D. Hebdige, op. cit., pp.57–58.

20 Ibid., pp.80–99.

21 C.T. Gilkes, 'From Slavery to Social Welfare: Racism and the Control of Black Women', in A. Swerdlow and H. Lessinger (eds) *Class, Race and Sex: The Dynamics of Control*, Boston, Massachusetts: G.K. Hall and Co., 1983: 288–300.

22 K. Marx and F. Engels, op.cit.

23 A. Gramsci, op.cit.

24 A. Gramsci, op.cit.

25 D. Gersh, op.cit., pp.163–164.

26 D. Gersh, op.cit., pp.163–164.

27 W.I. Thomas, 'The Relation of Research to the Social Process', in *Essays on Research in the Social Sciences*, Washington, DC: The Brookings Institution, 1931, p.189.

28 C.H. Cooley, *Human Nature and the Social Order*, New York: Charles Scribner's Sons, 1956.

29 D. Hebdige, op.cit., pp.73–89.

30 P.H. Collins, 1990, op. cit., pp.82–89; C.T. Gilkes, op.cit., pp.288–300; K.S. Jewell, op.cit., p.47; L.S. Robinson, 'Women, Media and the Dialectics of Resistance', in A. Swerdlow and H. Lessinger (eds) *Class, Race and Sex: The Dynamics of Control*, Boston, Massachusetts: G.K. Hall and Co., 1983, pp.308–324; P.B. Scott, 'Debunking Sapphire: Toward a Non-Racist and Non-Sexist Social Science' in G.T. Hull, P.B. Scott and B. Smith (eds) *All the Women are White, All the Blacks are Men, But Some of us are Brave: Black Women's Studies*, Old Westbury, New York: The Feminist Press, 1982, pp.85–92.

3 CULTURAL IMAGES AS SYMBOLS OF AFRICAN AMERICAN WOMANHOOD

1 D. Bogel, *Toms, Coons, Mulattoes, Mammies and Bucks: An Interpretation of Blacks in American Films*, New York: Viking Press, 1973; J.C. Bond, 'The Media Image of Black Women', *Freedomways*, First Quarter, 1975:

34–37; K.S. Jewell, An Analysis of the Visual Development of a Stereotype: The Media's Portrayal of Mammy and Aunt Jemima as Symbols of Black Womanhood, Dissertation, Columbus, Ohio: The Ohio State University, 1976; K.S. Jewell, 'Black Male/Female Conflict: Internalization of Negative Definitions transmitted through Imagery', *The Western Journal of Black Studies* 7:1, Spring 1983: 43–48; Verta Mae, *Thursdays and Every Other Sunday Off: A Domestic Rap*, New York: Doubleday and Co., 1972; J.S. Wood, 'The Black Female: Mammy, Jemima, Sapphire and other Images, in J.C. Smith (ed.) *Images of Blacks in American Culture*, Westport, Connecticut: Greenwood Press, 1988, pp.235–256.

2 Ibid.

3 C.T. Gilkes, 'From Slavery To Social Welfare: Racism and the Control of Black Women', in A. Swerdlow and H. Lessinger (eds) *Class, Race and Sex: The Dynamics of Control*, Boston, Massachusetts: G.K. Hall and Co., 1983 pp.288–300; K.S. Jewell, An Analysis of the Visual Development of a Stereotype: The Media's Portrayal of Mammy and Aunt Jemima as Symbols of Black Womanhood, Dissertation, Columbus, Ohio: The Ohio State University, 1976.

4 D. Bogel, op.cit., and K.S. Jewell, op. cit., 1976.

5 K.S. Jewell, 1976, ibid.

6 H. Wish, *Slavery in the South*, New York: The Noon Day Press, 1968.

7 Ibid.

8 K.S. Jewell, op.cit., 1976, p.15.

9 L. Banner, *American Beauty*, New York: Alfred A. Knopf, 1983, pp.112–114.

10 K.S. Jewell, op.cit., 1976, pp.20–23.

11 D. Bogel, op.cit.

12 J.A. Rogers, *Nature Knows No Color-Line*, New York: Helga M. Rogers, 1952.

13 Verta Mae, *Thursdays and Every Other Sunday Off: A Domestic Rap*, New York: Doubleday and Co., 1972.

14 Ibid.

15 S. Steele, *The Content of our Character: A Vision of Race in America*, New York: St Martin Press, 1990, pp.1–20.

16 G. Freyre, *The Masters and the Slaves*, New York: Alfred A. Knopf, 1966.

17 D. Bogel, op.cit.

18 N. Warren, 'From Uncle Tom to Cliff Huxtable, Aunt Jemima to Aunt Nell: Images of Blacks in Film and the Televison Industry', in J.C. Smith (ed.) *Images of Blacks in American Culture*, Westport, Connecticut, 1988, pp.51–117.

19 M.N. DePillars, African–American Artists and Art Students: A Morphological Study in the Urban Black Aesthetic, Dissertation, Pennsylvania State University, May, 1976; also see Jon Lockard's artwork of Aunt Jemima in K.S. Jewell, 1976, p.128.

20 K.S. Jewell, 1976, op.cit., p.128.

21 R. Hill, *The Strengths of Black Families*, New York: National Urban League, 1972; J. Scanzoni, 'Black Parental Values and Expectations of Children's Occupational and Educational Success', in H.P. McAdoo

212

and J.L. McAdoo (eds) *Black Children*, Beverly Hills: California, 1985: 113–122.
22 D. Hatchett, 'The Black Newspaper: Still Serving the Community', *The Crisis* 98:3, March 1991: 14–17; D.P. Johnson, 'Black Magazines: Optimism abounds despite Racism and Recession', *The Crisis* 98:3, March 1991: 18–21.
23 'Miss America Explains How and Why She Says No To Sex', *People*, November 26, 1984: 109–111.
24 S.L. Taylor, 'For Vanessa', *Essence*, October 1984: 79.

4 IMAGERY OF AFRICAN AMERICAN WOMANHOOD: UNDERLYING CONDITIONS – SOCIAL AND ECONOMIC CONSIDERATIONS

1 B.J. Lowenberg and R. Bogin (eds) *Black Women in Nineteenth-Century American Life*, University Park: Pennsylvania State University Press, 1976.
2 A.Y. Davis, *Women, Race and Class*, New York: Random House, pp.3–29.
3 J.W. Johnson, 'The Autobiography of an Ex-Colored Man', in *The Three Negro Classics*, New York: Avon Books, 1963, pp.478–479.
4 T. Kochman, *Black and White Styles in Conflict*, Chicago: The University of Chicago Press, 1981, p.55.
5 J. Kenyatta, *Facing Mount Kenya: The Tribal Life of the Gikuyu*, New York: AMS, 1978, pp.130–154.
6 D. Gregory, 'Rapping Back', *Essence*, August 1991: 61.
7 P.H. Collins, *Black Feminist Thought*, Boston, Massachusetts: Unwin Hyman, 1990; B. Hooks, *Feminist Theory: From Margin to Center*, Boston, Massachusetts: South End Press, 1984.
8 R.G. Dumas, 'Dilemmas of Black Females in Leadership', in L.F. Rose (ed.) *The Black Woman*, Beverly Hills, California: Sage Publications, 1982, pp.203–215.
9 R. Hill, *The Strengths of Black Families*, New York: National Urban League, 1972.
10 C.W. Franklin II and W. Pillow, 'The Black Male's Acceptance of the Prince Charming Ideal', in R. Staples (ed.) *The Black Family*, Belmont, California: Wadsworth Publishing Company, 1991, pp.124–130.
11 K.S. Jewell, *Survival of the Black Family: The Institutional Impact of U.S. Social Policy*, New York: Praeger, 1988.
12 B. Christian, *Black Women Novelists: The Development of a Tradition, 1892–1976*, Westport, Connecticut: Greenwood Press, 1980; A.B. Rushing, 'An Annotated Bibliography of Images of Black Women in Black Literature', *CLA Journal* 25, December 1981: 234–262; E. Schultz, 'Free in Fact and at Last: The Image of the Black Woman in Black Literature', in M. Springer (ed.) *What Manner of Woman*, New York: New York University, 1977: 316–342; Simms-Wood, 'The Black Female: Mammy, Jemima, Sapphire and other Images in J.C. Smith, *Images of Blacks in American Culture*, Westport, Connecticut: Greenwood Press, 1988, pp.235–256; M.H. Washington, 'Black

Women Image-Makers', *Black World* 13, August 1974: 10–18; and S. Towns, 'The Black Woman as Whore: Genesis of the Myth', *The Black Position* 3, 1974: 39–59.

13 K.S. Jewell, An Analysis of the Visual development of a Stereotype: The Media's Portrayal of Mammy and Aunt Jemima as Symbols of Black Womanhood, Dissertation, Columbus, Ohio: The Ohio State University, 1976.

14 M. Karenga. *Introduction to Black Studies*, Los Angeles, California: Kawaida Publications, 1987, p.91.

15 Ibid.

16 D. Hatchett, 'The Black Newspaper: Still Serving the Community', *The Crisis*, 98:3, March 1991: 14–17.

17 A. Cleft-Pellow, 'Literary Criticism and Black Imagery', in J.C. Smith (ed.) *Images of Blacks in American Culture*, Westport, Connecticut, Greenwood Press, 1988: 151–154.

5 CULTURAL IMAGERY OF AFRICAN AMERICAN WOMEN AND EMPIRICISM

1 United States Bureau of the Census, The Black Population in the United States: March, 1990 and 1989, Current Population Reports, Population Characteristics, Washington, DC: US Government Printing Office, Series P–20, No. 448, August 1991.

2 Ibid.

3 United States Bureau of the Census, 1991, op. cit.

4 K.S. Jewell, *Survival of the Black Family: The Institutional Impact of U.S. Social Policy*, New York: Praeger, 1988, p.76.

5 United States Bureau of the Census, 1991, op. cit.

6 J. Malveaux, 'The Economic Interests of Black and White Women: Are They Similar?' *The Review of Black Political Economy*, Summer 1985: 19.

7 Ibid., pp.13–22.

8 United States Bureau of the Census, 1991, op. cit.

9 United States Bureau of the Census, 1991, op. cit.

10 United States Bureau of the Census, 1991, op. cit.

11 United States Bureau of the Census, 1991, op. cit.

12 United States Bureau of the Census, 1991, op. cit.

13 United States Bureau of the Census, 1991, op. cit.

14 T. Boston, *Race, Class and Conservatism*, Boston, Massachusetts: Unwin Hyman, 1988, p.72.

15 B.A.P. Jones, 'Black Women and Labor Force Participation: An Analysis of Sluggish Growth Rates', in M.C. Simms and J.M. Malveaux, *Slipping through the Cracks: The Status of Black Women*, New Brunswick, New Jersey: Transaction Publishers, pp.11–31.

16 K. Fulbright, 'The Myth of the Double Advantage: Black Female Managers', in M.C. Simms and J.M. Malveaux (eds) *Slipping through the Cracks: The Status of Black Women*, New Brunswick, New Jersey: Transaction Publishers, pp.33–45.

17 E.C. Hughes, 'Dilemmas and Contradictions of Status,' *American Journal of Sociology* 50, 1945: 353–357.

18 C.E. Bennett, 'Student Race, Class and Academic History as Determinants of Teacher Expectations of Student Performance', *Journal of Black Psychology* 3, 1976: 71–87; J.E. Brophy, 'Research on the Self-fulfilling Prophecy and Teacher Expectations', *Journal of Educational Psychology*, 75:5, 1983: 631–661; J. Howard and R. Hammond, 'Rumors of Inferiority', *The New Republic*, September 1975: 17–21; J. Kunjubu, *Countering the Conspiracy to Destroy Young Black Boys*, Chicago, Illinois: Afro American Publishing Company, 1984; I. Katz, 'A Critique of Personality Approaches to Negro Performance with Research Suggestions', *Journal of Social Issues* 25:3, 1969: 13–27; C.B. Murray and H.H. Fairchild, 'Models of Black Adolescent Academic Underachievement', in R.L. Jones (ed.) *Black Adolescents*, Berkeley, California: Cobb and Henry, 1989: 229–245; and V. Washington, 'Teachers in Integrated Classrooms: Profiles of Attitudes, Perceptions and Behavior', *Elementary School Journal* 80:4, 1980: 192–201.

19 B.T. Dill, 'The Means to put my Children Through: Child-Rearing Goals and Strategies among Black Female Domestic Servants', in L.F. Rose (ed.) *The Black Woman*, Beverly Hills, California: Sage Publications, 1980: 114–116.

20 K. S. Jewell, op. cit., p.45.

21 A.O. Harrison, 'The Black Family's Socializing Environment: Self Esteem and Ethnic Attitude among Black Children', in H.P. McAdoo and J.L. McAdoo, *Black Children*, Beverly Hills, California: Sage Publications, 1985; R. Hill, *The Strengths of Black Families*, New York: National Urban League, 1972; H.P. McAdoo, 'Factors Related to Stability in Upwardly Mobile Black Families', *Journal of Marriage and the Family* 40, November 1978: 761–766; C. Stack, *All Our Kin: Strategies for Survival in a Black Community*, New York: Harper and Row, 1975.

22 L.W. Myers, *Black Women: Do They Cope Better?*, Engelwood Cliffs, New Jersey: Prentice-Hall, 1980.

23 K.S. Jewell, Divorced Women's Use of Institutional and Noninstitutional Counseling Services: an Exploratory Study, Final Report, Columbus, Ohio: Ohio Department of Mental Health, 1987.

24 P.M. Blau, *Exchange and Power in Social Life*, New York: Wiley and Sons, 1964.

25 D.K. Lewis, 'A Response to Inequality: Black Women, Racism, and Sexism', *Signs* 3:2, 1977: 343.

26 D.A. Bell, Jr., *Race, Racism and American Law*, Boston, Massachusetts: Little, Brown and Company, 1980, pp.24–28; also see K.S. Jewell, *Survival of the Black Family*, 1988, op. cit., p.135.

27 D. Cauchon, 'Undercover Tests Identify Bias', *USA Today*, September 26, 1991, p.3A.

28 K.S. Jewell, 'Black Male/Female Conflict: Internalization of Negative Definitions transmitted through Imagery', *The Western Journal of Black Studies* 7:1, Spring 1983: 46–48.

6 GENDER-ORIENTED SOCIAL POLICY: AN AGENDA FOR IMPROVING THE STATUS OF AFRICAN AMERICAN WOMEN

1 B. Friedan, *The Feminine Mystique*, New York: W.W. Norton Company, 1963; C. Delphy, 'Towards a Material Feminism', in E. Marks and I. DeCourtwon (eds) *New French Feminisms*, Amherst: University of Massachusetts Press, 1980; G. Lerner, 'Women's Rights and American Feminism', *American Scholar* 40, Spring 1971: 236; S. Stambler, *Women's Liberation: Blueprint for the Future*, New York: Ace Books, 1970.

2 United States Bureau of the Census, The Black Population in the United States: March 1990 and 1989, Current Population Reports, Population Characteristics, Washington, DC: US Government Printing Office, Series P-20, No. 448, August, 1991.

3 K.S. Jewell, *Survival of the Black Family: The Institutional Impact of U.S. Social Policy*, New York: Praeger, 1988, p.22.

4 Ibid., p.22.

5 K.S. Jewell, op. cit., p.22.

6 B. Valentine, 'Women on Welfare: Public Policy and Institutional Racism' in A. Swerdlow and H. Lessinger (eds) *Class, Race, and Sex: The Dynamics of Control*, Boston, Massachusetts: G.K. Hall and Co., 1983, p.281.

7 T.J. Hopkins, 'The Role of Community Agencies as Viewed by Black Families', *Journal of Orthopsychiatry* 42, 1972: 508–516.

8 S. Bahr, 'The Effects of Welfare on Marital Stability and Remarriage', *Journal of Marriage and the Family* 41, 1979: 553–560; T. Caplow, *Toward Social Hope*, New York: Basic Books, p.135; T. Caplow, 'The Loco Parent: Federal Policy and Family Life,' *Brigham Young University Law Review*, 1976: 709–714.

9 R. Hill, *Economic Policies and Black Progress: Myths and Realities*, Washington, DC: National Urban League Research Department, 1981, pp.53–63; B.R. Schiller, *The Economics of Poverty and Discrimination*, Engelwood Cliffs: Prentice Hall, 1989, p.174.

10 Ibid.

11 K.S. Jewell, op.cit., pp.52–53.

12 United States Bureau of the Census, op.cit.

13 R. Law, 'Public Policy and Health-Care Delivery: A Practitioner's Perspective', in M.C. Simms and J.M. Malveaux (eds) *Slipping Through the Cracks: The Status of Black Women*, New Brunswick, New Jersey: Transaction Publishers, 1989, pp.219–220.

14 Ibid.

15 United States Bureau of the Census, op. cit. U.S. National Health Center for Health Statistics of the United States; Annual and Unpublished Data, March, 1989.

16 Ibid.

17 L.C. Burbridge, 'Black Women in Employment and Training Programs', in M.C. Simms and J.M. Malveaux (eds) *Slipping Through*

the Cracks: The Status of Black Women, New Brunswick, New Jersey: Transaction Publishers, pp.131–137.

18 Ibid.

19 L.C. Burbridge, op. cit., p.97.

20 R. Taggart, *A Fisherman's Guide: An Assessment of Training and Remediation Strategies*, Kalamazoo: W.E. Upjohn Institute for Employment Research, 1981, p.33.

21 J.M. Jeffries, 'Discussion' in M.C. Simms and J.M. Malveaux (eds) *Slipping through the Cracks: The Status of Black Women*, Transaction Books, pp.131–137.

22 Ibid., p.136.

23 J.M. Jeffries, op. cit., p.136.

24 T. Gitlin, *The Whole World is Watching*, Berkeley, California: University of California Press, 1980.

25 M.B. Wilkerson, 'A Report on the Educational Status of Black Women during the UN Decade of Women, 1976–85', in M.C. Simms and J.M. Malveaux (eds) *Slipping through the Cracks: The Status of Black Women*, New Brunswick, New Jersey: Transaction Books, 1989, p.86.

26 Ibid.

27 United States Bureau of the Census, 'What's It Worth?: Educational Background and Economic Status', Current Population Reports, Household Economic Status, Washington, DC: US Government Printing Office, Series P-70, November 21, 1990.

28 Ibid.

29 M. Wilkerson, op. cit., p.88.

30 United States Bureau of the Census 1990 and 1989, 1991, op. cit.

31 K. Davidson, R.B. Ginsbury and H.H. Kay, *Text, Cases and Materials on Sex-Based Discrimination*, St Paul, Minnesota: West Publishing Company, 1974, pp.964–969; K. Lawrence and K.A. Klos, *Sex Discrimination in the Workplace*, Germantown, Maryland: Aspen Systems Corporation, 1978, pp.110–138.

32 R. Hill, 'What's ahead for Blacks?', *Ebony*, January 1980: 27–36.

7 THE US LEGAL SYSTEM: PROTECTING THE RIGHTS OF THE PRIVILEGED

1 T. Gitlin, *The Whole World is Watching*, Berkeley, California: University of California Press, 1980.

2 G. Tuchman, *Making News: A Study in the Construction of Reality*, New York: Free Press, 1978.

3 C. Epstein, 'Positive Effects of the Multiple Negative: Explaining the Success of Black Professional Women', *American Journal of Sociology*, January 1973: 913–935; C.P. Epstein, 'Black and Female: The Double Whammy', *Psychology Today*, August 1973: 57–61.

4 Ibid.

5 K. Marx and F. Engels, *The German Ideology*, Lawrence and Wishart, 1970.

6 J.H. Wilson, 'The Illusion of Change: Women and the American Revolution', in A.F. Young (ed.) *The American Revolution: Explorations in the History of American Radicalism*, Dekalb: Northern Illinois University Press, 1976, pp.385–443.
7 Ibid.
8 J.H. Wilson, op. cit., p.415.
9 E. Fox-Genovese, *Within the Plantation Household: Black and White Women of the Old South*, Chapel Hill, North Carolina: The University of North Carolina Press, 1988, p.199; G. Fitzhugh, *Sociology for the South*, New York: Burt Franklin, 1965, pp.213–216.
10 P. Williams, *The Alchemy of Race and Rights: Diary of a Law Professor*, Cambridge, Massachusetts: Harvard University Press, 1991, p.121.
11 P. Murray, 'The Liberation of Black Women', in M.L. Thompson (ed.) *Voices of the New Feminists*, Boston, Massachusetts: Beacon Press, 1970, p.90; also see J. Cole, 'Militant Black Women in Early U.S. History', *The Black Scholar* 9:7, 1978: 38–44; A. Davis, 'Reflections on the Black Woman's Role in the Community of Slaves', *The Black Scholar*, December 1971: 3–15; and P. Giddings, *When and Where I Enter: The Impact of Black Women on Race and Sex in America*, New York: William Morrow and Company, 1984, pp.58–65.
12 S. Lebsock, *The Free Women of Petersburg: Status and Culture in a Southern Town, 1784–1860*, New York: W.W. Norton and Company, 1984, pp.87–88.
13 Ibid.
14 J.E. White, 'The Pain of being Black', *Time*, September 16, 1991: 25–27.
15 R.H. Bork, *The Tempting of America: The Political Seduction of the Law*, New York: The Free Press, 1990, pp.115–116.
16 J.H. Wilson, op. cit., p.386.
17 J. Handler, *Law and the Search for Community*, Philadelphia, Pennsylvania: University of Pennsylvania Press, 1990.
18 D.A. Bell, Jr., *Race, Racism and American Law*, Boston: Little, Brown and Company, 1980, pp.656–661.
19 'Marshall's Retirement Jolts Black America,' *Jet*, Vol. 80, July 15, 1991, p.4.

8 DETERMINING ENTITLEMENTS: THE EXCLUSIONARY NATURE OF CULTURAL IMAGERY

1 W. Johnson, *The Social Services: An Introduction*, Itasca, Illinois: F.E. Peacock Publishers, 1982.
2 W.B. Miller, 'Lower Class Culture as a Generating Milieu of Gang Delinquency', in R. Giallombardo (ed.) *Juvenile Delinquency*, New York, John Wiley, 1976, pp.144 & 154; M. Wolfgang and F. Ferracuti, *The Subculture of Violence: Towards an Integrated Theory in Criminology*, London: Tavistock, 1967.
3 K.S. Jewell, *Survival of the Black Family: The Institutional Impact of U.S. Social Policy*, New York: Praeger, 1988, p.171.

4 United States Bureau of the Census, Consolidated Federal Funds Report, Fiscal Year 1990, Washington, DC: US Government Printing Office, Volume 1: County Areas, March, 1991.

5 F.J. Cook, *The Warfare State*, New York: The Macmillan Company, 1962; also see C.L. Mollenhoff, *The Pentagon*, New York: G.P. Putnam's Sons, 1967.

6 W. Williams, 'Do You Know Why We Need Poverty?' *The National Leader*, January 5, 1984:5.

7 Ibid., p.5.

8 E. Bonacich, 'Inequality in America: The Failure of the American System for People of Color', in M.L. Andersen and P.H. Collins (eds) *Race, Class, and Gender*, Belmont, California: Wadsworth Publishing Company, 1992, pp.96–110.

9 G. Will, 'Sexual Recklessness Causes Black Woes', *The Columbus Dispatch*, January 24, 1986, p.11A.

10 J.E. White, 'The Pain of being Black', *Time*, September 16, 1991: 25–26.

11 W.B. Miller, op. cit.

12 A. Davis, *Women, Culture and Politics*, New York: Random House, 1989.

13 G. Gilder, *Wealth and Poverty*, New York: Basic Books, 1981; L. Mead, *Beyond Entitlement*, New York: The Free Press, 1986; and C. Murray, *Losing Ground: American Social Policy, 1950–1980*, New York: Basic Books, 1984.

14 G. Gilder, op. cit.

15 W. Johnson, op. cit.

16 B.R. Schiller, *The Economics of Poverty and Discrimination*, Englewood Cliffs, New Jersey: Prentice Hall, 1989, pp.174–175.

17 J.D. McGhee, 'The Black Family Today and Tomorrow', *The State of Black America*, New York: National Urban League, 1985: 1–15.

18 United States Bureau of the Census, The Black Population in the United States: March 1990 and 1989, Current Population Reports, Population Characteristics, Washington, DC: US Government Printing Office, Series P-20, No. 448, August, 1991.

19 F. Piven and R. Cloward, *Regulating the Poor: The Functions of Public Welfare*, New York: Vintage, 1971.

20 B.R. Schiller, op.cit., p.173.

21 United States Bureau of the Census, 1990 and 1989, 1991 op. cit.

22 L. Weitzman, 'The Economics of Divorce: Social and Economic Consequences of Property, Alimony and Child Support Awards', UCLA Law Review 28, 1981: 1228.

23 United States Bureau of the Census, 1990 and 1989, 1991 op. cit.

24 Social Security Bulletin, Annual Statistical Supplement, U.S. Department of Health and Human Services, Social Security Administration, 1990; United States Department of Labor, Characteristics of the Uninsured Unemployment Report, Unpublished Report, ES203, 1985.

25 United States Bureau of the Census, Child Support and Alimony: 1985 (Supplemental Report), Current Population Reports, Series P-23, No. 154, Washington, DC: US Government Printing Office, 1985.

26 L. Burnham, 'Has Poverty Been Feminized in Black America?' in R. Lefkowitz and A. Withorn (eds) *For Crying Out Loud: Women and Poverty in the United States*, New York: The Pilgrim Press, 1986, pp.71–85; E. Higginbotham, 'We Were Never on a Pedestal: Women of Color Continue to Struggle with Poverty, Racism and Sexism', in R. Lefkowitz and A. Withorn (eds) *For Crying Out Loud: Women and Poverty in the United States*, New York: The Pilgrim Press, 1986, pp.101–112.
27 G.J. Duncan and S.D. Hoffman, 'A Reconsideration of the Economic Consequences of Marital Disruption', *Demography* 22, November 1985: 493–495.
28 W. Johnson, op. cit.
29 D. Glasgow, *The Black Underclass*, New York: Vintage Books, 1981.

9 A MICROCULTURAL RESPONSE: ALTERNATIVES TO MACROCULTURAL INSTITUTIONAL SUPPORT

1 H. McAdoo, 'Black Mothers and the Extended Family Support Network', in L.F. Rose (ed.) *The Black Woman*, Beverly Hills, California: Sage Publications, 1980, p.135.
2 S. Youngblood, 'Shakin the Mess Outa Misery', Play, in K. Perkins (ed.) *Black Female Playwrights*, 1989.
3 Verta Mae, *Thursdays and Every Other Sunday Off: A Domestic Rap*, New York: Doubleday and Company, 1972.
4 B. Landry, *The New Black Middle Class*, Berkeley, California: University of California Press, 1987, p.14.
5 B. Hooks, *Feminist Theory: From Margin to Center*, Boston: South End Press, 1985, p.15.
6 K.S. Jewell, Divorced Women's Use of Institutional and Noninstitutional Counseling Services: An Exploratory Study, Final Report, Columbus, Ohio: Ohio Department of Mental Health, August, 1987.
7 M.L Clark, 'Friendships and Peer Relations of Black Adolescents', in R.L. Jones (ed.) *Black Adolescents*, Berkeley, California: Cobb and Henry Publishers, 1989, pp.175–204.
8 M. Weinberg, *A Chance To Learn*, Cambridge: Cambridge University Press, 1977, p.87.
9 J. Kozol, *Savage Inequalities: Children in America's Schools*, New York: Crown Publishers, 1991.
10 J. Fleming, *Blacks in College: A Comparative Study of Students' Success in Black and White Institutions*, San Francisco: Jossey-Bass, 1984.
11 J. Katz, 'White Faculty Struggling with the Effects of Racism', in J.H. Cones, J.F. Noonan and D. Janha (eds) *Teaching Minority Students, New Directions for Teaching and Learning*, No. 16, San Francisco: Jossey-Bass, December 1983, p.33.
12 J. Fleming, op. cit.
13 B. Landry, op. cit., p.50.
14 N. Sudarkasa, 'Interpreting the African Heritage in Afro-American Family Organization', in H.P. McAdoo (ed.) *Black Families*, Newbury Park, California: Sage, 1989, p.37.

220

15 A. Billingsley, *Black Families in White America*, Englewood Cliffs, New Jersey: Prentice-Hall, 1968; A. Billingsley, *'Children of the Storm', Black Children and American Child Welfare*, New York: Harcourt Brace Jovanovich, 1972, p.46; R. Hill, *The Strengths of Black Families*, New York: National Urban League, 1972; K.S. Jewell, 'Use of Social Welfare Services and the Disintegration of the Black Nuclear Family', *The Western Journal of Black Studies* 8, Fall 1984: 192–198; C.A. McCray, 'The Black Woman and Family Roles', in L.F. Rose (ed.) *The Black Woman*, Beverly Hills, California: Sage Publications, 1980, pp.67–78; C. Stack, *All Our Kin: Strategies for Survival in a Black Community*, New York: Harper and Row, 1974.

16 C.A. McCray, op. cit., p.77.

17 H. McAdoo, op. cit., p.136.

18 A.W. Gouldner, 'The Norm of Reciprocity: A Preliminary Statement', *American Sociological Review*, 25, 1960: 161–178.

19 H. McAdoo, 'Transgenerational Patterns of Upward Mobility in African-American Families', in H.P. McAdoo, *Black Families*, Newbury Park, California: Sage Publications, 1988, p.166.

20 W.E.B. Dubois, 'The Souls of Black Folk', in *The Three Negro Classics*, New York: Avon Books, 1965.

21 C. Stack, op. cit.

22 C. Eric Lincoln, 'Black Studies and Cultural Continuity', *Black Scholar*, October, 1978: 12–18.

23 J.S. Butler, Book Review, of *Twentieth Century Dilemma, Twentieth Century Prognoses*, edited by Winston Van Horne and Thomas V. Tonnesen, Milwaukee: University of Wisconsin System Institute on Race and Ethnicity, 1989.

24 'Vanessa Williams: Success Is the Best', *Ebony*, April 1990: 52–56.

25 D. Norville, 'Vanessa Williams's Extraordinary Comeback', *McCall's*, April 1992: 100–103, 142–143.

10 REDEFINING IMAGES OF AFRICAN AMERICAN WOMANHOOD AND RESHAPING SOCIAL POLICY

1 J.C. Bond, 'The Media Image of Black Women', *Freedomways*, First Quarter, 1975: 34–37.

2 R.G. Dumas, 'Dilemmas of Black Females in Leadership, in L.F. Rose, *The Black Woman*, Beverly Hills, California: Sage Publications, 1980, pp.207–208.

3 R. Newby, Letter to Oprah Winfrey, *The Association of Black Sociologists Newsletter*, Spring 1987.

4 B. Lanker, *I Dream a World*, New York: Stewart, Tabori and Chang, 1989, p.27.

5 Ibid., p.27.

6 G. Simmel, *Conflict*, Englewood Cliffs, New Jersey: Prentice Hall, 1964.

BIBLIOGRAPHY

ADC Budgeting and Payment System, Income of a Stepparent, Unpublished Budgeting Methodology Guidelines, Ohio Department of Welfare Services May 1, 1991.

Alexander, C. and D. Weber, 'Social Welfare: Historical Dates', *Encyclopedia of Social Work*, 17, 1977: 1497–1503.

Asante, M.K., *Kemet, Afrocentricity and Knowledge*, Trenton, New Jersey: Africa World Press, 1990, p. 21.

Bahr, S., 'The Effects of Welfare on Marital Stability and Remarriage', *Journal of Marriage and the Family*, 41, 1979: 553–560.

Banner, L., *American Beauty*, New York: Alfred A. Knopf, 1983.

Beale, F., 'Double Jeopardy: To be Black and Female', in T. Cade (ed.) *The Black Woman*, New York: Signet, 1970.

Becker, H., *Art Worlds*, Berkeley, California: University of California Press, 1982.

Bell, D. A., Jr., *Race, Racism and American Law*, Boston: Little, Brown and Company, 1980.

Bennett, C.E., 'Student Race, Class and Academic History as Determinants of Teacher Expectations of Student Performance', *Journal of Black Psychology* 3, 1976: 71–87.

Billingsley, A., *Black Families in White America*, Englewood Cliffs, New Jersey: Prentice-Hall, 1968.

——, *Children of the Storm: Black Children and American Child Welfare*. New York: Harcourt Brace Jovanovich, 1972.

Blau, P.M., *Exchange and Power in Social Life*, New York: John Wiley and Sons, Inc., 1964.

Bloom, H., 'Estimating the Effect of Job Training Programs Using Longitudinal Data: Ashenfelter's Findings Reconsidered,' *Journal of Human Resources*, 19: 4, 1984.

Bogel, D., *Toms, Coons, Mulattos, Mammies and Bucks*, New York: The Viking Press, 1973.

Bonacich, E., 'Inequality in America: The Failure of the American System for People of Color', in M.L. Andersen and P.H. Collins (eds) *Race, Class, and Gender*, Belmont, California: Wadsworth Publishing Company, 1991, pp. 96–110.

Bond, J.C., 'The Media Image of Black Women', *Freedomways*, (First Quarter), 1975: 34–37.

Bork, R.H., *The Tempting of America: The Political Seduction of the Law*, New York: The Free Press, 1990.

222

BIBLIOGRAPHY

Boyd, H., 'The Black Press: A Long History of Service and Advocacy', *The Crisis*, March, 1991: 10–13.

Brophy, J.E., 'Research on the Self-fulfilling Prophecy and Teacher Expectations', *Journal of Educational Psychology* 75:5, 1983: 631–661.

Burbridge, L.C., 'Black Women in Employment and Training Programs', in M.C. Simms and J.M. Malveaux (eds) *Slipping through the Cracks: The Status of Black Women*, New Brunswick, New Jersey: Transaction, 1989: 97–114.

Burnham, L., 'Has Poverty Been Feminized in Black America?' in R. Lefkowitz and A. Withorn (eds) *For Crying Out Loud: Women and Poverty in the United States*, New York: The Pilgrim Press, 1986: 71–85.

Butler, J.S., Book Review of *Race:Twentieth-Century Dilemmas, Twentieth Century Prognoses*, edited by Winston A. Van Horne and Thomas V. Tonnesen, Milwaukee: University of Wisconsin System Institute on Race and Ethnicity, 1989, in *Contemporary Sociology: An International Journal of Reviews* Vol. 20, No. 2, March 1991, pp. 198–200.

Caplow, T., *Toward Social Hope*, New York: Basic Books, 1975, p.135.

——,'The Loco Parent: Federal Policy and Family Life,' *Brigham Young University Law Review*, 1976: 709–714.

Cauchon, D., 'Undercover Tests Identify Bias', *USA Today*, September 26, 1991: 3A.

Cherry, R., *Discrimination, Its Economic Impact on Blacks, Women and Jews*, Massachusetts: Lexington Books, 1989.

Christian, B., *Black Women Novelists: The Development of a Tradition, 1892–1976*, Westport, Connecticut: Greenwood Press, 1980.

Clark, M.L., 'Friendships and Peer Relations',%wn R. Jones (ed.) *Black Adolescents*, Berkeley, California: Cobb and Henry Publishers, 1989: 175–204.

Cleft-Pellow, A., 'Literary Criticism and Black Imagery', in J.C. Smith (ed.) *Images of Blacks in American Culture*, Westport, Connecticut: Greenwood Press, 1988: 151–154.

Cole, J., 'Militant Black Women in early U.S. History', *The Black Scholar* 9(7), 1978: 38–44.

Collins, P.H., 'Learning from the Outsider Within: The Sociological Significance of Black Feminist Thought, *Social Problems* 33 (6), 1986: S14–S32.

——, *Black Feminist Thought: Knowledge, Consciousness, and the Politics of Empowerment*, Cambridge, Massachusetts: Unwin Hyman, 1990.

Cook, F.J., *The Warfare State*, New York: The Macmillan Company, 1962.

Cooley, C.H., *Human Nature and the Social Order*, New York: Free Press, 1956.

Davidson, K., R.B. Ginsburg and H.H. Kay, *Text, Cases and Materials on Sex-Based Discrimination*, St Paul, Minnesota: West Publishing Company, 1974.

Davis, A.Y., 'Reflections on the Black Woman's Role in the Community of Slaves', *The Black Scholar*, December 1971: 3–15.

——, *Women, Race and Class*, New York: Random House, 1981.

——, *Women, Culture and Politics*, New York: Random House, 1989.

Delphy, C., 'Towards a Material Feminism', in E. Marks and I. DeCourtwon (eds) *New French Feminisms*, Amherst: University of Massachusetts Press, 1980.

DePillars, Murry N., African American Artists and Art Students: A Morphological Study in the Urban Black Aesthetic, Dissertation, Pennsylvania State University, 1976.

Dill, B.T., 'The Means to put my Children Through: Child- Rearing Goals and Strategies among Black Female Domestics', in L.F. Rose (ed.) *The Black Woman*, Beverly Hills, California: Sage Publications, 1980: 107–123.

——, 'Race, Class and Gender Prospects for an All-Inclusive Sisterhood', *Feminist Studies* 9, 1983: 131–150.

Dubois, W.E.B., 'The Souls of Black Folk', in *The Three Negro Classics*, New York: Avon Books, 1965.

Dumas, R.G., 'Dilemmas of Black Females in Leadership', in L.F. Rose (ed.) *The Black Woman*, Beverly Hills, California: Sage Publications, 1980: 203–215.

Duncan, G.J. and Hoffman, S.D., 'A Reconsideration of the Economic Consequences of Marital Disruption', *Demography* 22, November 1985: 493–495.

Epstein, C., 'Positive Effects of the Multiple Negative: Explaining the Success of Black Professional Women', *American Journal of Sociology* 78, 1973: 912–935.

Fitzhugh, G., *Sociology for the South*, New York: Burt Franklin, 1965, pp.213–216.

Fleming, J., *Blacks in College: A Comparative Study of Students' Success in Black and White Institutions*, San Francisco: Jossey-Bass, 1984.

Fox-Genovese, E., *Within the Plantation Household: Black and White Women of the Old South*, Chapel Hill: The University of North Carolina Press, 1988.

Franklin, C.W. II and W. Pillow, 'The Black Media's Acceptance of the Prince Charming Ideal', *Black Caucus* 13, Spring 1982: 3–7.

Franklin, J.H., *From Slavery to Freedom: A History of American Negroes*, New York: Alfred A. Knopf, 1948.

Frazier, E.F., *The Negro Family in the United States*, Chicago: University of Chicago, 1939.

Freyre, G., *The Masters and the Slaves*, New York: Alfred A. Knopf, 1966.

Friedan, B., *The Feminine Mystique*, New York: W.W. Norton and Company, 1963.

Fulbright, K., 'The Myth of the Double Advantage: Black Female Managers', in M.C. Simms and J.M. Malveaux (eds) *Slipping through the Cracks: The Status of Black Women*, New Brunswick, New Jersey: Transaction Publishers, pp. 33–45.

Gerbner, G. and L. Gross, 'The Scary World of TV's Heavy Viewer', *Psychology Today*, April 1976.

Gersh, D., 'The Corporate Elite and the Introduction of IQ Testing in American Public Schools', in M. Schwartz (ed.) *The Structure of Power in America: The Corporate Elite as a Ruling Class*, New York: Holmes and Meier Publishers, 1987: 163–184.

Giddings, P., *When and Where I Enter: The Impact of Black Women on Race and Sex in America*, New York: William Morrow and Company, 1984.

Gilder, G., *Wealth and Poverty*, New York: Basic Books, 1981.

Gilkes, C.T., 'From Slavery to Social Welfare: Racism and the Control of Black Women', in A. Swerdlow and H. Lessinger (eds) *Class, Race and Sex: The Dynamics of Control*, Boston: G.K. Hall and Company, 1983: 288–300.

Gitlin, T., *The Whole World is Watching*, Berkeley, California: University of California Press, 1980.

Glasgow, D., *The Black Underclass*, New York: Vintage Books, 1981.

Glazer, N. 'Beyond Income Maintenance', *The Public Interest* Summer, 1969, p.120.

Goffman, E., *Frame Analysis*, Philadelphia: University of Pennsylvania Press, 1974.

Goldstein, L. F., *The Constitutional Rights of Women: Cases in Law and Social Change*, New York: Longman, Inc., 1979.

Gouldner, A.W., 'The Norm of Reciprocity: Preliminary Statement', *American Sociological Review* 25, 1960: 161–178.

Gramsci, A. *Selections from the Prison Notebooks*, edited and translated by Q. Hoare and G. Smith, New York: International Publishers, 1971.

Gregory, D., 'Rapping Back', *Essence*, August 1991: 60–62.

Hall, S., 'Culture, the Media and Ideological Effect', in J. Curan, M. Gurevitch and J. Woollacott, *Mass Communications and Society*, Beverly Hills, California: Sage, 1973: 315–348.

Handler, J., *Law and the Search for Community*, Philadelphia, Pennsylvania: University of Pennsylvania Press, 1990.

Harper, H., 'Black Women and the Job Training Partnership Act,' in M.C. Simms and J.M. Malveaux (eds) *Slipping Through the Cracks: The Status of Black Women*, New Brunswick, New Jersey: Transaction Publishers, 1989, pp.115–129.

Headen, A.E. and Headen, S.W., 'General Health Conditions and Medical Insurance Issues Concerning Black Women,' in M.C. Simms and J.M. Malveaux (eds) *Slipping Through the Cracks: The Status of Black Women*, New Brunswick, New Jersey: Transaction Publishers, 1989, pp.183–197.

Hebdige, D., *Subculture: The Meaning of Style*, London: Methuen, 1979.

Higginbotham, E., 'We Were Never on a Pedestal: Women of Color Continue to Struggle with Poverty, Racism and Sexism', in R. Lefkowitz and A. Withorn (eds) *For Crying Out Loud: Women and Poverty in the United States*, New York: The Pilgrim Press, 1986: 101–112.

Hill, R., *The Strengths of Black Families*, New York: Emerson Hall, 1972.

——, *Economic Policies and Black Progress: Myths and Realities*, Washington, DC: National Urban League, 1981.

Hooks, B., *Ain't I a Woman: Black Women and Feminism*, Boston, Massachusetts: South End Press, 1981.

——, *Feminist Theory: From Margin To Center*, Boston: South End Press, 1984.

Hopkins, T.J., 'The Role of Community Agencies as Viewed by Black Families', *Journal of Orthopsychiatry* 42, 1972: 508–516.

Howard, J. and R. Hammond, 'Rumors of Inferiority', *The New Republic*, September 1975: 17–21.

Hughes, E.C., 'Dilemmas and Contradictions of Status', *American Journal of Sociology* 50, 1945: 353–357.

Jeffries, J.M., 'Education and Training, Discussion', in M.C. Simms and J.M. Malveaux (eds) *Slipping Through the Cracks: The Status of Black Women*, New Brunswick, New Jersey: Transaction Publishers, 1989: 131–137.

Jewell, K.S., An Analysis of the Visual Development of a Stereotype: The Media's Portrayal of Mammy and Aunt Jemima as Symbols of Black Womanhood, Ph.D. Dissertation, Ohio State University, 1976.

——, 'Black Male/Female Conflict: Internalization of Negative Definitions Transmitted through Imagery', *The Western Journal of Black Studies* 7(1), 1983: 43–48.

——, 'Use of Social Welfare Programs and the Disintegration of the Black Nuclear Family', *The Western Journal of Black Studies* 8, Winter 1984: 192–198.

Jewell, K.S., 'Will the Real Black, Afro-American, Mixed, Colored, Negro Please Stand Up? Impact of the Black Social Movement, Twenty Years Later', *Journal of Black Studies* 16, September 1985: 57–75.

——, Divorced Women's Use of Institutional and Noninstitutional Counseling Services: An Exploratory Study, Final Report, Ohio Department of Mental Health, August, 1987.

——, 'The Changing Character of Black Families: The Effects of Differential Social and Economic Gains', *Journal of Social and Behavioral Sciences* 33, 1988: 143–154.

——, *Survival of the Black Family: The Institutional Impact of U.S. Social Policy*, New York: Praeger, 1988.

Johnson, D.P., 'Black Magazines: Optimism abounds despite Racism and Recession', *The Crisis*, March 1991: 18–21.

Johnson, J.W., *The Autobiography of an Ex-Colored Man*, in *Three Negro Classics*, New York: Avon Books, 1970.

Johnson, W., *The Social Services: An Introduction*, Itasca, Illinois: F.E. Peacock Publishers, 1982.

Jones, B.A.P., 'Black Women and Labor Force Participation: An Analysis of Sluggish Growth Rates', in M.C. Simms and J.M. Malveaux, *Slipping through the Cracks: The Status of Black Women*, New Brunswick, New Jersey: Transaction Publishers, 1989: 11–31.

Kanter, R.M., *Men and Women of the Corporation*, New York: Basic Books, 1977.

Karenga, M., *Introduction to Black Studies*, Los Angeles, California: Kawaida Publications, 1987.

Katz, I., 'A Critique of Personality Approaches to Negro Performance with Research Suggestions', *Journal of Social Issues*, 25:3, 1969: 13–27.

Katz, J., 'White Faculty Struggling with the Effects of Racism', in J. H. Cones, J.F. Noonan and D. Janha (eds) *Teaching Minority Students, New Directions for Teaching and Learning*, No. 16, San Francisco: Jossey-Bass, December, 1983.

Kenyatta, Jomo. *Facing Mount Kenya: The Tribal Life of Gikuyu*, New York; AMS, 1978.

Kochman, T. *Black and White Styles in Conflict*, Chicago: The University of Chicago Press, 1981.

Kozol, J., *Savage Inequalities: Children in America's Schools*, New York: Crown Publishers, 1991.

Kunjubu, J., *Countering the Conspiracy to Destroy Young Black Boys*, Chicago, Illinois: Afro American Publishing Company, 1984.

Landry, B., *The New Black Middle Class*, Berkeley, California: University of California Press, 1987.

Lanker, B., *I Dream A World: Portraits of Black Women who Changed America*, New York: Stewart, Tabori and Chang, 1989.

Law, R., 'Public Policy and Health-Care Delivery: A Practitioner's Perspective', in M.C. Simms and J.M. Malveaux, *Slipping through the Cracks; The Status of Black Women*, New Brunswick, New Jersey: Transaction Publishers, 1989, pp. 217–225.

Lawrence, K. and K.A. Klos, *Sex Discrimination in the Workplace*, Germantown, Maryland: Aspen Systems Corporation, 1978.

Lebsock, S., *The Free Women of Petersburg*, New York: W.W. Norton and Company, 1984.

Lerner, G., 'Women's Rights and American Feminism, *American Scholar* 40, Spring 1971: 236.

Lerner, G., *Black Women In White America*, New York: Pantheon Books, 1972.

Levitan, S.A. and Johnson, C.M., *Beyond the Safety Net: Reviving the Promise of Opportunity in America*, Cambridge, Massachusetts: Ballinger Publishing Company, 1984.

Lewis, D.K., 'A Response to Inequality: Black Women, Racism and Sexism', *Signs*, Winter 1977: 339–360.

Lincoln, C.E., 'Black Studies and Cultural Continuity', *Black Scholar*, October 1978: 12–18.

Lowenberg, B.J. and R. Bogin (eds) *Black Women in Nineteenth Century American Life*, University Park: Pennsylvania State University Press, 1976.

Lyons, C., 'Blacks and 50 Years of TV: Ten Memorable Moments', *Ebony*, September 1989: 72–76.

McAdoo, H.P. 'Factors related to Stability in Upwardly Mobile Black Families', *Journal of Marriage and the Family* 40, November 1978: 761–766.

——, 'Black Mothers and the Extended Family Support Network', in L.F.R. (ed.) *The Black Woman*, Beverly Hills, California: Sage, 1980: 125–144.

——, 'Transgenerational Patterns of Upward Mobility in African American Families', in H.P. McAdoo, *Black Families*, Newbury Park, California: Sage Publications, 1988, pp. 148–168.

McCray, C.A., 'The Black Woman and Family Roles', in H.P. McAdoo (ed.) *Black Families*, Beverly Hills, California: Sage, 1981.

McGhee, J.D., 'The Black Family Today and Tomorrow', *The State of Black America*, New York: National Urban League, 1985: 1–15.

McQuail, D., 'The Influence and Effects of Mass Media' in J. Curan, M. Gutevitch and J. Woollacott (eds) *Mass Communications and Society*, 1979: 70–94.

Malveaux, J., 'The Economic Interests of Black and White Women: Are They Similar?', *The Review of Black Political Economy*, Summer 1985: 5–27.

——, 'Comparable Worth and its Impact on Black Women', in M.C. Simms and J.M. Malveaux (eds) *Slipping through the Cracks: The Status of Black Women*, New Brunswick, New Jersey: Transaction, 1989: 47–62.

Marcuse, H., *One Dimensional Man*, Routledge, 1964.

'Marshall's Retirement Jolts Black America', *Jet*, Vol. 80, July 15, 1991, p.4.

Marx, K. and F. Engels, *The German Ideology*, Lawrence and Wishart, 1970.

Mead, L. *Beyond Entitlement*, New York: The Free Press, 1986.

Merton, R.K., 'Patterns of Influence', in P. Lazarsfeld and F. Stanton (eds) *Communications Research 1948–1949*, New York: Harper, 1949.

Milbrand, R., *The State in Capitalist Society*, Weidenfeld and Nicolson, 1969.

Miller, W.B., 'Lower Class Culture as a Generating Milieu of Gang Delinquency', in R. Giallombardo (ed.) *Juvenile Delinquency*, New York: John Wiley, 1976.

Mills, C.W., *The Power Elite*, New York: Oxford University Press, 1956.

'Miss America Explains How and Why She Says No To Sex', *People*, November 26, 1984: 109–112.

Mollenhoff, C.L., *The Pentagon*, New York: G.P. Putnam's Sons, 1967.

Murray, C., *Losing Ground: American Social Policy, 1950–1980*, New York: Basic Books, 1984.

Murray, C.B. and H. Fairchild, 'Models of Black Adolescent Academic

Underachievement', in R.L. Jones (ed.) *Black Adolescents*, Berkeley, California: Cobbs & Henry, 1989: 229–245.
Murray, P., 'The Liberation of Black Women', in M.L. Thompson (ed.) *Voices of the New Feminists*, Boston: Beacon Press 1970: 88–102.
Myers, L.W., *Black Women: Do They Cope Better?*, Englewood Cliffs, New Jersey: Prentice-Hall, 1980.
Newby, R., Letter to Oprah Winfrey, *Association of Black Sociologists Newsletter*, Spring 1987.
Norville, D., 'Vanessa Williams's Extraordinary Comeback', *McCall's*, April 1992: 100–103, 142–143.
Penn-Tergborg, R., 'Survival Strategies among African American Women Workers: A Continuing Process', in Ruth Milkman (ed.) *Women, Work and Protest: A Century of U.S. Women's Labor History*, Boston: Routledge and Kegan Paul, 1985.
Piven, F. and Cloward, R., *Regulating the Poor: The Functions of Public Welfare*, New York: Vintage, 1971.
Robinson, L.S., 'Women, Media and the Dialectics of Resistance', in A. Swerdlow and H. Lessinger (eds) *Class, Race and Sex: The Dynamics of Control*, Boston: G.K. Hall, 1983: 308–324.
Rogers, J.A., *Nature Knows No Color-Line*, New York: Helga Rogers, 1952.
Rushing, A.B., 'An Annotated Bibliography of Images of Black Women in Black Literature', *CLA Journal* 25, December 1981.
Scanzoni, J. 'Black Parental Values and Expectations of Children's Occupational and Educational Success', in H.P. McAdoo and J.L. McAdoo (eds) *Black Children*, Beverly Hills, California: Sage Publications, 1985, pp. 113–122.
Schiller, B.R., *The Economics of Poverty and Discrimination*, Englewood Cliffs, New Jersey: Prentice Hall, 1989.
Schultz, E., 'Free in Fact at Last: The Image of Black Women in Black Literature', in M. Springer (ed.) *What Manner of Woman*, New York: New York University Press, 1977, pp. 316–342.
Scott, P.B., 'Debunking Sapphire: Toward a Non-Racist and Non-Sexist Social Science', in G.T. Hull, P.B. Scott and B. Smith (eds) *All the Women are White, All the Blacks are Men, But some of us are Brave: Black Women's Studies*, Westbury, New York: The Feminist Press, 1982: 85–92.
Simmel, G., *Conflict*, Englewood Cliffs, New Jersey: Prentice Hall, 1964.
Sims-Wood, J., 'The Black Female: Mammy, Jemima, Sapphire and other Images', in J.C. Smith (ed.) *Images of Blacks in American Culture: A Reference Guide to Information Sources*, Westport, Connecticut: Greenwood Press, 1988: 235–256.
Social Security Bulletin, Annual Statistical Supplement, U.S. Department of Health and Human Services Administration, 1990.
Sowell, T., *The Economics and Politics of Race*, New York: William Morrow and Company, 1983.
Stack, C., *All Our Kin: Strategies for Survival in a Black Community*, New York: Harper and Row, 1974.
Stambler, S., *Women's Liberation: Blueprint for the Future*, New York: Ace Books, 1970.
Steele, S., *The Content of our Character: A Vision of Race in America*, New York: St Martin Press, 1990.
Sudarkasa, N., 'Interpreting the African Heritage in Afro-American Family Organization', in H.P. McAdoo (ed.) *Black Families*, Beverly Hills, California: Sage, 1981: 37–53.
Taggart, R. *A Fisherman's Guide: An Assessment of Training and Remediation*

Strategies, Kalamazoo: W.E. Upjohn Institute for Employment Research, 1981.

Taylor, S.L., 'For Vanessa', *Essence*, October 1984: 79.

Thompson, J.B., 'Language and Power: A Critical Review of Studies in the Theory of Ideology', *Media, Culture and Society* 8, 1986: 41–64.

Towns, S. 'The Black Woman as Whore: Genesis of the Myth, *The Black Position* 3, 1974: 39–59.

Tuchman, G., *Making News: A Study in the Construction of Reality*, New York: Free Press, 1978.

——, 'Mass Media Institutions', in N.J. Smelser (ed.) *Handbook of Sociology*, Newbury Park, California: Sage, 1988: 601–626.

United States Bureau of the Census, Child Support and Alimony: 1985, Supplemental Report. Current Population Reports, Special Studies, Washington DC: US Government Printing Office, Series P-23, No. 154, July 1, 1985.

United States Bureau of the Census, Current Population Reports, Washington, DC: US Government Printing Office, Series P-25, No. 1018, November, 1989.

United States Bureau of the Census, The Black Population in the United States: March, 1988, Current Population Reports, Population Characteristics, Washington, DC: US Government Printing Office, Series P-20, No.442, November, 1989.

United States Bureau of the Census, 'What's It Worth?: Educational Background and Economic Status', Current Population Reports, Household Economic Studies, Washington, DC: US Government Printing Office, Series P-70, No. 21, 1990.

United States Bureau of the Census, Consolidated Federal Funds Report, Fiscal Year 1990, Washington, DC: US Government Printing Office, Volume 1: County Areas, March, 1991.

United States Bureau of the Census, 1987 Economic Censuses Survey of Minority-Owned Business Enterprises, Summary, Washington, DC: US Government Printing Office, MB87–4, August, 1991.

United States Bureau of the Census, 'The Black Population in the United States: March, 1990 and 1989', Current Population Reports, Population Characteristics, Washington, DC: US Government Printing Office, Series P-20, No. 448, August, 1991.

United States Department of Labor, Characteristics of the Insured Unemployed Report, Unpublished Report, ES203, 1985.

Valentine, B., 'Women on Welfare: Public Policy and Institutional Racism', in A. Swerdlow and H. Lessinger (eds) *Class, Race and Sex: The Dynamics of Control*, Boston: G.K. Hall, 1983: 276–287.

'Vanessa Williams: Success Is the Best', *Ebony*, April 1990: 52–96.

Verta Mae, *Thursdays and Every Other Sunday Off: A Domestic Rap*, New York: Doubleday and Company, 1972.

Warren, N., 'From Uncle Tom to Cliff Huxtable, Aunt Jemima to Aunt Nell: Images of Blacks in Film and the Television Industry', in J.C. Smith (ed.) *Images of Blacks in American Culture*, Westport, Connecticut, 1988, pp. 51–117.

Washington, M.H., 'Black Women Image-Makers', *Black World* 13, August 1974: 10–18.

Washington, V., 'Teachers in Integrated Classrooms: Profiles of Attitudes, Perceptions and Behavior, *Elementary School Journal* 80:4, 1980: 192–201.

Weinberg, M., *A Chance To Learn*, Cambridge: Cambridge University Press, 1977.

Weitzman, L., 'The Economics of Divorce: Social and Economic Consequences of Property, Alimony and Child Support Awards', *UCLA Law Review* 28, 1981: 1228.

Westergaard, J., 'Power, Class and the Media', in J. Curran, M. Gurevitch and J. Woolocott (eds) *Mass Communication and Society*, London: Edward Arnold Publishers, 1977.

White, J.E., 'The Pain of being Black', *Time*, September 16, 1991: 25–27.

Wilkerson, M., 'A Report on the Educational Status of Black Women during the UN Decade of Women, 1976–85', in M.C. Simms and J.M. Malveaux (eds) *Slipping through the Cracks: The Status of Black Women*, New Brunswick, New Jersey: Transaction, 1989: 97–114.

Will, G., 'Sexual Recklessness Causes Black Woes', *The Columbus Dispatch*, January 24, 1986.

Williams, P., *The Alchemy of Race and Rights: Diary of a Law Professor*, Cambridge, Massachusetts: Harvard University Press, 1991.

Williams, W., *The State Against Blacks*, New York: McGraw-Hill, 1982.

——, 'Do You Know Why We Need Poverty?', *The National Leader*, January 5, 1984:15.

Wilson, J.H., 'The Illusion of Change: Women and the American Revolution', in A.F. Young (ed.) *The American Revolution: Explorations in the History of American Radicalism*, Dekalb: Northern Illinois University Press, 1976: 385–443.

Wilson, W.J., *The Declining Significance of Race*, Chicago: University of Chicago Press, 1978.

Wish, H., *Slavery in the South*, New York: The Noon Day Press, 1968.

Wolfgang, M.E. and J. Ferracuti, *The Subculture of Violence*, London: Social Sciences Paperbacks, 1967.

Wood, J.S., 'The Black Female: Mammy, Jemima, Sapphire and other Images', in J.C. Smith (ed.) *Images of Blacks In American Culture*, Westport, Connecticut: Greenwood Press, 1988, pp. 235–256.

Youngblood, S., 'Shakin the Mess Outa Misery', Play, in K. Perkins (ed.) *Black Female Playwrights*, 1989.

NAME INDEX

SUBJECT INDEX